Developing Web Applications with Visual Basic .NET and ASP.NET

John Alexander
Billy Hollis

Wiley Computer Publishing

John Wiley & Sons, Inc.

Publisher: Robert Ipsen
Editor: Theresa Hudson
Developmental Editor: Kathryn A. Malm
Managing Editor: Angela Smith
New Media Editor: Brian Snapp
Text Design & Composition: John Wiley Composition Services

Designations used by companies to distinguish their products are often claimed as trademarks. In all instances where John Wiley & Sons, Inc., is aware of a claim, the product names appear in initial capital or ALL CAPITAL LETTERS. Readers, however, should contact the appropriate companies for more complete information regarding trademarks and registration.

This book is printed on acid-free paper. ♾

This publication is designed to provide accurate and authoritative information in regard to the subject matter covered. It is sold with the understanding that the publisher is not engaged in professional services. If professional advice or other expert assistance is required, the services of a competent professional person should be sought.

Library of Congress Cataloging-in-Publication Data:

ISBN: 0-471-08517-0

Printed in the United States of America.

10 9 8 7 6 5 4 3 2 1

To all our loved ones, those whom we hold so dear, and to those departed whom we miss. This is for you. Life is a measured gift, use it wisely and make it count.

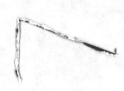

Contents

Acknowledgments

From John:

John would like to thank Valerie, Nathaniel, and Ian for sticking by him through the making of this book. Daddy promises not to lock himself in the basement any more.

Thanks to the contributors on the book: Cole Francis and Brian Wendt for the absolutely rocking job you guys did on this.

Thanks to Donis Marshall for the advice, guidance, assistance, and persistence throughout this process.

Thanks to the following folks at G.A. Sullivan: Greg Sullivan, Dave Smith, Don Benage, David Burgett, Matthew Baute, and Eric Brown. Dedication to quality is often given lip service, in the consulting industry but rarely followed through. I'm proud to be a part of this organization!

John also thanks the following folks at Microsoft that gave assistance, both directly and indirectly: Jennifer Ritzinger, David Lazar, Ari Bixhorn, Susan Warren, Dave Mendlen, Mike Iem, Scott Guthrie, Ilya Bukshteyn, Keith Ballinger, Chris Featherstone, and last but not least Steve Loethen.

And of course John would like to thank the Wiley Publishing crew that made this into what is now: Kathryn Malm, developmental editor extraordinaire, Terri Hudson, Ben Ryan, Jen Bergman, and his publisher, Robert Ipsen.

And finally thanks to Mom and Dad for the Commodore Vic-20 that started it all. . . .

From Billy:

Thanks, as usual, to my family for being forgiving enough to allow me the time to write another book. Cindy, Ansel, and Dyson have all been wonderful throughout my writing career.

I'd also like to offer appreciation to the folks at Microsoft that have given me invaluable assistance in the past few months, including, but not limited to, Mike Iem, Ari Bixhorn, and Jennifer Ritzinger. They exemplify the spirit of their company.

Introduction

Developing Web Applications with Visual Basic .NET and ASP.NET was born out of a desire to enable experienced Visual Basic developers to extend their knowledge and experience investment to the Web easily and seamlessly.

The thought behind this title is that the developer wouldn't need to master several technologies for ASP.NET development but could use the integrated tools and practical techniques to be productive quickly. It's also designed to be a code-based, hands-on introduction that will prepare, you, the reader for more focused titles.

Who Should Read This Book

If you are a Visual Basic programmer who has significant experience with:

- Event-driven programming (including working with forms and controls)
- COM component development
- Data access using ADO
- Basic familiarity with HTML, but little exposure to Web-related development concepts

then you should read this book. This book will help you to extend your existing knowledge investment to building Microsoft technology-centric Web Applications in .NET.

For the VB Developer, learning ASP Web development meant dealing with a variant of VB, a blurred line between code and content, component deployment issues, and bulky, interpreted solutions that are sometimes less-than-elegant.

In addition, the paradigm shift required for Web development meant rethinking traditional application design and architecture methods as well.

ASP.NET is an exciting new platform for developing, deploying, and running Web applications. It is a major enhancement of ASP; solving performance, scalability, and deployment challenges while strengthening the platform through its extensive compiled programming language support and a simplified, more powerful page model.

The integration of Web development features in Visual Basic .NET through its support of ASP.NET allows VB developers to make the transition more easily than ever before, without the use of separate tools or technologies. A major ASP.NET design goal was to create a similar programming model so that VB developers would have a shorter learning curve in building Web applications, thus solving many of the aforementioned problems using earlier technologies. This frees the developer to focus on the new concepts introduced by Web development without the need to learn multiple environments and tools in the process.

How This Book Is Organized

Chapter 1 provides a basis for introducing the vision of the Next Generation Web: Microsoft .NET! The developer is introduced to the .NET common language runtime and extensive language support. Next, Microsoft .NET Enterprise Servers (such as Commerce Server and BizTalk Server) are briefly discussed before descending to highlight the native underlying Internet related services exposed by Windows 2000. This discussion culminates in Chapter 1 with an overview of the programming enhancements and fundamental changes to Web development that ASP.NET provides. The point of this chapter is to start a foundation that will set the overall tone for the remainder of the book.

Chapter 2 begins with issues and concepts surrounding the impressive changes that especially impact ASP.NET development. Expanding the background in the previous chapter, now we start to explore the new features of the next version of Visual Basic. As the new environment features are highlighted, the reader will understand that the Visual Basic's RAD virtues have been extended for Web development.

Building on the changes introduced in Chapter 2, Chapter 3 continues with those changes in Visual Basic that pertain to Object-oriented development.

The focus of Chapter 4 is to acquaint the Visual Basic developer with DHTML for use in building ASP.NET Applications. Attention is given to illustrate the improvements brought about by the new server-side controls and the expanded flexibility that developers gain. Important for all levels of browser support, the ability of the server-side controls to automatically generate "uplevel" and "downlevel" HTML intelligently is shown as well.

Chapter 5 gives an overview of ASP.NET Pages, building on the knowledge of the previous preparatory chapters. As ASP.NET support is completely integrated into Visual Basic.NET, VB developers are able to effectively use their experience in making the transition to web development. Developers will also discover the ease of UI development through the use of WebForms, the use of the Code-behind method of writing ASP.NET Page code, and the simplified page object model. VB developers who have experience with WebClasses will appreciate the expanded capability and functionality of WebForms illustrated through several examples.

One of the exciting new features of ASP.NET is the ability to utilize and customize server-side controls. As control usage is natural to every VB developer, this knowledge will be extended to ASP.NET. Building on the discussion in Chapter 4 with HTMLControls, the focus in Chapter 6 now shifts to the Web-Controls, illustrating usage and function through practical examples. Since many of the WebControls will be familiar to the VB Developer from the start, the emphasis is on essential usage scenarios such as page navigation, validation, data access, and client-event handling topics. In addition, we've added a brief section on creating custom controls.

Chapter 7 deals with the second member of the ASP.NET platform: Web Services. Web Services can be used to enable remote access to internal systems from the Internet, thereby supporting integration and business-to-business applications. Developers will learn that Web Services are server objects that use the Simple Object Access Protocol (SOAP) (or HTTP-Get/Post) to accept requests and return results. They also discover that clients using the Service Description Language (SDL) discover these objects. The next topic is XML (the basis for SOAP and SDL) and its importance to Web Services as the common language of communication. The key concepts of these infrastructure technologies are touched upon before moving into a practical discussion of creating and testing a Web Service.

Chapter 8 begins with an overview of ADO.NET, the powerful yet simple-to-use data access toolset that is instrumental for creating rich Web applications. More than just a simple enhancement of Active Data Objects, ADO.NET brings true platform interoperability and scalable data access through the use of XML as the format for data transmission. The developer is reintroduced to the concept of data binding—from the server. The XML Designer and the ADO.NET Data Set Designer are examined in detail, with practical examples to illustrate usage. Special emphasis is placed on the fact that any COM+ object can be bound, in addition to traditional data stores. Formatting and error handling topics are also addressed in order to have a well-rounded understanding of this important subject.

ASP.NET simplifies configuration and deployment by improving the deployment process for both code and ASP.NET pages, and by providing extensible application configuration. Chapter 9 covers the differences between Application-level and Session-level scope. Next, proper usage and expanded support of the Application and Session objects are highlighted. Various scalability issues surrounding application design and maintenance are woven in throughout this section to underscore their importance, including data caching. As Security issues are on the mind of every developer, a primer on the ASP.NET Authentication/Authorization Services is of great importance. The chapter concludes with techniques for programmatically authorizing the user once authenticated.

Chapter 10 rounds out the title by providing a walkthough of a sample enterprise prototype application. Starting with design documents, we first discuss the requirements for the application and then move into an explanation of selected code listings. In addition, the data store and stored procedures are examined and explained, as is the presentation tier. A Web service for the client is also discussed.

Let's check out some background material on .NET and why it's important before moving on to Chapter 1.

.NET—Background and Purpose

.NET was introduced to the public in July 2000 at Microsoft's Professional Developers Conference. This technology had been in development for more than two years, under very heavy wraps. We had seen various aspects of what was to become .NET (at that time called "Next Generation Windows Services") at different times in the preceding year. The pieces, however, didn't reveal the overall plan. As we'll see in the following chapters, .NET makes our job as developers quite a bit easier for a multitude of tasks.

Microsoft .NET represents a revolution in application development—not just for Web application development, but for Windows apps as well. Moving information from anywhere to anywhere is the basic message of .NET. This means that that information should be able to flow from a mainframe to a phone or wireless device and anything in between. The key to making this information flow possible is Microsoft .NET's heavy reliance on standards-based protocols and formats, such as XML and SOAP. Another key factor is that .NET has been specifically designed with the Internet in mind.

To make the .NET vision a reality, companies must make many changes not just in technology, but also in philosophy. It can be a challenge for corporations to fully grasp the .NET vision, despite the many attempts to explain and demonstrate the different scenarios in which .NET is useful.

The best usage scenario I've seen in front of the public currently is in a TV commercial featuring lettuce. The scene begins with a shot of rotting lettuce sitting on a warehouse dock in the hot summer sun. The CIO (coincidentally visiting) confronts the warehouse foreman about the situation. The foreman explained that the delivery information was incorrect, that the distributor had been faxed, and they were waiting on a confirmation. The CIO then harangues the foreman about the fact that the company has computers that could solve this problem. The foreman replies, "Too bad they can't talk to my distributor." The commercial ends with a warehouse worker using a wireless device to reroute the lettuce on the fly, solving the problem and saving the lettuce. In 30 seconds, seamless communication between the partners in the business transaction is beautifully illustrated.

Before we can leap into the future, however, we need to understand where we've been. We're making the assumption that you've already read about the evolution of the database application from desktop to client/server to distributed. Let's take a quick look at the evolution of Web applications and learn why it's been such a long road. Until relatively recently the development environment, testing tools, and interoperability elements were comparatively primitive in light of what you've been used to as a Visual Basic developer.

Three Generations of Web Applications

The first generation of the Web application were Web pages and early dynamic systems that focused on exposing large amounts of static information through standard formats and protocols. Because the graphical nature of HTML was simple to understand and use, most anyone could publish a Web page. Vast numbers of users were empowered with the ability to publish and consume information on a wide scale.

However, as the demands for up-to-date content increased the challenges of providing this competitive edge with little more available than manual tools mounted. Single or limited user resources were limiting the refreshing of content on a timely basis. The use of client/server architecture began the rise of the shared resource, elevating departmental-level computing. However, this architecture relied on a fixed number of resource connections, so scalability was limited.

Client/server applications were amplified with Web browsers and server applications. The industry focused on rich OS and local services afforded by products like SQL Server, Exchange, and SNA Server. Web app developers took advantage of these local services and used HTML to "project" the UI to many types of clients. While this allowed for an explosion of information that was freely accessible, the static nature paved the way for the next generation. The absence of business efficiency meant that the main focus was on simply having an Internet presence ("brochure-ware because we gotta be there!"). The main metric of this time was the number of hits that the site received. The focus still wasn't on scalability; resources and connections were still directly tied together.

In 1996, Microsoft introduced a technology code-named "Denali" that changed Internet application development forever. The technology, of course, was Active Server Pages (ASP), and moved developers one step closer to Rapid Application Development for the Web. It was a huge kludge, and awkward and cumbersome, but, man, it was cool! Although there had been server-side technologies before ASP, none gave developers as much control and flexibility as the new offering.

Thus, the second generation was born, ushering in Windows DNA. Applications moved towards the *n*-tier architecture or distributed model. By freeing resource connections from direct communication with the business and presentation layer (the client), applications were able to provide greater scalability and performance while accessing enterprise data. In addition, the widespread use of a combination of "stateless" Web protocols with DNS and IP routing enabled scalability at quantum levels while improving the manageability and reliability of the applications themselves. While this was all well and good, debugging these applications was a pain in the registry, to put it mildly. With the separation of data and business logic, the applications themselves were improving, but the developer tools that spanned the different tiers and technologies were still in the dark ages. Developers also had to stay current on a plethora of different technologies to support and maintain these applications.

The need for interoperability between local and remote systems ushered in the modern age of Web applications. This new generation requires a standards-based mechanism to transmit data. And, as many have now learned, a business reason as well. Many Web sites and applications sprung up (literally overnight in some cases) without a clue or care on how to make a profit, made a ton of money in an IPO, and then spectacularly exploded when the .COM bubble burst. Applications become programmable Web Services, similar to those little plastic building blocks you may have used (or stepped on in the middle of the night) long ago. Web services permit applications to communicate, regardless of operating system or programming language, using the Internet as the medium. They are the "secret sauce" that finally will allow open communication between business entities, both internally and externally.

The key is that Web Services use protocols that are defined through public standards organizations such as the W3C. They enable not just the sharing of data, but can also invoke methods and utilize properties from other applications without concern about how the other applications were built.

.NET is about XML Web services. XML Web Services are programmatic. You can think of Web Services as components for the Internet. It is really standards-based reuse. Web Services allow you to expose code that implements business logic that can be re-used in multiple applications, but are based on vendor-independent Internet technologies and protocols such as HTTP, XML, SOAP,

and UDDI. They allow you to encapsulate code, publish interfaces, discover services, and communicate between the publisher and consumer of services, in much the same way as COM+ does, only using vendor-independent, standards-based technologies. True interoperability between disparate systems is a reality, thanks to .NET.

What's Wrong with COM?

So, what's wrong with COM? Nothing really . . . the Component Object Model is great for what it was designed for; providing an interface-based model of information communication between components *on a single machine*. In order to communicate between machines, the *Distributed Component Object Model*, or DCOM was created. DCOM added authentication in order to operate within the remote machines' security context via a Remote Procedure Call. Even so, the process of encapsulating and transporting parameters between the remote components (called marshalling) was very resource-intensive. If that wasn't enough, COM and DCOM were only supported on Windows-based systems, so all of the legacy corporate data on disparate systems had to be accessed indirectly through intermediate gateways such as SNA server (when it was available). COM added the attributes and benefits of Microsoft Transaction Server and gave birth to COM+.

So, is COM+ dead? *No!* Microsoft has put a tremendous amount of effort into COM+ interoperability within .NET. COM+ components appear as .NET assemblies through the wrappers that have been developed. So the question really isn't "What's wrong with COM?" as much as "What are the problems with getting information from anywhere to anywhere using current technology?"

The Internet isn't just a fad. Sure, the dot-com bubble has for the most part burst, but that doesn't mean that the Internet isn't a great medium for sharing information. There just has to be a valid and solid business reason for using it. As a Visual Basic Developer, you can extend the skills you've honed to utilize .NET in your solutions and applications. This and the remaining chapters will give you a solid understanding of developing Web applications while building on the knowledge you've gained as a Visual Basic developer. That said—let's go ahead and dig deeper. On to Chapter 1!

About the Authors

John Alexander is the Marketing Technologist for G.A. Sullivan. His broad project experience includes building solutions in several industries on platforms ranging from the mainframe to the Internet. A Microsoft Certified Solution Developer and Trainer with 19 certifications, John has also written Microsoft Official Curriculum (some of the earliest on Active Server Pages) and consults and teaches at sites from Seattle to Moscow. Highly experienced in software estimation, requirements gathering and definition, creating project plans, defining deliverables, and working on all phases of the software development life cycle, John prides himself on achieving solutions that exceed the client's expectations.

A featured speaker at conferences such as VB Connections, Web Tech-Ed 98, Developer Days, and VBITS, John has been nominated and chosen by Microsoft for the fourth straight year as a Microsoft Developer Network Regional Director. He is currently serving on the Microsoft virtual .NET Subject Matter Expert Team for DevDays 2001, has consulted as a technical adviser on *.NET e-Business Architecture* by G.A. Sullivan, published by SAMS, and has recently finished a speaking tour on .NET technologies. He is currently advising a major client on their first .NET project.

G. A. Sullivan is a global e-Business solution company. Since 1982, G. A. Sullivan professionals have consistently delivered complex enterprise solutions and provided strategic consulting to specific vertical industries. The company's focus is to drive maximum business results from technology investments.

G. A. Sullivan is a leader in implementing technology and providing business value using Microsoft's .NET platform. As one of Microsoft's leading development partners worldwide, G. A. Sullivan has proven experience as documented in numerous case studies. G. A. Sullivan's expertise is validated in their most recent technical book titled *.NET e-Business Architecture*, which documents best practices learned building an enterprise-class application utilizing the Microsoft .NET platform. Details are available at www.gasTIX.net.

G. A. Sullivan was among the first companies in the world to become a Microsoft Gold Certified Partner for E-Commerce Solutions. With 300 professionals across six U.S. and two European locations, G. A. Sullivan consistently ranks as one of the fastest growing technology companies in the United States. Learn more about G. A. Sullivan by visiting www.gasullivan.com.

Billy Hollis has been developing software for over twenty years. He has written for many technical publications, and is a frequent speaker at conferences, including Comdex, Microsoft's Professional Developers Conference (PDC), and the Visual Basic Insiders Technical Summit (VBITS). Billy is co-author of the first book ever published on Visual Basic .NET, *VB.NET Programming on the Public Beta*, and sole author of the book *Visual Basic 6:Design, Specification, and Objects*.

Billy is MSDN Regional Director of Developer Relations in Nashville, Tennessee for Microsoft, and was named Regional Director of the year for 2001. He is currently heavily involved in training, consultation, and software development on the Microsoft.NET platform

Cole Francis is a Senior Consultant for G.A. Sullivan in Kansas City, MO. He plays many roles as a consultant, including Business Analyst, Software Developer, and Quality Assurance. Cole is a Microsoft MCP, delivers occasional presentations for G.A. Sullivan, and has recently taken part in a Microsoft Case Study.

Cole would like to thank his wife, Tami, and his daughter, Kyrstin, for their ongoing dedication and support. Cole would also like to thank John Alexander for the opportunity to be a part of this book.

Brian Wendt is a consultant in Nashville, Tennessee. He has been working in the IT industry since 1983, previously in UNIX environments, and has spent the last ten years working with Microsoft technologies. He holds several Microsoft certifications including MCSD, MCDBA, and MCSE+Internet. In addition to .NET, his skills include C, C++, Microsoft SQL Server, ASP, Visual Basic, and JavaScript.

Getting Your Feet Wet with .NET

It is a very sad thing that nowadays there is so little useless information.
Oscar Wilde

Good ol' Oscar was right on the money in articulating the business challenge we are currently facing. We have tons of information sitting in many different sources, on as many platforms, without a universal mechanism to connect it all together. There has to be a standards-based set of open communication, regardless of the source, data, or destination. Enter .NET.

Many have heard of the .NET vision that has been put forth by Microsoft, but most don't fully grasp its significance. In a nutshell, .NET is Microsoft's vision for seamless communication that combines hardware, software, and philosophy. It is based on Extensible Markup Language (XML) Web services. What does this mean to you as a developer? In this chapter, we'll take a look at where .NET came from and the tools and technologies that are part of this vision.

This chapter focuses on understanding .NET, which will give you a big picture perspective; it expands on the background material in the Introduction (most of you skipped right to Chapter 1, so you should go back and read it sometime). It's helpful to understand .NET before you can use it effectively, hence the bit about getting your feet wet. We'll walk through the pieces and parts of the vision and the technologies used to make it a reality, round it out with a quick romp through ASP.NET, and try it out in a starting exercise before moving into Visual Basic .NET.

Core Components of .NET

The Microsoft .NET vision is realized through five separate pieces:

- Windows and the .NET Enterprise Servers
- .NET Framework
- Developer Tools
- .NET Foundation Services
- .NET User Experience

Figure 1.1 shows the relationship between the different components that comprise .NET and how they relate to current technology. As you can see in the figure, there are several parts missing from the current Microsoft technology (Windows DNA 2000) that would make our lives a lot easier, namely, Internet interoperability. Windows DNA 2000 hasn't gone anywhere. It's just been enhanced tremendously with Microsoft .NET. Notice that from the second to the third generation, the only piece that isn't enhanced is COM+. That's because we need to have smooth interoperability between COM+ objects and .NET. The other thing to be aware of is that both generations of applications still use the strong foundation of Windows. Let's take each part of the Microsoft .NET platform and explore it in the following sections.

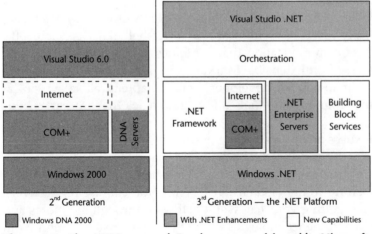

Figure 1.1 The .NET Framework Roadmap, as envisioned by Microsoft.

Windows and the .NET Enterprise Servers

In the .NET vision, the Windows operating system and the .NET Enterprise Servers provide the plumbing to make the end-to-end communication possible. Although none of the .NET Enterprise Servers support the .NET services directly at this time (mainly because they've yet to be released), several do support native XML, making it possible to create Web services in the Windows DNA 2000 world.

Windows 2000, Windows XP, and the forthcoming Windows .NET servers are the foundation on which the .NET vision becomes reality. Microsoft Windows native services allow the .NET Enterprise Servers to function as a common infrastructure for high-performance applications.

As a developer, you may be thinking, "Why should I care about servers?" These products allow you to extend your application development capabilities and help overcome challenges, things like communicating with legacy systems, hosting Web sites, translating disparate documents from outside your organization, load balancing your application for high availability, or communication with any other data store. As you read the following brief highlights of the .NET Enterprise Servers, see if you can apply them to your organization's challenges.

The .Net Enterprise Servers provide the complete application platform that allows Web services to function. Currently, the individual members comprising the Microsoft .NET Enterprise Servers are as follows:

- Application Center
- BizTalk Server 2000
- Commerce Server 2000
- Content Information Server
- Exchange Server 2000
- Host Integration Server 2000
- Internet Security and Acceleration Server 2000
- Mobile Information Server
- Sharepoint Portal Server 2000
- SQL Server 2000

Let's examine each of the servers briefly to see what each brings to the table. We'll go in alphabetical order so as not to offend any.

NOTE You might be wondering why the .NET rollout began without a Windows .NET server. It's simple. Although the initial .NET Framework rollout does affect the operating system by adding components to it, namely, the common language runtime, with the Windows Component Update that's included with Visual Studio .NET, both Windows 2000 and Windows XP incorporate parts of the .NET philosophy and foundation, with expanded support for underpinning technologies, such as XML.

Application Center

For Web sites that are built on Microsoft Windows 2000 and Microsoft Internet Information Services 5.0, Application Center provides management and deployment tools that assist with scalability and reliability. It's crucially important for mission-critical applications to have high availability, ensuring failover in case of hardware failure. Another factor is the ability for COM+ components to handle increasing workloads without failure. If those components were to fail, it would adversely affect performance and functionality, possibly even causing the Web site to crash.

For a developer, the Microsoft Application Center server makes the job of deploying and maintaining high-availability applications much, much easier. You can let the server handle the plumbing tasks of load balancing and focus on the application itself. One thing to keep in mind: If it isn't used properly, Application Center load balancing will negatively affect *throughput* (how much work gets done by the Web server) and *response time* (the amount of time to return user feedback) on Web sites where it is a high priority. By its very nature, component load balancing makes calls across the network, because the components involved are probably on different servers, and this in itself will affect throughput and response time. Weighing this with the benefits listed previously is an important factor in the architecture of a Web site.

BizTalk Server 2000

Microsoft BizTalk Server 2000 translates data between applications and organizations. It facilitates business-to-business communications and automates business processes. Microsoft BizTalk Server also provides services that can satisfy very stringent audit and tracking requirements and filtering and logging capabilities.

Microsoft BizTalk Server can parse documents in the following file formats right out of the box:

- XML

- Flat files (delimited or positional)

- EDI (ANSI X12 or UN/EDIFACT). X12 EDI, or Electronic Data Interchange, is currently the de facto standard for business-to-business electronic data exchange. It is governed by the American National Standards Institute (ANSI). The international counterpart to this is EDIFACT, which is governed by the United Nations.

Additional formats can be built using the parser SDK that is included with Microsoft BizTalk Server Enterprise Edition.

Microsoft BizTalk Server 2000 unites enterprise application integration and business-to-business integration through both its messaging and its orchestration pieces. It's been designed and built to utilize standards-based protocols such as Simple Object Access Protocol (SOAP) and XML to accomplish this. Another interesting feature of BizTalk Server 2000 is its ability to handle transactions that can span weeks or months, as opposed to just minutes or hours. It does this by dehydrating the transaction after a certain period of time—completely storing the transaction state in the database. Upon receipt of the other portion of the transaction, the state is retrieved from the database and rehydrated, regardless of the time needed to complete the transaction.

Of the .NET Enterprise Servers, Microsoft BizTalk Server 2000 allows disparate data sources to link together more seamlessly and easily than ever before. As a developer, you can take advantage of this on both external applications that connect businesses and internal applications.

Commerce Server 2000

Commerce Server 2000 enables scalable, maintainable, and available e-commerce sites by providing built-in ready-to-use resources for business-to-consumer and business-to-business Web application development. Commerce Server 2000 works with two complete solution sites that can easily be downloaded from the Microsoft Commerce Server site, which is currently at www.microsoft.com/commerceserver/downloads/solutionsites.asp. One solution site is for retail applications (B2C), and the other site is a starter for supplier applications (B2B). These sites actually have quite a bit of functionality and were specifically designed as a starting point. In addition, the sample Commerce Server 2000 site shows multilingual and multicurrency support. Best of all, it's a chocolate store. Download it currently from microsoft.com/downloads/release.asp?ReleaseID=31147. Resources such as these enable you to design, develop, and deploy an e-commerce solution quickly.

In addition to standing alone, Commerce Server 2000 is designed to operate with other .NET Enterprise Servers to extend its functionality. For example, you could use the document transfer capabilities of Microsoft Biztalk Server 2000 to exchange catalogs between trading partners in a B2B scenario or use Microsoft Host Integration Server 2000 to access product or inventory data on a legacy system.

I hope you can see from this short overview the power that developers have with not just Commerce Server, but also with the synergy of combining the strengths and features of the .NET Enterprise Servers into solutions that focus on solving the business problems of users and clients.

Exchange Server 2000

Microsoft Exchange Server 2000 is the developer's platform infrastructure for messaging and collaboration solutions. It is seamlessly integrated with Windows 2000 and introduces several new features for application developers. Some of the solutions you can leverage right out of the box with Microsoft Exchange Server 2000 are:

Messaging.   Using collaboration data objects, you can integrate applications with message stores and clients such as Microsoft Outlook. Developers can also link applications with Instant Messenger.

Calendar Applications.   Building custom calendar applications for the enterprise allows item saved at a personal level to be added to the enterprisewide calendar and categorized in meaningful ways.

Workflow or Real-Time Collaboration.   Collaboration solutions using Microsoft Project and Project Central allow for efficient scheduling of resources. Organizations can also manage workflow and have greater process control.

In addition to the solution development resources, Microsoft Exchange 2000 also has the Web Storage System, which can be accessed from several different development environments, including Office 2000/XP, Explorer, Web Browser, and Messaging Clients. The advantage of this data store as it relates to application development is its ability to handle semistructured data that is crucial when building knowledge management-type of solutions. This—along with the fact that Exchange 2000 enables URL addressing for resources, collaboration data objects support in ASP pages, and the ability to access ASP pages out of the Web store—makes it a very strong tool for developing messaging solutions of all kinds.

Host Integration Server 2000

Host Integration Server 2000, which is used for legacy host system integration, supplies secure access to host-based data and data translation between applications. This server allows a developer to choose the right technology for a given task, whether for simpler gateway integration or more complex programmatic access to applications, transactions, and legacy data stores, such as DB2. In addition, it also has the ability to do two-phase commit transactions between the mainframe and the windows environments.

Host Integration Server 2000 relies on technology being available on the host, so the majority of the time you won't have to deal with costly host application rewrites. Through the Open Transaction Manager Architecture (OTMA) server, existing legacy IMS implicit message queue-based transaction programs can use TCP/IP connectivity without being recompiled or redesigned.

Once the incoming information is transformed, BizTalk Server 2000 can use the Host Integration Server 2000 (HIS 2000) for either synchronous or (COM+)-based integration or asynchronous (Message Oriented Middleware, or MOM)-based integration through the MSMQ to MQSeries Bridge, allowing asynchronous document exchange.

Internet Security and Acceleration Server 2000

Internet Security and Acceleration Server (ISA) is a multilayered enterprise firewall and Web cache server built to provide policy-based access control, acceleration, and management of internetworking. The enterprise firewall capabilities of ISA help to protect network resources from threats such as external hackers, unauthorized access, and virus attacks. The Web cache facilitates an organization's ability to conserve network bandwidth and permits faster Web access by serving frequently used objects locally instead of externally.

As an Enterprise firewall, ISA provides Multilayered Firewall Protection in the following three ways:

Packet filtering determines which packets will be allowed to pass through to the secured proxy services.

Circuit filtering provides application-transparent circuit gateways for multiplatform access to several Internet services.

Application filtering allows ISA to interpret application protocol commands (e.g., HTTP, FTP, and Gopher) from client PCs. ISA Server also conceals the network topology and IP addresses from the outside network.

In addition to the multilayered firewall protection, Internet Security and Acceleration Server employs *Smart Application Filters,* which can accept, reject, redirect, and modify traffic through intelligent filtering of HTTP, FTP, SMTP email, H.323 conferencing, streaming media, and RPC content. ISA also makes use of rules-based *Server Publishing* to protect Web servers, email servers, and Web applications from external attacks.

As a Web cache server, ISA Server can be used as a forward cache, a reverse cache, or content distribution vehicle that uses fast RAM caching and efficient disk operations.

Developers can extend Internet Security and Acceleration Server through a collection of APIs and an SDK that can be used to develop additional Web and application filters, MMC snap-ins, reporting tools, scriptable commands, alert management, and more.

SQL Server 2000

Microsoft SQL Server 2000 includes significant enhancements that support the plumbing for .NET solutions and is an extremely powerful platform that developers can use not only as a data store but also to perform advanced data analysis. SQL Server 2000 builds on the advances introduced in SQL Server 7.0 and introduces inbound and outbound native support for XML. This is ideal for developing Web applications with dynamic data or business-to-business data processing, both situations that require the use of a platform-independent data transport mechanism.

Although there have been many enhancements to SQL Server in the current version, we will primarily focus on the ones that deal with XML because of the underlying support for Microsoft .NET.

T-SQL, or Transact-SQL, is the dialect of Structured Query Language used by Microsoft SQL Server. The FOR XML T-SQL language extension allows a SELECT statement to return the result set as XML. This is accomplished through the FOR XML clause, which retrieves XML data from the database engine. The FOR XML clause has three modes:

Raw.   The Raw mode returns one <row> element per row in the result set and has no support for nested elements. In the Raw mode columns and values returned in the result set are mapped to attributes and values on the <row>. The structure of the mode is very similar to comma-separated values (CSVs) but is in an XML format.

Auto.   In Auto mode, the Table/View name in database is used for the element name in the result set. You can choose between element attributes or subelements for the columns, with the names of the columns corresponding to the attribute or subelement names. Use the Elements to return subelements instead of attributes, which are the default. Auto mode supports nested XML output, which is determined by the ordering of the columns in your Select clause. Although sibling relationships are not supported in Auto mode, table and column aliases are.

Explicit. The Explicit mode provides complete control over the formatting of XML results. In this mode, columns can be individually mapped to either attributes or subelements and have complete support of nesting at any level. As would be expected with this level of control, sibling relationships and CDATA sections in XML output are fully supported.

XML views of SQL Server 2000 databases may be defined by using XML-Data Reduced (XDR) schemas to map the associated tables, views, and columns. The XML views can then be referenced in XPath queries, which are retrieved as XML documents directly from the database. In addition, you can expose XML document data as a relational resultset using the new OPENXML rowset function.

Now that we've examined the member .NET Enterprise Servers, let's go up a notch and learn about the .NET Framework and the developer tools that target it.

Sharepoint Portal Server 2000

Sharepoint Portal Server is an enterprise collaboration portal system. Documents can be categorized and stored internally within Sharepoint, and can also be accessed externally from whatever data store they reside in. For developers, Sharepoint adds collaboration functionality that allows for enterprise data access and indexing and can be customized based on the user's information needs with a dashboard-based portal.

Mobile Information Server

Mobile Information Server is just about that—serving up and extending information from .NET enterprise applications down to mobile devices from many vendors and wireless carriers. For the developer, this means you can extend your intranet or network to use a multitude of existing devices easily and seamlessly. From Outlook Mobile Access to your own custom applications, you can also use your existing skill sets and tools to create information solutions that are available anytime, anywhere.

Content Management Server

Content Management Server solves an (Internet) age-old problem—empowering the people who create the content to publish it to their page or site easily, without needing a tremendous amount of technical skill. This server also allows for dynamic content delivery based on the group accessing the site, and for sufficiently faster time to market for scalable Internet solutions.

.NET Framework

The .NET Framework is an environment for designing, developing, deploying, and running XML Web services, Web applications, NT services, and Windows applications, among others. The .NET Framework is separated into two parts: the *common language runtime* and the *class libraries*.

Let's explore the .NET Framework in a bit more detail before moving on. Figure 1.2 illustrates the major portions of the .NET Framework.

Common Language Runtime

You may or may not be aware of this, but runtimes have been around for quite a while. Some runtimes were interpreter based (Visual Basic, JAVA) and some were truly compiler based (C++, for example). In addition, the capabilities of runtimes varied greatly between languages, depending on their architecture. For example, some languages, such as SmallTalk, were totally object based, whereas others, such as COBOL, ignored them completely until relatively recently. Another challenge was the lack of portability between the languages. You couldn't take source code written in one language and run it through another's runtime.

The *common language runtime* has been specifically designed to address not only the preceding problems, but also quite a few more. It enables reliable applications by eliminating memory leaks. The concept of write-once, run-anywhere has been one of the most sought after treasures in application development. It's been tried before in different ways, but previous approaches always missed the mark. The common language runtime, on the other hand, advances us further down the road by providing a multilanguage execution environment that allows developers to build many different types of applications, from Web services to Windows applications to mobile applications and

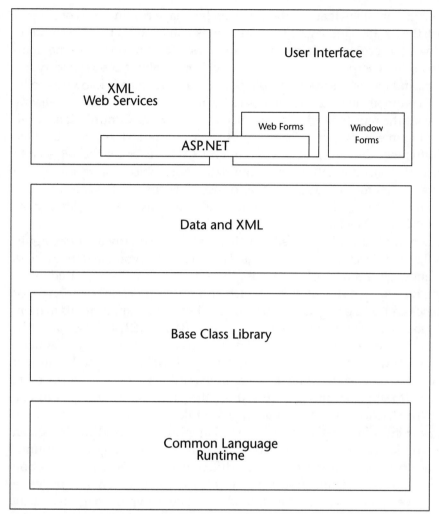

Figure 1.2   High-level parts of the .NET Framework.

everything in between. We can now create components and integrate them fully with Web services (and each other) without regard for programming languages. As we've heard before, we truly are now entering a state in which the language becomes a lifestyle choice.

Language compilers that use the common language runtime are considered *managed*; that is, the language's functionality is managed by the .NET Framework. In order for the runtime to provide services and resources to the managed code, the compiler must provide information about the related types, members, and references upon compilation. Data about data is known as *metadata*. The common language runtime uses the metadata in much the same way COM+ uses the registry and services such as the Service Control Manager to manage lifetime, locate and load classes, and set context boundaries. One major difference, however, is that although COM+ relies on the registry to store registration information and state data, .NET objects store this in the metadata, which resides locally to that object. This enables the common language runtime to manage object references automatically as well, releasing the object at the end of its lifetime.

Another advantage of managed code is the ability to tightly integrate applications that use objects across languages. This means that you can define a class in one language and derive a new class from it *in another language*, due to the common type system shared by all, which also makes possible cross-language inheritance and debugging. Currently, you can build .NET applications in more than 20 managed languages, including Visual Basic .NET, C#, Jscript .NET, Managed C++, and even COBOL. We'll delve further into this in just a moment.

Okay, so how does this work (in 60 words or less)? First, you design and write your source code, which is compiled into Microsoft Intermediate Language (MSIL) and then processed in the common language runtime through the class loader. Just-in-time (JIT) compilers compile the intermediary language (MSIL) into native code, which is highly optimized for the given platform or device and then executed through the common language runtime.

Having this common substrate that different languages can build upon offers tremendous advantages, such as inheritance between languages, a shared development environment, and consistent types that are easily mapped. If we break the common language runtime into functional areas, the groupings logically fall into what you see in Figure 1.3.

The common language runtime is Microsoft's implementation of the Common Language Infrastructure (CLI) specification released to ECMA. As such, the common language runtime represents a powerful platform for developing applications of all kinds. The CLI consists of the common intermediate language and the common type system.

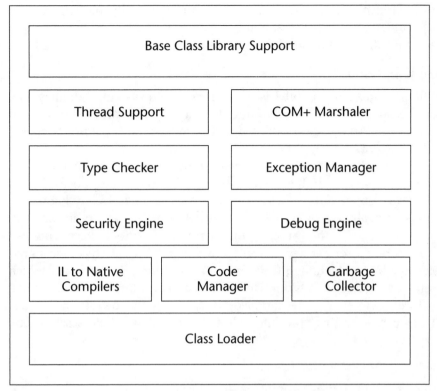

Figure 1.3 The .NET common language runtime diagram.

Common Intermediate Language

The common intermediate language specification is what powers the common language runtime. Microsoft's version is the Microsoft Intermediate Language, which all the .NET higher-level languages are compiled into in order to run on the common language runtime.

It may surprise you that Microsoft has submitted the core of the .NET Framework, the Common Language Infrastructure, to the European Computer Manufacturer's Association (the international standards body that also governs JavaScript) for standardization. Microsoft is fully participating in ECMA's standardization process, which means that ECMA and *not* Microsoft is key in controlling and maintaining the standard.

Common Type System

One of the key strengths of .NET is the common type system. It defines how types are declared and used by the runtime. The system is also the traffic cop in that it sets the rules that all the languages must follow within its object-oriented framework.

A great place to begin the discussion about types for those of us in the Visual Basic world is to start with the two major categories that are supported by the common type system: value types and reference types. We already know that you pass parameters either by reference or by value, so let's build on that. *Value types* are stored as the value, or contents, at the location. These types can either be inherent, user defined, or as enumerations. *Reference types* are stored as a reference to the location of the value. They can be self-describing, which can be either arrays or class types. These types derive from a single base type, *System.Object.* Reference types can also either be pointer or interface types. Class types can be further split into delegates, user-defined classes, and box value types:

Classes.   Template for the object

Interfaces.   Information to and from the object

Value types.   Categories of stored information

Delegates.   Representatives of the object (similar to function pointers)

Class Libraries

The class libraries are responsible for programmatic access to all available resources within .NET and include ASP.NET, Enterprise Services, ADO.NET, and Windows Forms. This is all well and good until you want to develop an application that uses the class libraries and runs in the common language runtime. For that, you need an environment to leverage this power, and Visual Studio .NET does just that.

For Web development, the class libraries can functionally be broken into three major areas:

Web services.   Responsible for all aspects of Web service communication and functionality.

User interface.   Responsible for communicating information to and from the user.

Data and XML.   Responsible for data communication and functionality.

As you can see in Figure 1.2, the class libraries sit on top of the Base Class Library (BCL), which sits on top of the common language runtime.

The BCL is really the heart of the .NET Framework. It provides the consistent base types that are used across all .NET-enabled languages. The classes are accessed by *namespaces*, which reside within *assemblies*. The unified class structure provides uniform access to the functionality exposed by the .NET platform, removing the requirement to master diverse technologies when writing applications. Mapping of data types enables the managed programming languages to be tightly and seamlessly integrated with the .NET Framework.

A namespace is a grouping of like objects. *Namespaces* make up the .NET Framework class library. They provide organization for all the resources available in the framework. They also provide scope, so you can have multiple classes within your application provided that each class resides in its own namespace and that it is properly qualified with the corresponding namespace. You can think of namespaces as giving similar functionality to that of aliases in SQL. The namespace name is actually part of the fully qualified type name and has the following syntax: namespace.typename. The two namespaces that Microsoft reserves are System and Microsoft. The System namespace contains thousands of subordinate objects. It holds the functionality of the Microsoft .NET Framework. The Microsoft namespace is used by product groups within Microsoft that target projects and applications that target the common language runtime.

The following code sample illustrates how namespaces are used within .NET:

```
Imports System.Web.Services
Imports System.Diagnostics
```

The *imports* keyword is used to access a namespace, which means that we don't have to qualify them when using types. This allows us to use the functionality contained in the assembly without having to load the source into the project. This is our class definition:

```
Public Class Service1
Inherits System.Web.Services.WebService
<webmethod()> Public Function TakeOrder(ByVal Order as String) as
Boolean
```

Notice in the following that Eventlog.writeentry has no namespace in front of it. If we hadn't imported the System.Diagnostic, we would have to use System.Diagnostics.EventLog.WriteEntry instead.

```
EventLog.WriteEntry ("OrdersReceived", "Order Received: " & Order)
Return True

End Function
```

Namespaces reside within assemblies. An *assembly* is a collection of one or more modules (classes, data sets, etc.) and is also referred to as a managed DLL, so there is a direct analogy between the two, so much so that the file extension is still .dll. One major difference to keep in mind, however, is that win32 and COM+ DLLs are compiled as native code, whereas .NET DLLs are managed and executed by the common language runtime.

You can define your own namespaces and create and compile your own assemblies as well. Each assembly has a *manifest*, which contains the information that describes the contents of the assembly, much like a project file does in earlier versions of Visual Basic. The manifest also describes the version, scope, and security information through its metadata. We've already talked about metadata, so let's apply it here. Assemblies emit metadata for versioning and to load and locate class types, expose interfaces, and resolve references and method invocations, to name a few. By containing all this information locally, there's no longer any need to rely on the registry to supply and store it. You add assemblies to your project by referencing them.

Assemblies can either be single or multifile and can be deployed by simply copying to a directory using the XCOPY console command, or by the more traditional deployment methods.

Developer Tools

Visual Studio .NET has been completely rebuilt from the ground up to take advantage of the .NET Framework and the common language runtime. Not only does it use a common foundation of resources, but it also allows for a multilanguage development environment. As you'll see later in this book, the ease in which applications are seamlessly deployed is a tremendous improvement.

One of Visual Studio .NET's main functions is to develop and also reuse XML Web services. XML Web services allow you to expose an application's functionality through the use of standard protocols such as the SOAP and XML. We'll focus on this in detail in Chapter 7.

We now have tools that use the power of the Microsoft .NET Framework, but we aren't limited to a single language. Thanks to the common language runtime, organizations can take advantage of the benefits provided, while still leveraging their language investments. Some of the languages are (in addition to Visual Basic .NET, C#, Jscript.NET, and J#) Perl, COBOL, Python, ADA, and many others. For this discussion, however, we are going to focus on the languages that have been created and supported by Microsoft, starting with Visual Basic .NET.

NOTE **A good thing about .NET is that all languages under the umbrella are first-class players. This may seem like a very brief overview, but I want to stay focused on Visual Basic .NET and ASP.NET.**

Visual Basic .NET. Visual Basic developers can now rapidly develop applications for the Web and smart devices, just like they've always been able to do for Microsoft Windows. This is in no small thanks to the reengineering of Windows Forms and the addition of Mobile Web Forms, and the Smart Device Extensions Toolkit. Like the other member languages within .NET, Visual Basic .NET can seamlessly interoperate within the Visual Studio .NET multilanguage environment.

Microsoft Visual Basic .NET has also been totally rearchitected and rebuilt to use the Microsoft .NET Framework. You wanted objects, and you've got them. *Everything* is now an object. As a result, developers using Visual Basic .NET now have direct access to the rich set of unified libraries that provides access to everything under the sun.

We'll see exactly how Visual Basic has changed as we explore the new language features in Chapter 2 and then expand on this in Chapter 3 by examining the new object-oriented features.

C#. C# is an entirely new programming language built especially to leverage the .NET Framework. In fact, you could say it's the first .NET-only language. It's been designed specifically to augment the strengths of Visual Basic and JAVA and eliminate the weaknesses of other languages like Visual C++. It also borrows heavily from Visual Basic's Rapid Application Development environment. Microsoft is using C# extensively both internally and in the creation of its products.

Jscript .NET. Jscript .NET is the .NET-enabled version of the popular scripting language and is undoubtedly the most dramatic change in functionality since it's introduction in 1996. One nice thing that the development team strove for was that any enhancements to Jscript would work within the existing language requirements. Now Jscript is a truly compiled language. Everything's an object now, and classes and packages have now been added. With the classes comes inheritance, and because Jscript .NET is a full member of .NET, classes from other languages can be inherited as well.

Managed C++.   Under .NET, C++ comes in two flavors: managed and unmanaged. Managed C++ uses the .NET Framework and the common language runtime for execution. Unmanaged C++, in this brave new world, targets the Visual C++ compiler and, as such, is totally compatible with previous versions.

.NET Foundation Services

.NET Foundation Services are designed to provide the plumbing for applications needing authentication and notification services of all shapes and sizes. In other words, they are consumer-focused Web services. Microsoft .NET My Services is the first set of user-centric Web services that Microsoft is building. These services allow users to have access to their data regardless of device, platform, or application. .NET My Services, which will centralize all your information in a single place, are being described as the passport to the future. It's really all about giving you control over your information when, where, and how you see fit.

Security is paramount to .NET My Services because it creates a virtual identity for you through the Passport authentication service. Notice that the identity is the key concept in .NET My Services, as shown in Figure 1.4. Everything else hangs from it.

The initial set of .NET My Services will include:

.NET Presence.   Contains the information about where users are to receive their alerts and is very similar to user status in Messenger.

.NET Location.   Contains the user's physical location. Location examples include At Home or At Work to enhance the Presence service by providing additional information.

.NET Services.   Lists and coordinates the services to which a user has subscribed.

.NET Notifications.   Sends a notification about an important event to a subscription on any device, any time, anywhere. Users specify .NET Presence settings (such as a cell phone if offline) to make themselves available to these notifications, if they opt to.

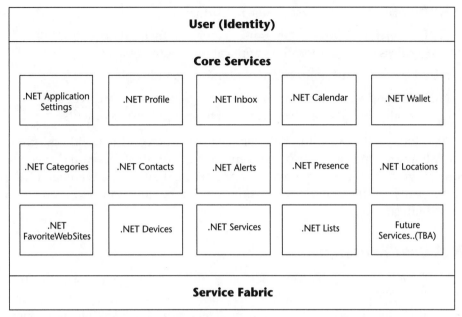

Figure 1.4 .NET My Services and service fabric.

.NET Calendar.   Stores the user's calendar information centrally so that work, family, and personal information can be accessed by users and those they choose to share it with. The access can range from full to limited (such as meeting information) to simply free/busy data.

.NET Contacts.   Lets users store their contact information and share it with those they choose.

.NET Inbox.   Gives users access to their email on any computer or device upon a successful sign in to .NET My Services.

.NET Documents.   Provides users with secure storage for their documents and enables virtual file access upon a successful sign in to .NET - My Services.

.NET Wallet.   Enables the user to store payment account and shipping information used for online purchasing.

.NET ApplicationSettings.   Stores user application settings so that any device automatically adjusts to what is stored upon user sign in.

.NET Profile.   Stores personal user information.

.NET FavoriteWebSites.   Gives users access to their favorite Web links regardless of device, location, application, or other software client.

.NET Lists.   Lets users store any kind of relevant list.

.NET Categories.   A standardized list of categories that are available across all .NET My Services and used to group data documents.

Even though these are the first services that Microsoft is building, others will follow and open a whole new revenue stream for the Web. As a developer, you can get into the act by creating applications that take advantage of the functionality in these services or using them in conjunction with your own home-built services.

.Net User Experience

We've talked about the servers, the tools, and the building block services that Microsoft .NET provides. That is all well and good, but without devices and clients that can take advantage of the applications and services we developers create, the whole vision would seem to be in vain. The devices run clients, which in turn provide user experiences.

Smart Devices

Smart devices are just that: They're smart, smart about the way information is presented and gathered. Examples of these devices include desktop, laptop, and workstation PCs; and cell phones, handhelds, tablet PCs, and game consoles (as well as the XBOX). Taking advantage of the huge amount of information that can be harnessed through the lower levels of .NET platform, smart devices are smart in the following areas of interaction:

Identity Interaction.   They know your preferences and personal information.

Network Interaction.   They know the infrastructure and servers proving the information.

Information Interaction.   They are intuitive about the information and the context in which it's received.

Device Interaction.   They can recognize and interact with other devices.

Software Interaction.   Similar to the hardware infrastructure interaction, they take advantage of the information provided by software and services, in accordance with user preferences and authentication.

Clients

Smart devices are only one of the endpoints in the .NET platform that harness and leverage the information provided into something that we can effectively use. Let's take a look at another endpoint—clients. You might have always thought of clients as the hardware on this end, namely, your desktop machine. But end users interact with computers through clients, software that translates our actions into what the hardware can understand. Clients run on everything from smart devices like PCs and PDAs to industrial controls and home appliances, hence the need for client software for the .NET platform.

Smart Devices + Clients = User Experiences

The user *experiences* the product of the interaction of the smart devices and the clients. Through seamless interaction, and a user-centric design, the technology now bends to the desires of the user rather than the other way around. For example, if you are traveling on business, your travel agent can update your calendar and send you an alert if your flight is delayed. Coworkers or clients could receive an alert as well and access your calendar to determine when you'll arrive.

So that's the tour of the parts that make up the .NET vision. Now that we've explored it, let's get a quick introduction to ASP.NET, which will be greatly expanded on as we progress through the rest of the book.

Introduction to ASP.NET

Unless you've been living in a cave for the last year or so, you've most likely heard about the next generation of active server pages, ASP.NET. But do you understand the implications of this technology? You've grown up as a developer with a very rich development environment, easy database connectivity, and an integrated debugging tool. Menus, however, left a lot to be desired. Until now, you've most likely avoided ASP development because it is so clumsy, and the tools are much more primitive than what you're used to.

Up until now ASP has been the best and most widely used technology for Web development that we've had to work with. It's just that when you have an architecture that mixes layout (HTML) and logic (scripts), has code that must be interpreted and browser compatibility issues, and doesn't allow you, among other things, to support 24x7 applications, you can get cranky. That's really all changed now that Microsoft Visual Studio .NET brings the RAD environment to Web development.

How does ASP.NET fix the preceding problems? Well, just like you're used to in Visual Basic, ASP.NET allows you to cleanly separate presentation and business logic, thereby simplifying maintenance tasks. By using the services provided by the .NET Framework, you don't have to rely on a grab bag of different technologies. And because your code is compiled the first time a page is requested instead of when it is interpreted, there will be impressive performance gains. Another improvement that ASP.NET brings to the table is state management built right in, which includes Web farm support. Caching is very important in Web applications to increase speed, and now that is very easy to take advantage of at several levels within ASP.NET. Finally, one last important benefit is the ability to update files while the server is running.

As illustrated in Figure 1.5, ASP.NET applications no longer run in the context of IIS; now they use the functionality of the .NET Framework to satisfy the requests of the Web client through the HTTP runtime. Here is the process in a nutshell. The incoming request is processed by the HTTP runtime, which then resolves the requested URL to the corresponding application for processing. Requests pass through a number of HTTP modules, which developers can create to modify the requests on the fly. Request handlers pass a specific URL request to an application.

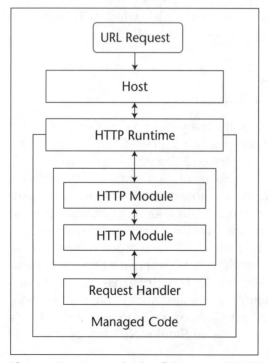

Figure 1.5 Communication flow among ASP.NET components.

The heart of ASP.NET is System.Web. It's actually contained in System.Web.dll. System.Web is responsible for the Web-related tasks in the .NET Framework. As you'll discover in the following chapters, whether they discuss Web forms (Chapter 5), Web controls (Chapter 6), or Web services (Chapter 7), all of this functionality flows from this portion of the .NET Framework. The heart of this functionality is contained in the System.Web namespace, as illustrated in Figure 1.6.

Your First ASP.NET Application

Let's try this out. The sample application that Chapter 10 is based on uses the Northwind sample database included with Microsoft SQL Server 2000. Thus it seems fitting to use it for our first application. We are going to create a Web form with a data grid control on it that shows selected Northwind employee information. We will also data bind the grid to an ADO.NET data set. Notice how similar building Web applications in Visual Basic .NET is to what you've done in the past with Windows applications:

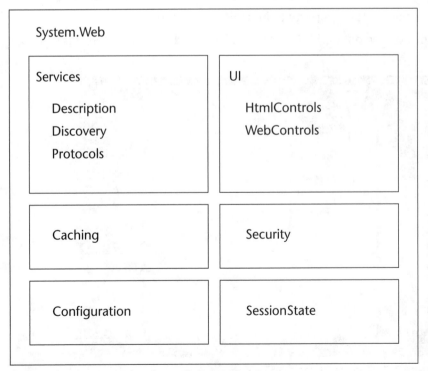

Figure 1.6 System.Web, where all the magic happens.

Open the Web Application Project

1. Open Visual Studio .Net and select an ASP.NET Web application.

2. Name it EmployeesVB.

3. Notice that the Web form looks very similar to Visual Basic forms, as shown in Figure 1.7.

4. Double-click on the Web form to access the code window.

5. Place the cursor at the beginning of the Public Class WebForm line. Hit Enter twice to add two lines at the very top.

6. Type the following code:

```
Imports System.Data
Imports System.Data.SqlClient
```

7. Click the WebForm1 tab at the top of the code window to access the Web form.

8. Click on the toolbar and add a label, command button, and data grid, as shown in Figure 1.8.

9. Click on the label. Locate the text property in the Properties box.

10. Change the text property to NorthWind Employees.

11. Click on the data grid. Locate the ID property in the Properties box.

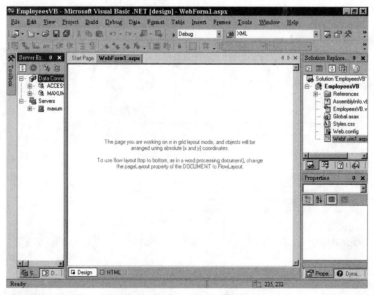

Figure 1.7   The Visual Basic .NET IDE.

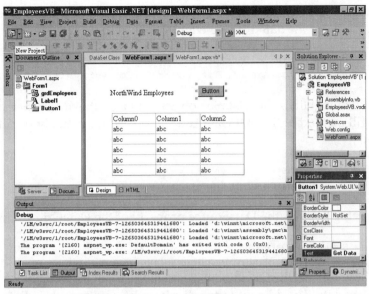

Figure 1.8   Adding controls to the Web form.

12. Change the ID property to grdEmployees.

13. Click on the Command button. Locate the text property in the Properties box.

14. Change the text property to Get Data.

15. Double-click on the Command button to access the Code window.

16. Type the following code in the Button1_Click Event:

```
Dim DS As DataSet
Dim MyConnection As SqlConnection
Dim MyCommand As SqlDataAdapter
MyConnection = New
SqlConnection("server=localhost;uid=sa;pwd=;database=northwind")
MyCommand = New SqlDataAdapter("select firstname as 'First Name',
lastname as 'Last Name', Title from Employees", MyConnection)
DS = New DataSet("Employees")
MyCommand.Fill(DS)
grdEmployees.DataSource = DS
grdEmployees.DataBind()
```

Now let's talk a little about what we've just typed. In the following line, we are creating a database connection object:

```
MyConnection = New
SqlConnection("server=localhost;uid=sa;pwd=;database=northwind")
```

In the following line, the SQLDataAdapter object is using MyConnection and a SQL query for the data that we want:

```
MyCommand = New SqlDataAdapter("select firstname as 'First
Name', lastname as 'Last Name', Title from Employees", MyConnection)
```

In the following line, the DataSet object replaces the RecordSet object. Notice the fill method of the SQLDataAdapter object. It's actually populating the data set:

```
DS = New DataSet("Employees")
MyCommand.Fill(DS)
```

The following line sets the DataSource property of the DataGrid control:

```
grdEmployees.DataSource = DS
```

In the following line, the DataBind method of the DataGrid control loads the data grid with data. The data grid then displays the data as an HTML table:

```
grdEmployees.DataBind()
```

Now, click File and then click Save Employees VB.aspx. Push Cntl-F8 to build and browse. The output should look like Figure 1.9.

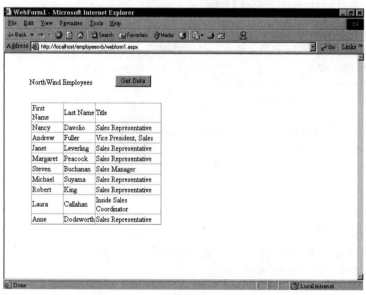

Figure 1.9 ASP.NET page output.

Wrapping Up

This chapter should have given you a better understanding of what .NET is, why we need it, and how it relates to what you've done before. In Chapter 2, you'll learn about the new features and enhancements in Microsoft Visual Basic .NET. And it will continue to just get better from there. We'll explore object-oriented enhancements, Web development, Web applications, controls, and ADO before focusing on configuration and deployment. This is the first step in the journey. After this the path will widen on a trail of progressive revelation about .NET. And, yes, you'll do much more coding very soon. Enjoy.

The Development Environment and Language Changes

If it keeps up, man will atrophy all his limbs but the push-button finger.
Frank Lloyd Wright

Before getting started on the new Web development capabilities in Visual Basic .NET, you need to know about the important differences between it and previous versions of Visual Basic. There are three major areas to cover:

- The new Visual Studio .NET development environment (usually referred to as the IDE, for Integrated Development Environment)

- Syntax changes and additions in the Visual Basic language that are not related to object orientation

- The new object-oriented capabilities of Visual Basic .NET

This chapter will cover the first two of these categories, and the third chapter will get into the object-oriented changes.

The New Development Environment

When you first fire up Visual Studio .NET, you get a new Start Page that has a number of useful new capabilities. If you have just installed Visual Studio .NET, you'll see the My Profile tab, shown in Figure 2.1. It lets you change various things about the layout and usage of the development environment.

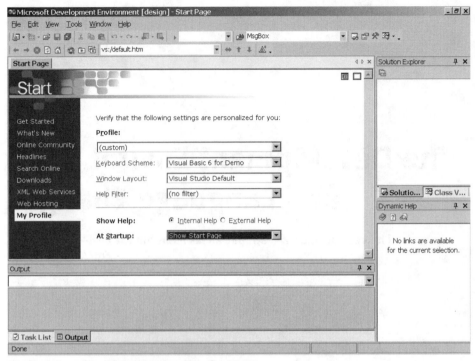

Figure 2.1 MyProfile tab in Visual Studio .NET.

You should select an appropriate profile before continuing. For most VB developers, the easiest path is to select the Visual Basic Developer profile, which configures the environment with layout and behavior that is similar to Visual Basic 6. The position of the windows and the keystrokes used for various purposes will mirror those in VB6, so you'll be able to dive right in and get to work.

Other tabs on the Start Page give access to lists of new features and changes in Visual Studio .NET (taken from the help files) and news about .NET (taken from the Web). There's also a tab that points you to some interesting services, including free trial memberships at sites that can host your Visual Studio .NET Web projects. Using these hosting sites is easy, and if you do not already have a good hosting option, you should try one of them.

On succeeding times that you use Visual Studio .NET, the Start Page will contain a list of recent projects that you've worked on and options to call up an existing project or start a new one. The Start Page is shown in Figure 2.2.

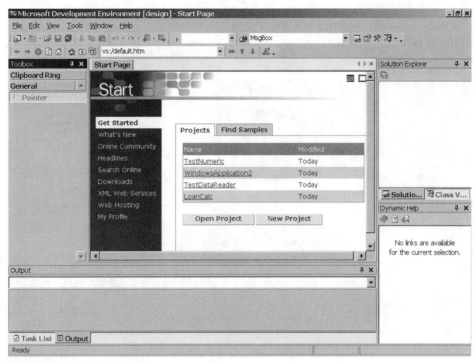

Figure 2.2   The Start Page.

An IDE Nickel Tour

A tour through the Visual Studio .NET IDE is an interesting mixture of familiar elements and new, unfamiliar ones. There's so much new functionality that it can take a while to examine it all. Let's hit the high points first.

The general layout of Visual Studio .NET has one big functional difference from VB6. Instead of using a Multiple Document Interface (MDI) model layout for multiple windows, the Visual Studio .NET environment uses tabs to allow an area to contain multiple windows. (The VB6-style MDI layout is available and can be turned on in Tools, Options. However, the old SDI layout arrangement from VB6 and earlier is not available in Visual Basic .NET.) Figure 2.3 is an example of the IDE with several of the tabbed areas highlighted.

This tabbed design for the various screen areas allows a lot of functionality to be packed into a tight space. For example, the same area (marked with a 1 in the figure) is used for the toolbox and the Server Explorer (both of which will be discussed soon). And the area used for code windows and form design (marked with a 2 in the image) also displays the Start Page and help pages.

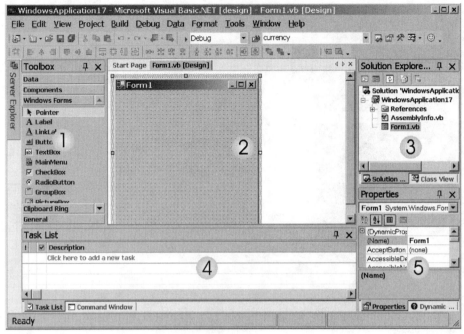

Figure 2.3 The new IDE in Visual Studio .NET.

The area used for form design, code, help files, and so on, is usually called the Designer pane. It is always part of the IDE and is surrounded by windows on the left, right, and bottom.

On the left (area 1 in Figure 2.3) are the toolbox and Server Explorer. On the right (area 3) are the Solution Explorer (the replacement for Visual Basic 6's Project Explorer), a class viewer, and access to help files. At the bottom (area 4) are the Task List, the Output Window, and a variety of debug-related windows that we will discuss later. In the bottom right (area 5) is the area for the Property Window and Dynamic Help.

Managing this many windows can be a challenge, especially because different ones are important at different times in the development process. So the environment includes some capabilities to alter behavior and appearance of all the windows that reside on the edge of the Designer pane. These windows can be pulled out of their default tabbed areas and made free floating, for example. When necessary, they can be dropped back into their original areas, and their tab will be restored. (You may have to practice this dropping operation a bit to get comfortable with it.)

Another behavioral option is to set windows to auto-hide. You do this by clicking on the pushpin icon in the upper right corner of the windows. When such a window is in auto-hide mode (indicated by the pushpin being horizontal), only the tabs for these windows show up at the edge of the screen. When a tab is selected, the associated window slides into view and can be used. When you click somewhere else in the environment, the window slides back to its hidden position. Figure 2.4 shows all the edge windows in auto-hide mode but with the Toolbox pulled out.

The Designer Pane

The place where you'll spend most of your time in the IDE is the Designer pane. This contains code windows for code editing, form design surfaces, and component design surfaces (a new concept in Visual Studio .NET). It also displays help topics.

The Designer pane is tabbed along the top. There is a tab for each currently active window in the pane. If you have a Web form as part of your solution, and you look at the layout of the Web form, there will be a tab for that. If you look at the code behind the Web form, there will be another tab for that. And the IDE starts off with a tab in the Designer pane for the Start Page. Figure 2.5 is a view of a typical Designer pane with several tabs.

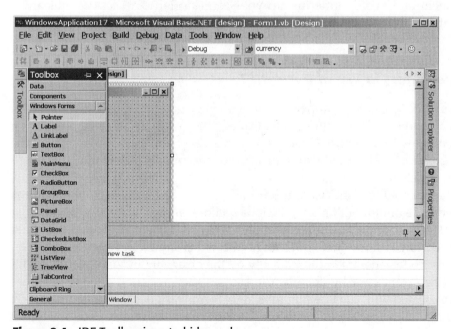

Figure 2.4 IDE Toolbox in auto-hide mode.

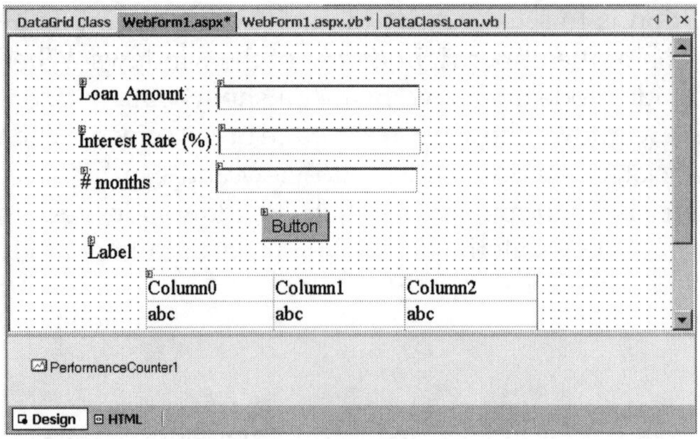

Figure 2.5 The Designer pane with tabs.

The figure shows another interesting aspect to the Designer pane. If you place a control on a form that has no visible manifestation (such as the PerformanceCounter1 control in the screen in the figure), it does not appear directly on the form, as in VB6. Instead, it appears in a part of the Designer pane that is called the component tray and is directly beneath the form's design surface. Quite a number of these controls are available, so it's nice to have a special area for them and avoid cluttering up your form design surface. (We talk more about performance counters in the section on the Server Explorer.)

Code Editors in Visual Basic .NET

Code editing windows appear in the Designer pane, too, and the editors in Visual Studio .NET are quite sophisticated. They are very smart about placing parentheses in appropriate places if you leave them out, for example. The Visual Basic .NET editor also reformats code to proper indentation automatically, which is a big timesaver.

The code editors in Visual Studio .NET have one very nice new feature, called code outlining. It allows various sections of code to be made hidden or visible by clicking some minus and plus signs on the left edge of the screen. A code-editing window with outlining indicated is shown in Figure 2.6.

Most code generated automatically by the designers in Visual Studio .NET is hidden from view by default. You can see such a section of code in Figure 2.6, indicated with the line that says Web Form Designer Generated Code. By default you can hide and show your own individual routines. You can also set your own regions to show and hide with the #Region directive.

```
    Protected WithEvents txtInterestRate As System.Web.UI.WebControl
⊞  Web Form Designer Generated Code

⊞     Private Sub Page_Load(ByVal sender As System.Object, ByVal e As

⊟     Private Sub Button1_Click(ByVal sender As System.Object, ByVal e
           Dim dblLoanAmount As Double
           Dim intMonths As Integer
           Dim dblInterestRate As Double

           dblLoanAmount = CDbl(txtLoanAmount.Text)
           intMonths = CInt(txtNumberOfMonths.Text)
           dblInterestRate = CDbl(txtInterestRate.Text)

           Dim dblPaymentAmount As Double
           Dim dblMonthlyInterestRate As Double = dblInterestRate / 120
           dblPaymentAmount = -Pmt(dblMonthlyInterestRate, intMonths, d
           lblPaymentAMount.Text = CStr(dblPaymentAmount)
```

Figure 2.6   The new code outlining feature in the Code Editor.

Toolbox

The toolbox also acts a lot like the one in VB6. It looks a bit different because the controls in the toolbox are listed in a linear arrangement with the name of the control beside the icon, unlike the icon-only display in VB6. You'll also see a lot more tabs in the toolbox, and organizing your controls in the tabs is more important because you'll be dealing with a lot more controls in Visual Basic .NET, as we'll see later.

Property Window

The Property window in Visual Basic .NET looks and acts a lot like the one in VB6, but you'll find some properties changed. Caption in VB6 becomes Text in Visual Basic .NET, for example. And Height and Width are not top-level properties but instead are found under the Size property. But such differences are very minor.

Dynamic Help

One difference of the Property window is that it shares space on the screen with another window called Dynamic Help. The two views are accessible through tabs at the bottom of the window.

Dynamic Help is a feature of the IDE that continuously monitors what you are doing and tries to guess what help topics you might be interested in. It displays those help topics in a list. If you feel a bit lost at any point in development and are not sure where to go in the help system, you might want to check Dynamic Help for suggestions.

You can turn off Dynamic Help in the IDE options (accessible by choosing Tools, Options). This can help make the IDE's performance a bit snappier on slower machines.

Solution Explorer

The Solution Explorer will look quite familiar to Visual Interdev users, and it is generally similar to the Project Explorer in VB6. The Solution Explorer has to be more flexible than the Project Explorer because a .NET solution can contain more than just the files associated with a single project. A solution can also contain:

- Additional related projects in the Visual Basic .NET language
- Projects or languages in other languages
- Items that are useful for the solution, such as graphic images, HTML files, and XML files
- Configuration files for the solution or for individual projects (we'll see a lot about the Web.config files for Web projects later)
- A list of references to other modules or to other services such as Web services

You'll do a lot of the management of your solutions by right-clicking on something in the Solution Explorer. For example, you can right-click on a Web form and select an option to make it the startup page for a project.

Figure 2.7 shows a Solution Explorer window with a number of different types of items in it.

Figure 2.7 The Solution Explorer window.

The Solution Explorer shares a region of the screen with several other windows. These only come up if you request them. The windows that can appear in the same region as the Solution Explorer include:

- The Class View
- The Resource View
- Index to Help
- The Macro Explorer

We won't discuss all of these because some are self-explanatory, and others are a bit advanced for a nickel tour. But you are encouraged to check out all the windows available in the IDE.

These windows share space on the screen via a tabbed arrangement. The bottom of the region of the screen where the Solution Explorer appears becomes tabbed when more than one window from the preceding list is active. You can then switch among these windows with the tabs.

Class View

One of the windows sharing space with the Solution Explorer is the Class View. This window is basically an object browser for your solution. You can review the components and classes in your solution, and their object interfaces, using the Class View.

Task List

Another feature that will look familiar to Interdev users but will be a welcome addition for VB users is the Task List. This appears by default in a window under the Designer pane. It contains a list of tasks that need to be accomplished. Clicking on a task takes you directly to the location where that task needs to be accomplished.

Where do the tasks come from? Some are generated by the IDE. For example, build errors are listed in the Task List, and clicking on one will take you to the place in the code with the error. You can generate your own tasks by inserting a comment that begins with a certain string of letters (called a token). Some of the tokens that are automatically available when you install Visual Studio .NET include TODO and HACK. For example, if you insert the following comment somewhere in your source code, the Task List will contain that to-do item, as shown in Figure 2.8.

```
'TODO: I've got some work to do here.
```

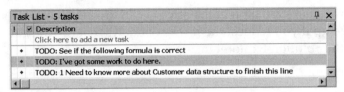

Figure 2.8 To-do item in code on the Task List window.

As with build errors, if you click on a to-do task (or any other task generated by a comment token), you are taken directly to that location in the code.

You can also add new tasks that do not appear in code. The window in the figure shows a place to click to do that. You can set the Task List to show different types of tasks. And you can create your own tokens, such as a DEMO token to show code that was added just for a demo and needs to be removed later. Spend some time playing around with the Task List. It is definitely your friend.

Output Window

Sharing space with the Task List is the Output window. This takes on some of the functions of the Debug window in VB6. You can write text into it during program execution, for example. However, you don't write text into it with Debug.Print. Instead, you use Console.Writeline.

Command Window

Another window sharing space with the Task List is the Command window. This has some of the functions of the Immediate window in VB6. For example, using a command line, you can access most options normally selected on a menu. It is also used, in its Immediate mode, to evaluate expressions and change the value in variables during debugging.

Server Explorer

We've left one of the best new features of the IDE to the end of the tour. The Server Explorer is a new feature that helps you get to a wide variety of server resources, including:

- Databases
- Data connections

- Data structures
- Data in tables and views
- Message queues
- Performance counters
- Event logs
- Windows services

If you are not familiar with message queues, performance counters, event logs, and the like, you should invest some time in learning more about server-based resources. They can be very useful.

The great thing about the Server Explorer is that it exposes most of these items in a way that makes it easy to use them in your code. For example, to use a performance counter, you just select the one you want and drag it onto your design surface. You get a control that encapsulates the interface to that performance counter. You can then change properties on the performance counter and use it in your code. We'll see more about using the items in the Server Explore in Chapter 8.

You can even create new performance counters from the Server Explorer. It simplifies the use of system resources and makes it unnecessary to keep many external tools, such as the SQL Enterprise Manager, continuously loaded. You should definitely spend some time investigating the Server Explorer. It can save you lots of time and frustration.

Other Nice Features of the IDE

We don't want to get bogged down at this point in everything the IDE does (it does a lot), but here are a few more IDE capabilities you may want to explore on your own:

- Macros and the macro development environment
- Toolbars, a couple dozen of them, in fact
- Editors for HTML and XML
- Viewing or changing data that's in an XML file using a grid—without coding a line

And in the chapter on data, we'll look at some of the wizards in the IDE for automatically creating lots of standard data-related code.

Taking It Out for a Spin:
Your Hello, World! Program

Next we're going to create a Hello, World program. This will show off the IDE and illustrate some of the major differences in Visual Basic .NET. Because the focus of this book is Web development, our Hello, World program will be Web based.

You must have an appropriate configuration for Visual Basic .NET to run any Web-based programs. In particular, Visual Studio .NET must be installed appropriately, and Internet Information Server (IIS) must be loaded and running. If you took the default options when installing the operating system and Visual Studio .NET, this configuration should be in place for you.

In this example, we will create a Web Form that has two controls:

- A label that contains some text for us to change

- A button to change the text in the label and submit the page

To see the Hello, World program in action, take the following steps:

1. Start up Visual Studio .NET. You'll see the Start Page. Click the button labeled New Project. (If you are already running Visual Studio .NET, you can start a new project by selecting File, New, Project.) You will see a screen that looks much like Figure 2.9.

2. Make sure the Visual Basic Projects folder on the left is highlighted, and click on the ASP.NET Web application project type on the right. In the Location text box, enter an appropriate name for your project, such as HelloWorld.

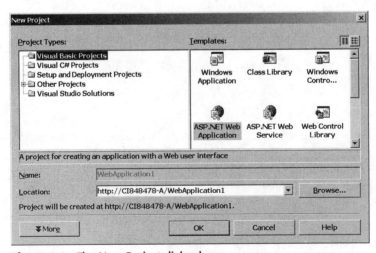

Figure 2.9 The New Project dialog box.

3. Press OK. Visual Studio .NET will then set up the Web project. This process creates a lot more files than are needed for a typical Visual Basic forms project. Note that the directory to hold these files is, by default, created off of the root directory of your Web site. If you are not familiar with Web technologies in general, and this is confusing to you, you'll want to pay special attention to Chapter 4. For now, don't worry about it because it just means that Visual Studio .NET takes care of a lot behind the scenes to make a Web site ready for your development.

4. You'll get a screen to design your first Web Form. It will look much like Figure 2.10, though there may be variations depending on your Visual Studio profile. If you are using the Visual Basic developer profile (as suggested earlier in the chapter), your screen should look very close to this one.

NOTE Note the differences between what you see here and the way Visual Basic 6 would look for regular forms-based development.

- You can see the extra files created for the project, shown in the Solution Explorer in the upper-right portion of the screen.

- The design surface is all white, befitting a Web page, and there is a note about layout options for Web forms controls.

- Below the design surface are two tabs that will be familiar to Visual Interdev users. One shows the visual layout of the form (the Design tab), and the other shows the HTML that is used to create that layout. We won't be using the HTML tab in this example; however, it is used at other places in the book.

- The toolbox contains a different set of controls.

Despite the differences, you'll find that the environment responds very much like VB6 forms-based development.

5. Click and drag a Label control onto the design surface and release it. The Label control will appear on the form. Its properties will appear in the Property window.

6. In the Property window, change the Text property for the control to "Greeting goes here."

7. Drag a Button control onto the form. In the Property window, change its Text property to "Update Greeting."

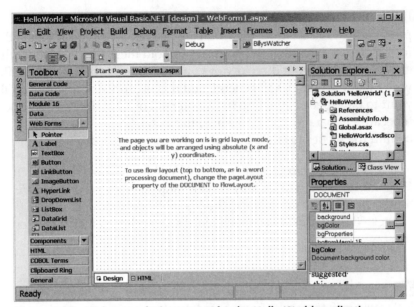

Figure 2.10 Web Form design screen for the Hello World application.

8. Now it's time to fix up the button so that it changes the text in the label control to Hello, World. Double-click on the button, and an event routine will come up, just as with Visual Basic forms. In the event routine, type in the following code:

```
Label1.Text = "Hello, World!!"
```

9. We are now ready to test this Web Form. Press the Run icon in the toolbar. It may take a while to see the resulting screen, especially if this is the first time you have shown a Web Form. The screen that comes up is in Internet Explorer (unless your default browser has been set to something else), and it looks like Figure 2.11.

10. Now press the button. The label will change to say Hello, World!!.

This very short exercise has demonstrated some key ideas about doing Web development with Web Forms and Visual Basic .NET. You have now seen that controls on Web Forms act very much like controls on VB6 forms, with properties to set behavior and event code behind the controls to take actions. If you've ever used Active Server Pages, you were probably surprised at how much easier it was to get a Web page with some logic behind it up and going.

Chapters 5 and 6 go into much more detail about Web Forms and the controls that go on them, so we'll leave further discussion to that point and get back to talking about the environment and changes to Visual Basic.

Figure 2.11   Running the Hello, World application.

Debugging

The last part of the IDE we need to take a look at is how it handles debugging. If you have set your profile to Visual Basic developer, setting breakpoints and stepping through code is very much VB6. If you are using a different profile, the keys may be different, but the actions are generally the same. The following discussion assumes you are using the Visual Basic developer profile and refers to keystrokes used in that profile.

Setting Breakpoints and Stepping through Code

To set a breakpoint in Visual Basic .NET, position the cursor on the line where the breakpoint needs to be and press F9. Then when the program runs and hits that line, execution will be suspended and the code window will show up with that line highlighted. At that point, you can use the following keys to control execution:

F8.   Step through the code one line at a time, going into other routines as necessary.

Shift-F8.   Step through the code one line at a time, but don't step into functions or other routines. When a line calls a function, this kind of step will just run the function and return.

Ctrl-Shift-F8. Step out of a routine. Use this when you've seen all you want to inside a routine such as a function and you want debugging to resume with the next line in the routine that called it.

There are some nice enhancements over VB6. For example, if you right-click on a breakpoint and select Breakpoint Properties, you get access to capabilities such as only breaking after the line has been executed some specified number of times. This allows you to skip through, say, the first four executions of the breakpoint and only break on the fifth execution.

Debug-Related Windows

Once a program is running, various other windows become available for debugging purposes. These windows show up in the same area of the screen as the Task List and the Command window and are accessible via tabs at the bottom of this area. Available windows include:

Call Stack. Lists the procedures that are currently calling other procedures and waiting for their return. There is a similar capability in VB6 that was accessed with a menu option on the View menu.

Breakpoints. Gives some nice alternatives for creation and management of breakpoints. Instead of going to a breakpoint in code, you can refer to it in this window. You are able to change properties of the breakpoint, such as whether it is currently active and how many times it has to be hit before a break.

Locals. Used to monitor the value of all variables that are currently in scope. It has a tree-control interface, similar to the equivalent function in VB6.

Autos. Displays variables used in the statement currently being executed and the statement just before it. These variables are identified and listed for you automatically, (which is where the name of the window comes from). The variables can be displayed in regular format or in hexadecimal, and you can copy a variable to use somewhere else, such as in a Watch window (discussed soon).

Figure 2.12 is a sample screen, showing some code being stepped through, and the Autos and Breakpoints windows. Other debug-related windows would be accessible through the tabs under the Autos and Breakpoints windows.

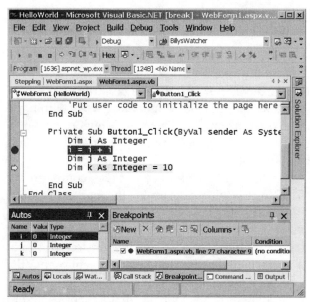

Figure 2.12   Debugging screen in Visual Studio .NET.

Setting and Using Watches

There are also four Watch windows in this same area of the screen, called Watch 1 to Watch 4. Each can hold a set of variables or expressions that you would like to monitor. Variables are added to the windows in a couple of ways. They can be copied in the Autos window and then pasted into a Watch window. Or, when a line of code is being executed, the Debug, QuickWatch command puts up a dialog box showing variables in the line, and you can add them to the Watch window.

Typically, you use a Watch window to monitor the value of a variable. Variables can also have their values changed with Watch windows. Values can be displayed in regular form or in hexadecimal.

Visual Basic .NET Language Enhancements

Contrary to what some authors have said, Visual Basic .NET is still Visual Basic. But it's true that there are major adjustments. To get all the things we Visual Basic users wanted—Web interface development, inheritance, structured exception handling, and so on—Microsoft had to make Visual Basic work within the larger .NET environment. This caused incompatibilities with previous versions. To cite a quick example, Visual Basic .NET had to support .NET data types, and these have some variations from the data types supported by VB6.

When Microsoft realized that it would be necessary to break compatibility with earlier versions, it decided to use this opportunity to clean up the language a bit. Visual Basic is descended from QuickBASIC, which is itself descended from earlier BASIC versions. Programming has changed a lot over the years. Because of this, and because there have been many versions of Visual Basic, there are a number of areas of redundant or obsolete syntax in VB6. Visual Basic .NET deals with many of these issues by cleaning up the syntax.

This section will deal with the changes to Visual Basic that are not related to objects and classes. Those changes will be covered in the next chapter. Also, the list of changes in this chapter is not intended to be exhaustive. It contains what we think are the most important changes you need to know about.

Data Type Changes

Some of the most important changes to understand are changes to data types. Fortunately, these changes are not huge and are pretty easy to absorb.

As we mentioned, data type changes are necessary because Visual Basic .NET must work within the .NET Framework. In .NET, there is a standard set of data types that all .NET-compliant languages must support. You can check the documentation for a complete list of data types supported, but I will give a summary of the changes from VB6 data types.

Integer Types

The most visible changes concern types that support signed whole numbers, which are often called integer types. Table 2.1 summarizes the changes.

Besides getting used to typing in different types when you code, the biggest problem that these changes cause is that they can break calls to routines in DLLs or the Windows API that are expecting certain lengths. If you are using the Upgrade wizard to transfer code into Visual Basic .NET, it will fix these changes for you (along with a lot of others), but code that is cut and pasted needs to have these data types adjusted manually.

Table 2.1   Changes in Integer Data Types from VB6 to Visual Basic .NET

OLD (VB6) TYPE	NEW TYPE	REFERS TO . NET TYPE OF	SIZE	RANGE
Integer	Short	Int16	16 bits	_32,768 to 32,767
Long	Integer	Int32	32 bits	_2,147,483,648 to 2,147,483,647
(not available)	Long	Int64	64 bits	_9,223,372,036,854,775,808 to 9,223,372,036,854,775,807

Note that for integer types, there is a distinction between what Visual Basic calls the type and what .NET calls the type. This is represented by the two columns in the table with headings New Visual Basic .NET type and Refers to .NET type of. This distinction is normally not important, but there are a few instances in which it is. We will see one example in Chapter 8, covering data access, in which setting the data type for a data column requires using the .NET name instead of the Visual Basic .NET name.

Even though Short is only 16 bits and Integer is 32 bits, the Integer type is actually slightly more efficient in this era of 32-bit processors and operating systems. The only advantage of Short is to save memory.

Strings

The String data type in Visual Basic .NET is used almost exactly the same as the String data type in VB6. Strings are variable length and are concatenated with the ampersand, for example. However, the string is handled a bit differently internally, and you need to be aware of the changes.

First, all strings are Unicode by default, so you don't do anything special to get Unicode support. But the major difference is that when a string is changed, the changed version is *always* copied into a new String type. That is, strings are not manipulated in place. Even minor operations on the string require memory copies of the entire string.

This has a significant impact on performance. Many string operations that performed quite acceptably in VB6 may be too slow in Visual Basic .NET. The fix for this is to use what's known as a StringBuilder class. We won't go into the details here, but you should be aware of the need for using StringBuilder when doing intense string manipulation.

Variant Is Now Object

The Variant data type does not exist in Visual Basic .NET because it is not needed. In .NET, everything, including data types such as Integers and String, are descended from a generic Object type. Thus the Object type can handle all of the functions of the old Variant type and offers even more flexibility.

To start out, you can just use the Object type where you would have used the Variant type in VB6 and not worry about the nuances. The next chapter will further discuss object-related changes in Visual Basic .NET, and we will take up the Object type in a bit more detail.

Currency Is Now Decimal

The Currency type in Visual Basic .NET is also no longer available. It should be replaced in most circumstances with the Decimal data type (which is 96 bits, enough for financial calculations). The new 64-bit Long may also be useful in some logic doing currency manipulations because it is not subject to the size limitations of the old 32-bit Long.

The Decimal data type in Visual Basic .NET works a bit differently from the Decimal type in VB6. In VB6, Decimal was actually a subtype of Variant; that is, you couldn't declare a type to be Decimal. Instead, it was necessary to declare it as Variant and then set the subtype within Variant to Decimal. However, in Visual Basic. NET a variable can be declared as Decimal because that is one of the standard data types.

As in VB6, the Format function can be used to format a currency value for output.

Dates

The Date type has some slight differences in Visual Basic .NET. Internally, it is no longer stored in a Double type. Instead, Date is a base type in .NET, and is stored in an 8-bit integer type. There are functions (ToDouble and FromADate) to convert back and forth.

Character Type and Character Arrays

Another new data type called Char is available for storage of a single character. It is really 2 bytes long because it holds Unicode character values. Char was included as a base type in .NET because C-oriented languages use it heavily in the form of arrays of characters (which they often use in place of strings). You don't necessarily have to use the Char type much because variable-length strings are as good or better than character arrays in most circumstances. But there are some design scenarios in which character arrays offer better access or performance, so you should be aware of their availability.

User-Defined Types Changed to Structures

In Visual Basic 6.0, a user-defined type (often abbreviated as a UDT) is a special data structure that is defined with the Type ... End Type construct. Such a type is publicly available, and an instance of a UDT has all of its elements (members) available. Here's an example of a UDT in VB6:

```
Type Customer
    CustID As Integer
    CustPhone As String
    CustStatus As Boolean
End Type
```

The closest equivalent to a UDT in Visual Basic .NET is a structure. Visual Basic .NET has no Type statement. Instead, a structure is declared using the Structure ... End Structure syntax.

In a major difference from VB6, every member of a structure must be declared as one of the following: Dim, Public, Protected, Friend, Protected Friend, or Private. Dim and Public both indicate public access, and the others give various restrictions on access. Suppose we would like to create a structure that is equivalent to the UDT in the previous example. Such an equivalent, with the necessary declaration modifiers, might look like this:

```
Structure Customer
    Public CustID As Integer      ' Must declare access, _
                                    even if Public.
    Dim CustPhone As String       ' Still defaults to Public access.
    Private CustStatus As Boolean ' Can be Private inside Structure.
End Structure
```

In this case we are making CustStatus private to the Structure. You might wonder what good that does. In a VB6 UDT, a private element would be completely pointless because nothing could get to it. But structures are more flexible than UDTs. For example, structures can expose properties, events, and methods. The code for these elements could refer to one of the private elements such as the CustStatus element. There is an example of such a structure in Chapter 3.

The syntax for accessing a structure is object syntax and is very similar to the syntax for accessing user-defined types in VB6 and earlier.

Fixed-Length Strings

Another data type not supported in .NET is fixed-length strings. It does not have a replacement that is a base type in .NET. However, there is a compatibility class that looks and acts like a fixed-length string.

You have to change your code a bit to use it, however. Instead of declaring a fixed-length string like this:

```
Dim sMyFixedLengthString As String*20
```

you would have to declare it as:

```
Dim sMyFixedLengthString As New VB6.FixedLengthString(20)
```

You also would need to vary your syntax to put strings into one of these objects if you are using strict type checking (with Option Strict set to On). We discuss strict type checking and Option Strict in the next chapter. Unfortunately, this replacement does not work for all cases. Fixed-length strings are often used in two scenarios in which the compatibility object fails to offer a solution:

- Fixed-length strings in user-defined types to simulate fixed length records
- Fixed length strings as array arguments called to the Win32 API

In the first scenario, the problem is that structures (the replacement for UDTs in Visual Basic .NET, discussed previously) can only take base types as subelements. Because there is no base type for fixed-length strings, they cannot be used. The work-around is to use character arrays (from the Char type discussed previously) or use variable-length strings and include logic to check and adjust the length to a certain size.

The API situation is a bit trickier, and we won't get into it in this book. But you'll find that you won't need to worry about that very much because there are far fewer situations in Visual Basic .NET where calls to the API are necessary. In most cases, the .NET Framework classes furnish access to API functionality without having to go directly to the API.

Variable Declaration Changes

Visual Basic has always had syntax for declaring variables that was a little quirky compared to other languages. In .NET, Visual Basic is being brought more into line with the way other languages declare variables. For example, consider the following variable declaration line:

```
Dim A, B As Integer
```

This syntax is valid in both VB6 and Visual Basic .NET, but it has different results. In VB6, variable A becomes a Variant, and B is an Integer. However, in Visual Basic .NET, both A and B are initialized as Integer. This is more consistent with the way other languages handle variable declaration.

Perhaps the biggest change to variable declaration is the ability to set initial values of declared variables. Here's some sample syntax:

```
Public strCompany As String = "ABC Company"
Dim intHoursAvailable As Integer = 10
Dim intMinutesAvailable As Integer = intHoursAvailable * 60
```

For initializing to constant values, the preceding examples show that you can just put = {constant value} after the regular declaration. For initializing to calculated values, any elements used in the calculation must have been declared and initialized to their own values. So intMinutesAvailable can be initialized to an expression that contains the previously declared intHoursAvailable.

Changes to Arrays

There are some minor differences in declaring and using arrays from what you are used to in Visual Basic .NET.

Option Base Gone

In VB6, arrays can be set to start with index 0 or index 1; 0 is the default. The statement Option Base 1 sets arrays to begin at element 1.

In Visual Basic .NET, the Option Base statement is not supported. Arrays must begin at element 0. In VB6, you could declare the bounds for an array like this:

```
Dim nNumbers(3 To 12) As Integer
```

This syntax is not available in Visual Basic .NET. All arrays must begin at element 0.

Fixed Number of Dimensions

In VB6, a Redim statement could actually change the number of dimensions of an array (sometimes called the rank of the array). In Visual Basic .NET, no such capability is available. The number of dimensions must be specified when an array is declared, and cannot be changed.

Initializing Array Values

Just as you can place initial values in individual variables (covered above), you can also place initial values in arrays. The values are in a list enclosed by braces. Here's an example:

```
Dim nNumbers() As Integer = {3, 4, 5, 6}
```

Note that you cannot specify the size of an array declared this way. The compiler figures out the size from the list of elements you include. In the preceding case, the array will be four elements—nNumbers(0), nNumbers(1), nNumbers(2), and nNumbers(3).

A similar example using strings looks like this:

```
Dim s() As String = {"John", "Paul", "Jones"}
```

In this case, s(0) is initialized to "John", s(1) to "Paul", and s(2) to "Jones".

Redim Cannot Be Used as a Declaration

In VB6, you could initially declare an array with ReDim instead of Dim. That's not possible in Visual Basic .NET. You can declare an array with no size and then give it a size later, like this:

```
Dim t() As Integer
ReDim t(5)
t(5) = 7
```

But you can't make that initial declaration in the first line of the example with ReDim, the way you could in VB6. (In this case, the rank of the array is assumed to be 1.)

Changes from Early Betas

If you saw or read about early betas of Visual Basic .NET, you might have heard that arrays were declared differently in Visual Basic .NET, and that they did not have the topmost element that you were accustomed to in VB6 and earlier. This was true in those early betas, but it is no longer true. If you didn't hear anything about that, you can just ignore this paragraph.

New Arithmetic Statements

For more concise syntax, Visual Basic .NET offers several new operators for functions like incrementing and decrementing a variable. Here are examples of the ones you are likely to use most often. For these examples, assume that the variable iIndex is an Integer, and sName is a String.

iIndex += 1   This statement increases the value of iIndex by 1.

iIndex -= 5   This statement decreases the value of iIndex by 5.

iIndex *= 2   This statement doubles the value of iIndex.

sName &= ", Jr."   This statement appends the string ", Jr." to the end of the string variable sName.

Changes in the Way Variables Are Scoped

In VB6, a variable can be declared anywhere inside a procedure, and it is then available for access anywhere else in that procedure. That is, a variable declared inside a procedure is said to have procedure scope.

If the variable is declared inside a code block such as a For loop, a While loop, or an If block, the variable is still accessible in the rest of the procedure outside the block. Here's an example in VB6:

```
Dim bContinue As Boolean
bContinue = True
While bContinue
    Dim sMessage As String
    sMessage = sMessage & "."
    If Len(sMessage) > 100 Then
        bContinue = False
    End If
Wend
MsgBox sMessage
```

This will work. The MsgBox will display a string with 101 periods in it when the loop is finished, because the variable sMessage is available outside the loop, even though it was declared inside the loop.

Scoping rules are different in Visual Basic .NET. A variable declared inside a code block is only available inside that block. That is, it has block scope. The preceding VB6 example would not work in Visual Basic .NET and would need to change to something like this:

```
Dim bContinue As Boolean
bContinue = True
Dim sMessage As String
While bContinue
    sMessage = sMessage & "."
    If Len(sMessage) > 100 Then
        bContinue = False
    End If
End While
MsgBox sMessage
```

Block scope works a bit differently from procedure scope. If a variable is declared inside a block, it does not lose its value when the block is exited. The value is still there in case the block is reentered. Even though the value is not lost, the variable cannot be referenced from outside the block.

Miscellaneous Changes

There are number of minor syntactical changes you should know about that didn't fit in any of the other categories. This section covers these miscellaneous changes.

Changes in Using Parentheses

There are a number of places in VB6 where parentheses are optional, or even not allowed, that require parentheses in Visual Basic .NET. For example, if a subroutine is called without the Call keyword in front of it in VB6, parentheses are not used around the argument list for the subroutine. However, all subroutine calls in Visual Basic .NET require parentheses around the argument lists.

Similarly, some built-in functions in VB6, such as the Date function, did not take any parentheses. But in Visual Basic .NET, all function calls must be followed by parentheses, even for an empty argument list.

To illustrate, here's some VB6 code that will need to be changed in Visual Basic .NET:

```
MsgBox "Hello, World"
Dim sDate As String
sDate = Date
```

These will not work in the new Visual Basic because the compiler now requires the developer to always include parentheses for subroutine and function calls. The equivalent working versions of these examples in Visual Basic .NET are:

```
MsgBox ("Hello, World")
Dim sDate As String
sDate = Date()
```

This is not as big an adjustment for you as a developer as you might think, however. The Visual Basic .NET editor is very smart about parentheses. If you leave them off and type in the VB6 code example, the editor will actually insert the appropriate parentheses for you as soon as you leave the line.

Parameters Are ByVal by Default

In VB6, arguments in an argument list that are not declared to be either ByVal or ByRef are ByRef by default. This means that arguments without a ByVal can be changed by the called function or subroutine, and the changes will affect the variables in the calling routine. (That's why it's good practice to always include ByRef or ByVal explicitly.)

The default changes in Visual Basic .NET and becomes ByVal instead. This is arguably a better default to use, but if you cut and paste code from Visual Basic 6 that does not explicitly have ByRef or ByVal in its argument lists, you might get some unexpected behavior in Visual Basic .NET. The changes that were propagated back into the calling routine in VB6 will not be propagated back in Visual Basic .NET.

Optional Parameters Must Have Default Value

Optional parameters are still supported in Visual Basic .NET, but they now require a default value in the argument list where the parameters are declared. The Is Missing construct is no longer available to see if a parameter is missing and supply a default value. Note, however, that the availability of overloaded functions (discussed in the next chapter) make the use of optional parameters in argument lists less common.

Keywords Moved to Framework Class Methods and Properties

The Visual Basic language has always had a lot of keywords. Such operations as squaring a number, for example, used a language keyword (Sqr). The design philosophy is different in .NET. To make such functionality available to all languages, common operations such as squaring a number are encapsulated in classes in the .NET Framework. To use the operation, you thus need to know which class to use and the namespace in which that class is defined. (We'll take up namespaces in detail in Chapter 3.)

Table 2.2 lists some of the VB6 keywords that have been replaced, with their new name and location.

Table 2.2   VB6 Keywords Replaced by Elements of the .NET Framework Classes

KEYWORD	LOCATION IN VISUAL BASIC .NET (NAMESPACE)	METHOD / PROPERTY
Circle	System.Drawing.Graphics	DrawEllipse
Line	System.Drawing.Graphics	DrawLine
Atn	System.Math	Atan
Sgn	System.Math	Sign

continues

Table 2.2 (Continued)

KEYWORD	LOCATION IN VISUAL BASIC .NET (NAMESPACE)	METHOD / PROPERTY
Sqr	System.Math	Sqrt
Rnd	System.Random	Next
Lset	System.String	PadRight
Rset	System.String	PadLeft
DoEvents	System.Windows.Forms.Application	DoEvents
VarType	System.Object	GetType (returns an object of class Type, which has properties to get information)
Date	System.DateTime	Today
Time	System.DateTime	TimeOfDay
Date$	{built-in availability in VB.NET}	DateString
Time$	{built-in availability in VB.NET}	TimeString

The list in the table is not exhaustive. If you notice that a keyword you are accustomed to using in VB6 is not available as a keyword in Visual Basic .NET, it's likely that there is a replacement for it. So don't just assume you can't do it. Check your documentation for alternatives.

In some cases, you may not notice the difference. If appropriate namespaces have been declared, you can use such members as Now and Timer by just referring to them, and the code looks like you're using keywords even though they are actually members of a class.

Retired and Obsolete Keywords

The process of cleaning up the syntax of Visual Basic resulted in a number of older keywords that are no longer needed. A few newer ones are also replaced to be more consistent with the way .NET does things. Here are the main keywords that are no longer available (not counting the ones such as Option Base that we've already covered in this chapter):

- Gosub
- On x GoTo ... (often referred to as computed GoTo's)
- Let (as in Let i = i + 1)

- VarPtr, ObjPtr, StrPtr
- DefBool, DefByte, DefInt, DefLng, DefCur, DefSng, DefDbl, DefDec, DefDate, DefStr, DefObj, DefVar (all of which set aside first letters of variables to declare their type)
- Wend (changed to End While)

Also note that because Gosub is no longer used, the keyword Return is available for a new use. In VB6, you returned the value of a function or property like this:

```
Public Function DoubledNumber(i As Integer) As Integer
    DoubledNumber = i * 2
End Function
```

This still works, but you have another alternative. You can use the Return keyword to return the value, like this:

```
Public Function DoubledNumber(i As Integer) As Integer
    Return i * 2
End Function
```

This is somewhat preferred because if you change the name of the function, you don't have to change that line of code to take the new function name into account.

The Empty and Null keywords are no longer used in Visual Basic .NET. Both can be replaced in code with the Nothing keyword. Note that Null is still a reserved word in Visual Basic .NET, even though it doesn't do anything and will generate a syntax error if you try to use it. This helps avoid confusion with its former meanings.

Error-Handling Changes

Most of us hate to write error-handling code in VB6. It's messy coding, mostly because the error-handling syntax in VB6 is derived from BASIC languages from the 1980s (or earlier).

A Quick Overview of Error Handling in Visual Basic 6

In VB6, a typical routine with error-handling code looks like this:

```
Private Function OpenFile(sFileName As String) As Boolean

On Error GoTo ErrHandler:
```

```
Open sFileName For Random As #1
OpenFile = True
Exit Sub

ErrHandler:
Select Case Err.Number
    Case 53  ' File not found
        MsgBox "File not found"
    Case Else
        MsgBox "Other error"
End Select
OpenFile = False

End Function
```

The top of the routine points to a section of code called an error handler, which is usually placed at the bottom of the routine. The error handler gets control as soon as an error is detected in the routine, and it looks at the error number to see what to do. The error number is available as a property of the Err object, which is a globally available object that holds error information in VB6.

If the error handler can take care of the error without breaking execution, it can resume execution with the line of code that generated the error (Resume) or the one after that (Resume Next) or at a particular location (Resume {LineLabel}).

This structure becomes more complex if the error handling needs to vary in the routine. Multiple On Error GoTo... statements must be used to send errors to various error handlers, like this:

```
Private Function OpenFile(sFileName As String) As Boolean

On Error GoTo ErrHandler1
' Do calculations here
Dim i As Integer
i = Len(sFileName)
Dim j As Integer
j = 100 \ i

On Error GoTo ErrHandler2
Open sFileName For Random As #1
OpenFile = True
Exit Function

ErrHandler1:
Select Case Err.Number
    Case 6  ' Overflow
        MsgBox "Overflow"
    Case Else
        MsgBox "Other error"
End Select
```

```
OpenFile = False
Exit Function

ErrHandler2:
Select Case Err.Number
    Case 53  ' File not found
        MsgBox "File not found"
    Case Else
        MsgBox "Other error"
End Select
OpenFile = False

End Function
```

With this setup, it is easy to get confused about what should happen under various conditions. It's also necessary to remember to change the error-handling pointer as necessary, or errors will be incorrectly processed.

The New Way in .NET—Structured Exception Handling

Visual Basic .NET still supports these old error-handling techniques, but that's really for compatibility with old code. There's a much better way to manage errors in Visual Basic .NET called structured exception handling.

The first difference to understand is that structured exception handling does not use error numbers and the Err object. In .NET, errors in code cause an object to be generated. The object is called an exception, and it loosely corresponds to the Err object in VB6.

However, where there is only one global Err object in VB6, there are many types of exception objects in Visual Basic .NET. For example, if a divide-by-zero is done in code, an OverflowException is generated. There are several dozen types of exception classes in Visual Basic .NET, and in addition to using the ones that are available in the .NET Framework, you can inherit from a class called ApplicationException and then create your own exception classes (see the next chapter for a discussion of inheritance).

Having many types of exceptions in Visual Basic .NET enables different types of errors to be trapped with different error handlers. This is a major advance over VB6. The syntax to do that is discussed in the following section.

Structured Exception-Handling Keywords in Visual Basic .NET

Structured exception handling depends on several new keywords in Visual Basic .NET. They are:

Try.   Begin a section of code in which an error might occur. This section of code is often called a Try block.

Catch.   Begin an error handler. Catch comes after a Try block, and it receives control when an error is encountered in the Try block. A Try structure can have more than one Catch block, with each one catching a different type of exception.

Finally.   Contains code that runs when the Try block finishes normally, or if the Catch block receives control and then finishes. That is, the code in the Finally block always runs, regardless of whether an error has been detected.

Throw.   Generates an error. This is similar to Err.Raise in VB6. It's usually done in a Catch block when the error should be kicked back to a calling routine. Note that a Throw statement, like an Err.Raise, ends execution of the error handler; that is, there is no more code in the Catch block after the Throw statement is executed. However, Throw does not prevent code in the Finally block from running. That code still runs before the error is kicked back to the calling routine.

Some typical simple structured exception-handling code in Visual Basic .NET looks like this:

```
Private Sub GetAverage(iItems As Integer, iTotal as Integer) as Single
    ' Code that might throw an exception is wrapped in a Try block
    Try

        Dim sngAverage As Single

        ' This will cause an exception to be thrown if iItems = 0
        sngAverage = CSng(iTotal / iItems)

        ' This only executes if the line above generated no error
        MessageBox.Show("Calculation successful")
        Return sngAverage

    Catch exc As Exception
        ' If the calculation failed, we get here
        MessageBox.Show("Calculation unsuccessful - exception caught")
        Return 0
    End Try

End Sub
```

In this code, we are trapping all the errors with a single generic exception type, and we don't have any Finally logic. The following is a more complex example:

```
Private Sub GetAverage(iItems As Integer, iTotal as Integer) as Single
    ' Code that might throw an exception is wrapped in a Try block
    Try

        Dim sngAverage As Single

        ' This will cause an exception to be thrown
        sngAverage = CSng(iTotal / iItems)

        ' This only executes if the line above generated no error
        MessageBox.Show("Calculation successful")
        Return sngAverage

    Catch excOverflow As OverflowException
        ' We'll get here with an OverflowException in the Try block
        MessageBox.Show("Calculation generated Overflow Exception")
        Return 0

    Catch exc As Exception
        ' We'll get here when any exception is thrown and not caught in
        ' a previous Catch block
        MessageBox.Show("Calculation failed - generic exception caught")
        Return 0
    Finally
        ' Code in the Finally block will always run.
        MessageBox.Show("We always get here, with or without an error")
    End Try
End Sub
```

In this code, there are multiple Catch blocks for different types of exceptions. If an exception is generated, .NET will go down the Catch blocks looking for a matching exception type. That means the Catch blocks should go from specific types first to more generic types later.

This type of code structure is especially relevant for data-handling code, and we'll see more of it in Chapter 8. A Catch block for data errors can be written with completely different exception handling than other types of exception.

You'll understand more about structured exception handling if you see it in action. To do that, you can type in the code in the previous listing (or get it from the Web site) and run it. Set a breakpoint early in the code and then step through the code line by line.

It's also educational to place the code in a subroutine or function, insert a Throw into the Catch block, and then call that routine from somewhere else. This gives you a better idea about how Throw works.

Here's how the code would change with the Throw statement added:

```
Private Sub GetAverage(iItems As Integer, iTotal as Integer) as Single
    ' Code that might throw an exception is wrapped in a Try block
    Try

        Dim sngAverage As Single

        ' This will cause an exception to be thrown
        sngAverage = CSng(iTotal / iItems)

        ' This only executes if the line above generated no error
        MessageBox.Show("Calculation successful")
        Return sngAverage

    Catch excOverflow As OverflowException
        ' We'll get here with an OverflowException in the Try block
        MessageBox.Show("Calculation generated Overflow Exception")
        Throw excOverflow
        MsgBox("More logic after the thrown - never executed")

    Catch exc As Exception
        ' We'll get here when any exception is thrown and not caught in
        ' a previous Catch block
        MessageBox.Show("Calculation failed - generic exception caught")
        Throw exc
    Finally
        ' Code in the Finally block will always run, even if
        ' an exception was thrown in a Catch block
        MessageBox.Show("We always get here, with or without an error")
    End Try
End Sub
```

Here is some typical code to call the preceding subroutine. You can place this code in a button's click event to test it out.

```
Try
    Dim sngAvg As Single
    sngAvg = GetAverage(0, 100)
Catch exc As Exception
    MsgBox("Back in the click event after an error")
Finally
    MsgBox("Finally block in click event")
End Try
```

This type of error handling offers more flexibility with cleaner logic than the On Error constructs in VB6. You should definitely invest enough time to understand structured exception handling before beginning serious development in Visual Basic .NET.

Wrapping Up

There are a lot of changes in Visual Basic .NET from previous versions. However, as this chapter has shown, most of them don't take a lot of effort to absorb. And the changes are well worth it to integrate Visual Basic into the .NET Framework, thus giving Visual Basic .NET the power to do Web development in a way that is far beyond anything available in VB6.

We are not quite finished with the changes in Visual Basic .NET, however. The next chapter discusses all the changes related to object technologies, including such subjects as inheritance, function overloading, and changes in object syntax.

Object-Oriented Changes in Visual Basic .NET

Change is the only constant. Hanging on is the only sin.
Denise McCluggage, U.S. race car driver

In the previous chapter, we discussed many changes in the Visual Basic language and development environment when moving from VB6 to Visual Basic .NET. But there is another group of related changes that require quite a bit of discussion. These are the changes related to object orientation. All of those changes are collected and discussed in this chapter.

The changes discussed in the previous chapter did not, for the most part, introduce new programming concepts. Even something as new as structured exception handling can be compared to previous capabilities of VB6. However, some of the concepts in this chapter have no parallel in earlier versions of Visual Basic. It will be necessary to explain and discuss some highly abstract concepts.

It is important to understand that this chapter is not intended to serve as a beginning tutorial on object-oriented concepts. There are a number of books that do that, and it is a transition that takes more than reading a single chapter and doing a few examples. So the first thing we need to do is to find out if you, as an individual reader, are ready to tackle this chapter.

Type of Developers

Both Visual Basic and Active Server Pages have always been object based. Forms and controls could always be considered objects, all the way back to Visual Basic 1.0. Later versions of Visual Basic and Active Server Pages added

65

a number of new objects, such as data access objects and the Application, Response, and Session objects in ASP. Such objects have properties, methods, and events, and learning to manipulate these programming elements has always been essential to success as a Visual Basic or ASP developer.

However, with version Visual Basic 4.0, new object capabilities were added to Visual Basic. It became possible to create new objects in Visual Basic, using classes. These classes could have properties, methods, and events defined for them by the Visual Basic developer. In addition, forms could also, for the first time, have new properties and methods added by the developer.

With VBScript 5.0 in Active Server Pages, a subset of these same object-oriented capabilities became available. Classes could be written with properties and methods, although events were not supported. Lack of compilation to separate modules also limited the ability to share encapsulated logic in VBScript.

These changes moved Visual Basic and VBScript from being object-based languages to being object-oriented ones. Although they did not have all the capabilities of an object-oriented language (inheritance being the biggest omission), it was possible to do some semblance of object-oriented development with Visual Basic and, to a lesser extent, with VBScript.

Some developers embraced these new techniques. Others did not. That split persists down to the present. Visual Basic and ASP developers can be roughly divided into those developers who learned object-oriented techniques and those that didn't.

Which Type Are You?

If your main development experience has been in Active Server Pages, using VBScript, you probably have not learned very much about object-oriented concepts. The changes in VBScript to support creation of classes were done fairly recently, and implementing classes in a script-based language is less than ideal. If you fall into this category, you may need additional grounding in object-oriented concepts for this chapter to be useful.

If you are a Visual Basic developer, here's a quick way to estimate how far you are along the object-oriented path. If you have designed and written some class modules (.CLS files) in a production project, you're in pretty good shape. You have had to learn the basis of properties, methods, and events. If you've never written a class file yourself, but only used classes created by other developers, you are probably more like the ASP developers, and you also need additional exposure to object-oriented concepts before getting the most from this chapter.

At press time there were no good options for an introduction to object-oriented concepts in Visual Basic .NET. However, a good conceptual introduction that you might want to check out is *The Object Primer* by Scott Ambler

(Cambridge University Press, 2001). It is not specific to a particular language or platform and presents object concepts from the ground up.

For those who are ready to plunge ahead with the object-oriented changes in Visual Basic .NET, let's get started.

Namespaces

In working with classes, one of the first problems you face is how to identify them. This is not much of a problem for classes you create in your own projects—you just refer to the class name. But as classes are distributed into libraries, this is not good enough. It becomes all too easy for class names to overlap. For example, you might have a Customer class in two different libraries. How can you unambiguously refer to the one you want?

In .NET (and in some other object-oriented environments) this problem is addressed with the concept of namespaces. Namespaces were discussed briefly in Chapter 1. Now we are ready to explore the concept in more depth.

A namespace is quite similar in concept to a directory or subdirectory in a file system. With a file system, it is possible to have files with the same name, but you can unambiguously identify the one you want by giving a full path name in a hierarchical set of directories. Likewise, namespaces form a hierarchical structure that has locations in it for groups of related classes. You can unambiguously identify the class you want by specifying a path for it in the namespace hierarchy.

For example, .NET has a namespace called System. Within this namespace are many additional namespaces. Two of those namespaces are called Web and Windows. The one identified as Web is referred to in a .NET program as:

```
System.Web
```

And the one for Windows is referred to as:

```
System.Windows
```

The System.Web namespace has a namespace within it called UI, and there is a class in that namespace called Control. This class is related to server controls that go on Web pages. To refer to this class unambiguously in code, you need the reference:

```
System.Web.UI.Control
```

The System.Windows namespace in turn has a namespace called Forms, and within that namespace is a class called Control. This class is related to controls that appear on Windows Forms. The class is referred to in code as:

```
System.Windows.Forms.Control
```

So we have two classes both named Control that serve different purposes. That's okay because they reside in different namespaces. The namespace hierarchy plus the actual class name gives us an unambiguous reference.

Using and Defining Namespaces

You'll spend a lot of time getting to know the various namespaces in the .NET Framework. The classes in them provide you with a ton of prewritten functionality. The base classes were discussed briefly in Chapter 1, and you'll see references to various base classes for different purposes throughout the book.

In addition to using the predefined namespaces (and classes in them), you'll also need to define your own namespaces. When you start up a project, it will have its own namespace defined for it by default, and that namespace will only contain classes in that project. However, you can have multiple projects share a namespace, or you can have a single project implement more than one namespace.

To do this, you need the Namespace keyword. Classes are defined within a namespace with the following syntax:

```
Namespace MyNamespace
    Class MySimpleClass
    ' logic to implement MySimpleClass
    End Class

    Class MyOtherClass
    'logic to implement MyOtherClass
    End Class
End Namespace
```

Now the classes are referenced in code with the identifiers:

```
MyNamespace.MySimpleClass
MyNamespace.MyOtherClass
```

You can also nest namespaces. Suppose we wanted MySimpleClass and MyOtherClass to be in the same root namespace (MyNameSpace) but in different subnamespaces within MyNamespace. Then the syntax would look like this:

```
Namespace MyNamespace
    Namespace MyFirstSubNamespace
        Class MySimpleClass
        ' logic to implement MySimpleClass
        End Class
    End Namespace
```

```
      Namespace MySecondSubNamespace
          Class MyOtherClass
          'logic to implement MyOtherClass
          End Class
      End Namespace
  End Namespace
```

In this case, the classes would be referred to in code with:

```
MyNamespace.MyFirstSubNamespace.MySimpleClass
MyNamespace.MySecondSubNamespace.MyOtherClass
```

Now suppose we wanted to split up MySimpleClass and MyOtherClass into different modules. We could use syntax like this in the first module:

```
Namespace MyNamespace.MyFirstSubNamespace
    Class MySimpleClass
    ' logic to implement MySimpleClass
    End Class
End Namespace
```

And the second module would look like this:

```
Namespace MyNamespace.MySecondSubNamespace
    Class MyOtherClass
    ' logic to implement MyOtherClass
    End Class
End Namespace
```

The references to the classes would still look the same as before:

```
MyNamespace.MyFirstSubNamespace.MySimpleClass
MyNamespace.MySecondSubNamespace.MyOtherClass
```

Using a Namespace in Your Program

In the VB6 world, you were familiar with the idea of creating references to class libraries in DLL and OCX files. Before you could use a class, you had to go to the Add Reference dialog box and point to the class.

A very similar process is used in Visual Basic .NET. Suppose the set of classes in MyNamespace is in a DLL called MyNamespace.DLL. Further, MyNamespace.DLL is in a directory named C:\MyVBNETModules. Then to use classes from MyNamespace in your program, you'll need to add a reference to the DLL.

To do that, access the Project, Add Reference menu option. You'll get a dialog box that looks like Figure 3.1.

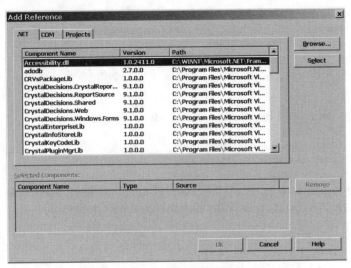

Figure 3.1 Adding a reference to a .NET DLL.

The libraries that are already listed are those that .NET knows about because they are globally available. All the .NET Framework base classes, for example, are somewhere in this list. But your classes are not available by default unless you have deployed them a certain way (deployment is discussed in Chapter 9).

The Browse button can be used to point to your own DLLs. When you press it, you get a typical File Open dialog box, and you can point at your DLL. At that point, the component will show up in the table at the bottom of the dialog box shown in the figure, and when you press OK, the classes in the component can be referred to in your project (using their full namespace path).

Shortening Namespace and Class References

Although the detailed way to reference classes, using an entire namespace path, is unambiguous, it can get tedious to keep typing in long namespace references in code. To make code more concise, you can refer to a namespace at the beginning of a module with an Imports statement. Then the classes in the namespace become available in code without typing in the entire namespace path. You can use a class by just typing the class name.

Here's an example. Let's assume we have a DLL that contains two classes—MyNamespace.MyFirstSubNamespace.MySimpleClass and MyNamespace.

MySecondSubNamespace.MyOtherClass (as in the example we looked at previously). After referring to MyNamespace.DLL as described previously, you could immediately refer to MySimpleClass in a declaration statement like this:

```
Dim x As MyNamespace.MyFirstSubNamespace.MySimpleClass
```

But this is fairly clumsy. If we are using MySimpleClass a lot, we could put the following line at the beginning of our module:

```
Imports MyNamespace.MyFirstSubNamespace
```

Now the preceding line becomes:

```
Dim x As MySimpleClass
```

This is a lot cleaner and easier to read and is generally preferred.

There is only one problem. If another namespace that your program knows about already has a class named MySimpleClass, there is ambiguity. Which MySimpleClass does the previous line mean in that case?

If there is such ambiguity, the solution is to use the full namespace path to refer to the class in code. That is, on class names that exist in more than one imported namespace, you must use the full namespace path for that particular class (but not necessarily for other classes in the namespace that are not ambiguous).

If you do have the ambiguity problem, you can still abbreviate the namespace to make it easier to refer to. If you change your Imports statement to look like this:

```
Imports MyNS = MyNamespace.MyFirstSubNamespace
```

you can declare your class with this line:

```
Dim x As MyNS.MySimpleClass
```

This works even if there is a class named MySimpleClass in some other available namespace.

If there are several ways to unambiguously refer to a class in code, it does not matter which of them you use. The code will behave exactly the same. For example, if we are using the MyNS alias, the following two lines have exactly the same effect in code:

```
Dim x As MyNS.MySimpleClass
Dim x As MyNamespace.MyFirstSubNamespace.MySimpleClass
```

Some Naming Conventions

Microsoft has two namespace root names: System and Microsoft. The System namespace is for the basic .NET Framework classes. These classes will probably migrate to other .NET platforms and are associated with .NET, not with Windows or other Microsoft products.

The Microsoft namespace is for classes related to Microsoft products that work with .NET. For example, the special classes that work in Visual Basic to replicate some of the functionality with VB6 are in this namespace.

It is no accident that this namespace is called Microsoft. If you follow the suggested naming conventions for .NET, your organization should have its own root namespace, and it would typically be related to the organization name. All the classes you produce should be in that root namespace. Keep in mind that you can have as many subnamespaces as you want, just like you can have as many subdirectories as you need in a file system.

Such a naming convention keeps the possibility for namespace collisions to a minimum. If you just called a namespace Data, for example, you might get a library from someone else at some point that also had a Data namespace. But if your namespace is ABCCompany.Data, that possibility is eliminated (unless some other company with a similar name picks the same root namespace).

Object-Related Changes to Visual Basic Syntax

Before we get into the really major changes concerning objects in Visual Basic .NET, let's go over some of the minor changes in object syntax that are helpful to know. Understanding these changes will make it easy to explain the big changes later in the chapter. These changes include:

- Removal of default properties, unless they are indexed properties
- No more need to use the Set keyword when dealing with object references
- A different syntax for property procedures
- A new function (CType) to cast objects to a particular type
- Changes in event handler syntax

Let's look at each of these in turn.

Removal of Default Properties

Let's consider a line of code in VB6 or earlier. In this example, assume that strAddress is a string variable and txtAddress is a text box:

```
' in VB6, this places the Text property of txtAddress in strAddress
strAddress = txtAddress
```

In VB6 and earlier, the text box control has a default property, namely, the text it holds. The Visual Basic compiler recognizes this and compiles the preceding line as if it were written:

```
strAddress = txtAddress.Text
```

In Visual Basic .NET, such default properties are not available. The .NET Framework itself does not support marking a property as a default property (unless it has an index, as I'll explain soon). So that first line of code will no longer work in Visual Basic .NET. The second form will be required.

This should not have too much of a negative impact on most professional developers because good coding practices have long recommended against using default properties. The resulting code is not easy to read and can be misinterpreted. However, one syntax form that contains a default property is in common use. It is often seen in working with ADO code, for instance, as in the following example:

```
' Works In VB6
strAddress = rsMyRecordSet("Address")
```

This code contains *two* references to default properties. Some programmers may not even be aware that this code compiles as if it were written in this long form:

```
' Works In VB6 and VB.NET
strAddress = rsMyRecordSet.Fields("Address").Value
```

The Fields collection is the default property of the Recordset object, and the Value property is the default property of a Field object.

The Value property works just like the Text property of the text box in our previous example. That means that when changing over to Visual Basic .NET, it is necessary to insert the Value property to make the code compile. However, the Fields collection is a different matter. This default property takes an argument, namely, the key to the collection that is used to retrieve a single element (which is Address in the preceding example). Visual Basic .NET makes an exception for properties that are indexed in this fashion. Such default properties can be inferred by the compiler because it notes the parameter that is included for the default property. So, even in Visual Basic .NET, the preceding example can be written as:

```
' Works In VB6 and VB.NET
strAddress = rsMyRecordSet("Address").Value
```

No More Set

The changes just discussed for default properties allow another change that is definitely an improvement. In VB4 through VB6 it was necessary to set all object references with the Set keyword. That is, to set an object reference to a text box, those versions of Visual Basic require syntax like this:

```
Set txtID = txtOldID    ' VB6 and earlier style
```

This would make the txtID and txtOldID object variables refer to the same object instance.

Without the Set, the code means something entirely different. As we discussed previously, the following code causes the Text property of txtOldID to be assigned to the Text property of txtID:

```
txtID = txtOldID    ' Means something different in VB6 and VB.NET
```

The Set keyword was needed in VB6 and earlier to make these two cases (assigning an object reference and assigning a default property) look different in code. But in Visual Basic .NET, the default property no longer exists. So the Set becomes superfluous. The preceding line of code (without the Set) can be used in Visual Basic .NET, but it sets an object reference.

Property Procedure Changes

Suppose I want to create a property named CustomerID for one of my classes in VB6. The property needs to be of Integer type. Typical code in VB6 for the property would look like this:

```
' Property procedures In VB6 (this code does not work in VB.NET)
Private mintCustomerID as Integer

Public Property Get CustomerID() As Integer
    CustomerID = mintCustomerID
End Property

Public Property Let CustomerID(nNewValue As Integer)
    mintCustomerID = nNewValue
End Property
```

Most developers would place these two routines together, but VB6 does not require that. They could be widely separated in the code, and they would still work. Also, one of them could be left out. If the Get property procedure were left out, the property would be a write-only property because it could only be set and not read. Likewise, if the Let procedure were left out, the property would be read only.

A property in VB6 could have up to three separate property procedures (Let, Get, and Set), although it was only required to use one. The Set versus Let distinction was needed for the same reason that Set was needed for object references—to eliminate ambiguity between setting default properties and setting object references.

In Visual Basic .NET, we have a new ballgame. Let property procedures are not needed because there's no need to differentiate between object references and common variables. Set and Get procedures are then tied together with some new syntax, which resembles equivalent syntax in C#. Here's an example for the CustomerID property:

```
Private mintCustomerID as Integer

Public Property CustomerID() As Integer

    Get
        Return mintCustomerID
    End Get

    Set (ByVal Value As Integer)
        mintCustomerID = Value
    End Set

End Property
```

This is cleaner than the equivalent VB6 (and earlier) syntax. It also removes a lot of pitfalls, such as changing the data type for a Get but forgetting to do so for the equivalent Let.

With this syntax, you can't make a property read-only by merely leaving out the Set procedure. Instead, the ReadOnly keyword is used at the beginning of the property declaration, and then the Set block can be left out. If we made the preceding CustomerID property read-only, it would look like this:

```
Private mintCustomerID as Integer

Public ReadOnly Property CustomerID() As Integer

    Get
        Return mintCustomerID
    End Get

End Property
```

In this case, the module containing the property would be the only code that could change the property value, by changing the value of mintCustomerID.

There is also a WriteOnly keyword to make a property write-only, in which case the Get block is left out. The preceding example in write-only form looks like this:

```
Private mintCustomerID as Integer

Public WriteOnly Property CustomerID() As Integer

    Set (ByVal Value As Integer)
       mintCustomerID = Value
    End Set

End Property
```

Option Strict

Experienced Visual Basic developers know all about the importance of a directive called Option Explicit. I think some of them have it tattooed on their arms. It was never the default up to VB6, but pros knew to turn it on as soon as they installed Visual Basic.

Visual Basic .NET finally makes Option Explicit the default, so you don't have to turn in on anymore. But a new directive called Option Strict has been created. I think that most developers will want to become just as fanatical about turning it on as they have been in the past about Option Explicit.

You can set Option Strict the same way as Option Explicit, by making Option Strict the first line of code in a module. You can also set it on for all modules in a project in the project properties dialog box. Right-click on the project in the Solution Explorer and select Properties. Then select the Build option on the left-hand side of the screen. The dialog box should look like Figure 3.2.

Note the setting for Option Strict in the middle of the page.

When Option Strict is turned on, the Visual Basic compiler no longer allows some types of automatic data type conversions. In particular, any type of implicit conversion that might result in loss of data or a conflict in object types is disallowed. Here's an example:

```
' Does not work with Option Strict On
Dim lngX As Long = 100
Dim intY As Integer
intY = lngX
```

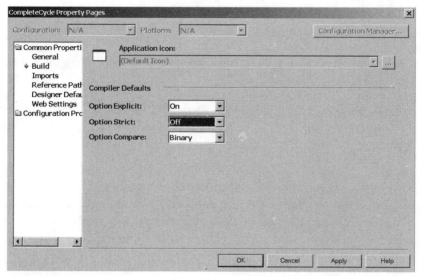

Figure 3.2 Setting Object Strict in the project properties dialog box.

If Option Strict is turned off, this code will compile and run with no errors. However, if Option Strict is turned on, the code will generate a syntax error in the last line. Because a Long data type might have a value that is too big to fit in an Integer, the implicit conversion from Long to Integer is disallowed. (If Option Strict is turned off, and the Long is too big to fit in an Integer, there will be a runtime error.)

To fix that syntax error, you must explicitly tell the compiler that you really want to make the conversion. To do that, the CInt function could be used to explicitly convert the Long to an Integer, so the last line would be changed to:

```
intY = CInt(lngX)
```

Conversion functions, such as CInt, and CSng, have been available in previous versions of Visual Basic, but they are now more important because they are used more often when Option Strict is turned on.

Option Strict also disallows late binding, so if you must have late binding in your code, you'll have to turn Option Strict off.

CType Statement

You might be asking yourself why the previous section is in a chapter on object-oriented changes. The reason is that if Option Strict is set to On, one of its most importance consequences is to disallow many implicit conversions between object types when setting object references. The guiding principle is the same as previously: If an implicit conversion might have a data type problem as runtime, it is disallowed.

Here is an example of code that will work whether Option Strict is set to either Off or On:

```
' This code works with Option Strict On or Off
Dim objForm As Object
Dim frmForm As New Form1
objForm = frmForm
```

Placing a reference to a Form object into an object variable of type Object is always going to work, so Option Strict has no effect on that syntax. That is, going from a specific type to a more generic type never has a problem.

Going the other way is a different story. Here's an example:

```
' This code has a syntax error if Option Strict is On
Dim objForm As Object
objForm = New Form1
Dim frmForm As Form
frmForm = objForm
```

If you have Option Strict set to On, this code will be marked with a syntax error on the last line. That conversion is going from a generic type to a more specific type, so it could theoretically fail. The CType function is available to use in such situations. It performs an explicit casting to a particular object type. If the last line is changed as follows, the code will run properly, even with Option Strict set to On.

```
frmForm = CType(objForm, Form)
```

As this example shows, to use CType, you must supply the object variable that is holding the reference to the instance you want to cast and the type to which you want to cast it. In this case, we are casting to the type Form.

Event Handler Changes

Events in Visual Basic .NET work syntactically very much as they did in VB6. A class implements an event by declaring the event at the beginning of the class and then raising the event as appropriate in the class's routines. However, the way events are handled in the code that instantiates and uses such classes has changed.

At first you might not notice the changes. The way that events are handled looks superficially the same. If an object has events (because it is declared using the keyword WithEvents), it appears in the left-hand drop-down list of the code editor. If the object is highlighted in that list, its events appear in the right-hand drop-down list. VB6 developers are very accustomed to treating controls this way, but the procedure is the same for any object instantiated from a class with events.

In VB6, an event for a control or class instance had a standard name. It consisted of the object name, an underscore, and the event name. So the click event for a text box named txtName would be txtName_Click. This convention is carried forth in Visual Basic .NET. However, there's a big difference. In VB6, the event could only have that name. In Visual Basic .NET, such a name is merely the default—an event can have any name desired.

The difference can be seen when the entire declaration of an event is examined. Here is the txtName_Click event in VB6:

```
' VB6 version of the click event
Private Sub txtName_Click()

End Sub
```

Things are not quite so simple in Visual Basic .NET. Here is the equivalent click event:

```
' VB.NET version of the click event
Private Sub txtName_Click(ByVal sender As Object, _
        ByVal e As System.EventArgs) Handles txtName.Click

End Sub
```

A few things jump out about this new version. First, the click event has parameters. This makes it easier to find out more about what's going on in the click event. (You can examine the parameters on your own. They vary a lot from event to event, so we won't discuss them in detail here.)

Second, the declaration ends with Handles txtName.Click. That is where the event is actually hooked into the routine. The name at the beginning (txtName_Click) is just assigned by the development environment as a convenience. It doesn't have to be that name; it can be assigned any name you like. As long as the Handles txtName.Click appears at the end, the event will still get fired when the text box is clicked.

All event routines in Visual Basic .NET must have this assignment at the end to hook the event to a particular event in a particular class. Just naming an event with the conventional name does not hook the event in automatically, as it did in VB6.

Delegates

There's actually a lot going on under the covers in the way events are handled using the preceding syntax. What Visual Basic .NET is really doing is creating an object called a delegate, which is an intermediary that hooks events in a class to routines in the calling code.

Delegates can be used for many additional techniques involving events and other parts of an object interface. For example, they can be used to hook events from multiple instances of a class into the same event handler. Delegates are a bit advanced for an introductory chapter such as this. However, you should be aware that Visual Basic .NET has many more options for handling events than VB6 does and be ready to learn techniques to handle those options when you need them.

Object-Oriented Enhancements in Visual Basic .NET

Now that we have gotten some of the more prosaic changes out of the way, we are ready to discuss new functionality. Visual Basic developers have been waiting a long time for full object-oriented capabilities, and finally with Visual Basic .NET, we get them.

In Visual Basic .NET, the syntax of Visual Basic has changed, and a number of new keywords have been added. Visual Basic .NET now becomes a true object-oriented language. For example, there is no syntactical difference between a form module and a class module in Visual Basic .NET. They both use the same object-based syntax, and the form is only differentiated by inheriting a form class from the library of base classes. (We don't cover forms in this book because it is aimed at learning Internet development, but this is still a good illustration of just how different Visual Basic .NET is from VB6.)

A Word to the Wise

All tools can be misused. When powerful tools are misused, the consequences can be significant. Object orientation is a powerful programming tool, and it can definitely be misused. We will be noting in the following discussion some of the more common ways object-oriented techniques can be abused. But a couple of general warnings are appropriate at this point.

At the beginning of the chapter, we discussed the fact that those developers with little background in object-oriented concepts would have a difficult time assimilating all the material in this chapter. Let's reiterate that warning. The discussion that follows presumes that you already know the basics of properties, methods, instantiating an object, and similar concepts in VB6. The discussion builds on that base because we can't do an object-oriented tutorial in one chapter.

Also, you should be aware that these object-oriented capabilities, as powerful as they are, should not be used indiscriminately. To cite an analogy, I have a power drill that I like a lot. But I don't use it to pound nails. I have a hammer for that. Just because you gain access to new tools does not mean your old tools are suddenly useless. I've seen designs where the developer thought every variable had to be in an object and where object hierarchies six or eight levels deep were constructed. Don't do that. Use these techniques gradually, and integrate them into your development. That doesn't mean to be shy about trying them, but don't abandon proven techniques you already know, either.

Why Is It Considered Object Oriented Now?

Before we can get to the syntax additions and changes that implement the new object capabilities in Visual Basic .NET, we need to be clear on some basic object concepts. There are four that are considered key to object orientation:

- Abstraction
- Encapsulation
- Inheritance
- Polymorphism

Because readers are presumed to have some understanding of object concepts in VB6, we don't have to talk in too much detail about encapsulation. Even very basic object capabilities, such as the classes in VB6, implement encapsulation pretty well. But we will need to discuss the other concepts, particularly inheritance, in more detail.

Abstraction

Abstraction is the simplest of these concepts and also the most widely available. It basically means the ability to represent a functional concept in code and hide the implementation of that functionality in a black box.

In its broadest sense, any structured programming language allows abstraction. A function, for example, operates as a black box, taking some arguments for input and returning some value without exposing the details of how the value is generated. However, in object-oriented terms, abstraction means a bit more. A single function may not be enough to represent a large concept. To do that, you need the capability to tie many functions together in a related fashion. That is, you need the concept of a class that ties the various abstracted elements of an entity into one single representation.

With its ability to create classes, Visual Basic has had abstraction since version 4, so we won't spend as much time on abstraction as on the other object concepts. However, there are some enhancements that are abstraction-related that we'll be looking at later in the chapter.

Encapsulation

Encapsulation is the object concept that deals with the idea of an interface. In particular, encapsulation demands that an interface to a set of functionality should be separate from the implementation of that functionality. If an interface is defined and consumed, the consumer should not know or care if the implementation behind the interface changes.

VB4 and up also supported encapsulation. A class could be created, and calling code only needed to be concerned with the interface to the class. Changing the way a method was implemented in code did not require any changes in the code calling the class, as long as the interface did not change.

Polymorphism

Abstraction and encapsulation tell us something about the basic structure of an object and its interface. The next two concepts, inheritance and polymorphism, make provision for using interfaces and classes in more complex ways.

Polymorphism extends the concept of an interface beyond a single class and into related classes. We may have a set of classes that all need a method to save their contents, for example. We could implement a Save method on each class. If we use exactly the same interface for Save on each class, we are allowing the Save method to exhibit polymorphism. A collection of objects of different types can all have a Save method. The elements of this collection can then all be treated the same way by code that needs to call the Save method.

There are actually two ways that Visual Basic has supported polymorphism in the past. Late binding to an interface allowed calling the same method on different classes, as long as each class used the same argument list for the method. It was also possible to create a standalone interface and then implement that interface in different classes. In this case, the polymorphic methods could be used with early binding.

All of these capabilities are still intact in Visual Basic .NET.

Inheritance

Inheritance is the big dog in Visual Basic .NET object-oriented improvements because it is the one that Visual Basic has never had before. Experienced object-oriented developers have wanted inheritance ever since VB4 left it out. It is possible to do sophisticated object-based development without inheritance, but there are drawbacks. Certain situations simply cry out for inheritance as the easy, elegant way to accomplish needed object designs. We will see an example later after we have covered the new syntax for inheritance.

So what is inheritance? The easiest way to explain it is to go through a conceptual example. Consider the following typical programming scenario. You have a payroll application, and there are several types of employees: full-time, part-time, hourly, and salaried. You would like to create a set of objects to handle all these types in the payroll application.

Using Visual Basic 6 or earlier versions, one solution would be to create a single Employee class and then set up a property for that class that indicated the subtype (full time hourly, for example). Then the logic in the Employee class would need lots of Select Case logic to change its behavior depending on the subtype of employee. The Calculate method, for example, would have a Select Case that selected the algorithm for calculating pay based on the employee type.

This is a classic example of where the concept of inheritance is useful. Using inheritance, you could create a base class called Employee, which contained all the generic employee functionality. That would include properties for data such as name and department. However, the Employee class might not have a Calculate method because that varies with employee type.

Then you could create subclasses for each subtype of employee. Each subclass would inherit from the base class, thereby gaining all of its functionality. Subclasses would therefore have properties for name and department without having any code for them. As soon as a subclass indicates that it inherits from the Employee base class, it would immediately possess the entire object interface of the Employee class. And that's not just the form of the interface (which you could get in VB6 by defining an interface and implementing it). It also includes all of the logic behind properties and methods. If the ZipCode property in the Employee base class has validation logic to accept only certain formats of zip code, all the subclasses also have this data validation functionality for the ZipCode property.

Then functionality specific to the subtype could be added to the subclass. For instance, each subclass could implement a Calculate method to calculate pay for that employee type. An hourly employee would need a property for the number of hours worked, which is required for calculation of pay for that type of employee. All of the special logic and special properties and methods specific to that subtype of employee would be encapsulated into this one subclass.

Figure 3.3 shows the relationships among the base Employee class and the subclasses. This type of design has many advantages. It is easier to add new subtypes of employee, for instance. But perhaps the biggest advantage is that if something in the base Employee class is changed, all of the subclasses immediately respond to the changes. This is called implementation inheritance.

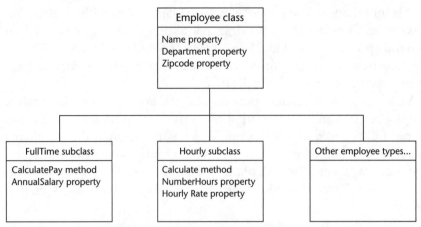

Figure 3.3   The Employee class and its subclasses.

For example, suppose your company operates only in America, and the ZipCode property therefore requires numeric digits. You could have your Employee base class do the data validation to ensure this. Later, your company might open a Canadian operation. In that case, the ZipCode property would need to accept a different format to store Canadian postal codes. This logic could be added to the base Employee class, and all subclasses would immediately have it.

There are variations on this design. The base employee class could be functional for a generic employee with a Calculate method that only worked for a full-time salaried employee. Then the subclasses could override the Calculate method with their own ways of calculating pay for other employee types.

This conceptual design, in which generic functionality is abstracted to a base class and specific functionality is encapsulated in subclasses, takes a while to get used to. It's worth the effort. Some common programming needs are well satisfied by this capability. We will see the syntax for using inheritance in Visual Basic .NET code later in this chapter.

Changes in Syntax for Classes

Later in the chapter, we discuss the syntax for the new capabilities such as inheritance. But first, we need to cover changes in the way classes are created in Visual Basic .NET versus VB6.

One big improvement is the ability to place more than one class in a physical source code file. We touched on this in an example early in the chapter, when we discussed namespaces. Within a source module, a class is begun with the Class keyword and ends with the End Class statement. Here is an example:

```
Public Class MySimpleClass
    ' Class members and routines go here
    Public Sub MyMethod()
        Console.Writeline("I'm a method")
    End Sub
End Class


' Other classes if needed--we can include
' as many as we need.

Public Class MyOtherClass
    ' Class members and routines go here
    ' ...
End Class
```

These classes are by default in the project's default namespace. If we want them to be in a different namespace, we place a Namespace statement at the beginning of the classes specifying the namespace desired and then place an End Namespace statement after all of the classes in the namespace, as shown earlier in the chapter.

Methods in classes are handled the same way as in VB6, by creating a Public Sub or Public Function. Events for classes are also created the same way as in VB6. Properties are handled with the new syntax for properties discussed earlier in the chapter.

Overloading

Methods do have one significant new feature in Visual Basic .NET. Multiple versions of the same method can exist in a class, as long as each version has a different argument list. This feature is called method overloading. Here is a typical scenario where this feature is helpful.

Suppose our class needs a method named Display to display data to some device. Such a method might need to accept either integers or strings and to have different logic for generating output for these two data types. To create such a method, we create two versions of the Display method, each with its own logic for display of data. To indicate that the method is overloaded, we use the Overloads keyword. Here are shell code fragments that show the declaration of the two versions of the Display method:

```
Overloads Sub Display(ByVal iNumber As Integer)
    ' display routine that handles number goes here
End Sub

Overloads Sub Display(ByVal sString As String)
    ' display routine that handles string goes here
End Sub
```

The methods must have some difference in the parameter list to be eligible for overloading. The difference can be a different number of parameters, different types of parameters, or both. The set of parameters for a particular version of a method, including the types of the parameters, is sometimes called the method's "signature."

Without overloading, getting the Display functionality previously mentioned would have required one of two more complex techniques. Two separate display routines could be constructed with different names, one for a number and one for a string. Or optional parameters could be used, but it would be necessary for the programmer using the routine to keep the order and type of parameters straight. Overloaded methods are much cleaner than either of these techniques.

As you use the .NET Framework, you will notice that many of the .NET Framework classes contain overloaded methods. The fact that a method is overloaded is noted in the Intellisense window. A sample screen containing Intellisense for an overloaded method is shown in Figure 3.4.

Note the part of the screen indicated by the black arrow that says 2 of 4. This part of the Intellisense tooltip window is calling your attention to the fact that the method being accessed is the second of four overloaded methods. The up and down arrows next to the 2 of 4 allow you to cycle through the other overloaded versions and to show their parameter lists. (This method happens to be a constructor method. Such methods are discussed a bit later in the chapter under the heading *Constructors*.)

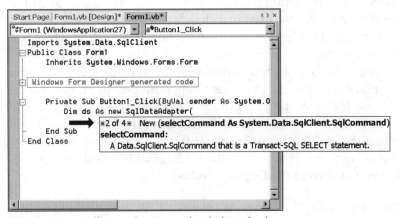

Figure 3.4   Intellisense for an overloaded method.

Declaration and Instantiation

Instantiation of a class in Visual Basic .NET is done with syntax similar to that in VB6, although there are notable differences. You could declare an instance of a class named MySimpleClass in VB6 with a line like this:

```
Dim objMyObject As New MySimpleClass    ' instantiation in VB6
```

However, this syntax has a big drawback. VB6 did not instantiate the class when this line was executed. Instead, actual instantiation was delayed until some reference was made to the class, such as trying to set a property of the class. Because such a reference could be considerably separated in the code from the preceding line, most developers preferred to instantiate a class like this in VB6:

```
Dim objMyObject As MySimpleClass    ' other way to instantiate in VB6
Set objMyObject = New MySimpleClass
```

In this case, instantiation was definitely carried out by the second line, so the developer knew exactly where instantiation would appear.

Both techniques work in Visual Basic .NET, but the difference is that the first technique also instantiates the object immediately. There is no delay in instantiation until the first reference. That means that the reasons for avoiding the first technique in VB6 no longer apply in Visual Basic .NET, and you will see it used as the preferred way to instantiate an object in most Visual Basic .NET sample code.

It was sometimes inappropriate in VB6 to instantiate with New. The most commonly used alternative was the CreateObject function, which does not exist in Visual Basic .NET and is not needed. The New operator is used for almost all class instantiations in Visual Basic .NET. (There are a few exceptions to this, and there is a CreateInstance method of a class called the Assembly class that can also be used to create an instance of a class. However, the circumstances under which this technique is used are quite limited.)

Constructors

Even though the same basic syntax shown for instantiation works in both VB6, and Visual Basic .NET, there is one major addition to Visual Basic .NET syntax for instantiation. The easiest way to explain it is to start with the closest available VB6 counterpart.

When a class was instantiated in VB6, the first thing that happened in the class code was the firing of the Class_Initialize event. This event contained code that needed to be run when a new instance of the class was created. However, VB6 had no way to pass parameters to Class_Initialize. If an instance of a class needed some parameters to tell it how to act, a different method or property had to be implemented to pass that information into the class. (I typically used a method named Load for this in VB6.)

In Visual Basic .NET, Class_Initialize does not exist. Instead, the class has a method called a constructor. The name of the method is New. This method is the first code executed in a new instance of a Visual Basic .NET class, just like Class_Initialize was the first code run in VB6.

Because New is a method, it can have parameters. When you create a New method for one of your classes in Visual Basic .NET, you can give it any parameters you like (or none, if it doesn't need any). Such a constructor is sometimes called a parameterized constructor.

If a class has a New method with no parameters, then the code to instantiate a class in Visual Basic .NET is very similar to the equivalent code in VB6:

```
Dim objMyObject As New MySimpleClass()    ' instantiation in VB.NET
```

The only difference from equivalent syntax in VB6 is the set of parentheses at the end of the line. Note that if you leave these off when typing in the line, they will be added automatically by the VB code editor.

Again, this example shows a New method with no parameters. If the New method for a class has parameters, you must supply those parameters when an object is declared and instantiated. For example, suppose a class named Customer has a New method that requires a customer ID, like this:

```
Public Sub New(nCustomerID As Integer)
    ' Use CustomerID to initialize the data in the object
    mnCustomerID = nCustomerID    ' save customer ID for property
    GetCustomerData(nCustomerID)
End Sub
```

For such a class, you must supply the customer ID at instantiation. Here's an example:

```
Dim nCustID As Integer = 5
Dim objCustomer As New Customer(nCustID)
```

This generates an instance of the Customer class for the customer with an ID of 5.

> **NOTE** Constructors are optional. Just like you could leave out the
> Class_Terminate event for a class in VB6, you can also leave off the New
> constructor in Visual Basic .NET. If you leave off the constructor, no code
> in the class is run when the class is instantiated.

Overloaded Constructors

Now let's combine two concepts we've discussed in this section, overloading
and constructors. We discussed the fact that methods can be overloaded so that
there are multiple versions of the method that take different parameters. Well,
a constructor is just a method with a special name. It, too, can be overloaded.
That means you can create several New methods in a class, each with a different parameter list. Such constructors are referred to as overloaded constructors.

There is one minor syntactical difference. When a normal method is overloaded, all versions of the method are declared with the Overloads keyword.
However, constructors can never have the Overloads keyword in their declaration. For example, we might enhance our Customer class so that we can either
pass in a customer ID, as before, or leave it off. If it is left off, this means that we
are starting up a brand new customer, and an ID needs to be generated automatically. Now our two constructors for the class could look something like this:

```
Public Sub New(nCustomerID As Integer)
    ' Use CustomerID to initialize the data in the object
    mnCustomerID = nCustomerID      ' save customer ID for property
    GetCustomerData(nCustomerID)
End Sub

Public Sub New()
    ' Get a new CustomerID for a brand new customer
    mnCustomerID = GenerateNewCustID()
    SetDefaultFields()
End Sub
```

Now we can still instantiate an existing customer with this code:

```
Dim nCustID As Integer = 5
Dim objCustomer As New Customer(nCustID)
```

Or we can instantiate a brand new customer and have an ID generated with
this code:

```
Dim objCustomer As New Customer()
```

You can have as many overloaded constructors as you need. I've seen classes in the .NET Framework with as many as 16 overloaded constructors. Perhaps that should be dubbed overloading overkill. To help those who consume your classes, it's good practice to keep the number down to just those constructors you really need.

Life Cycle of an Object

In the previous chapter, we discussed many changes related to the fact that Visual Basic .NET must fit within the .NET Framework. Another such change is the way an object's life cycle is managed in Visual Basic .NET.

In VB6, we have a fair amount of control over phases of an object's life span. We were able to write code affecting the life cycle in several places, with the most commonly used being:

Class_Initialize event.   First code in a class to run when an instance was created

Class_Terminate event.   Ran automatically as soon as an object's reference count reached zero

We have seen that the replacement for the Class_Initialize event is a constructor. So what's the replacement for the Class_Terminate event? The answer to that question is a bit complex.

The closest analog to Class_Terminate is a method on a class called a destructor. It is named Finalize. However, there's a big difference. The execution of Class_Terminate was predictable and only depended on conditions in the application. Execution of Finalize is less predictable and depends on external conditions.

The reason is that the way memory for objects is reclaimed (a process called garbage collection) has changed in .NET. Finalize runs when an object is garbage-collected. But an object is not necessarily garbage collected when the reference count reaches zero. The CLR determines when garbage collection runs depending on, among other things, when more memory for objects is needed. Because of this, there may be an indefinite amount of time after an object's reference count reaches zero before the Finalize method is run. With such a potential delay, it is usually unwise to put much code in the Finalize method. Instead, it is considered good practice to write a different method, normally called Dispose, to take care of an object's cleanup chores (releasing database connections, for example). Then the code that created the object is responsible for calling Dispose at the right time.

The reason for the change is not arbitrary. Some of the biggest benefits of .NET arise from its sophisticated garbage collection. But object cleanup was easier in previous Visual Basic versions than it is Visual Basic .NET.

Inheritance Syntax
in Visual Basic .NET

Earlier in the chapter, we discussed the conceptual nature of inheritance. Now, having gotten some of the other object enhancements of Visual Basic .NET under our belt, we are ready to tackle the syntax used to do inheritance.

We saw earlier how a class is defined in code in Visual Basic .NET:

```
Public Class MySimpleClass
    ' Class members and routines go here
    Public Sub MyMethod()
        Console.Writeline("I'm a method")
    End Sub
End Class
```

In this case, MySimpleClass only has the methods and properties defined for it in the class. (This is not quite true, as we will see a bit further in this chapter in the section *Everything's an Object*. But it will suffice for our discussion at this point.)

Now suppose we want MySimpleClass to be a subclass of some other class. As we discussed earlier, that would give MySimpleClass all of the object interface and capabilities of the parent class, and then we would just add the functionality that needed to be specific to MySimpleClass.

Let's call the base class MyBaseClass; suppose it looks like this:

```
Public Class MyBaseClass
    ' Class members and routines go here
    Public Sub New()
        ' initialization logic goes here
        Console.Writeline("Cranking up an instance of MyBaseClass...")
    End Sub

    Public Sub MethodInBaseClass()
        Console.Writeline("I'm a method in the base class")
    End Sub
End Class
```

To make MySimpleClass a subclass of MyBaseClass, we use the Inherits keyword, and MySimpleClass changes (shown in bold) to look like this:

```
Public Class MySimpleClass
    Inherits MyBaseClass

    ' Class members and routines go here
    Public Sub MyMethod()
        Console.Writeline("I'm a method")
    End Sub
End Class
```

Note the second line. Once MySimpleClass has this line added, it instantly gains all of the functionality of MyBaseClass. Suppose we now declare an instance of MySimpleClass with this line:

```
Dim objX As New MySimpleClass
```

Checking Intellisense for objX reveals that objX has a method named MethodInBaseClass. When that method is accessed, no code runs in the class MySimpleClass. Instead, code runs in MyBaseClass because that's where MethodInBaseClass is.

MySimpleClass also gains a constructor (New subroutine) by inheriting from MyBaseClass because the base class has one. When the line of code shown executes, the New subroutine in MyBaseClass executes and performs any setup logic necessary.

If you are new to the concept of inheritance, it's a good exercise to go through the preceding code. To do so, take the following steps:

1. Start up an ASP.NET Web Application project. Name it something appropriate, such as TestInheritance.

2. Select Project, Add Class from the menu, and name the new class MyClasses.vb.

3. Place the code shown above for MySimpleClass and MyBaseClass in the class module.

4. Go to the blank WebForm1 created for the project. Place a button on this form. Double-click the button and place this code in the button's click event:

```
Dim objX As New MyClasses.MySimpleClass()
objX.MyMethod()
objX.MethodInBaseClass()
```

Run the project, and when the Web Form comes up in the browser, click the button. If you like, you can set a breakpoint on the first line in the code in step 4 and watch the code execute.

NOTE By default, the Console.Writeline statements in this example do not write to the Output window because this is a Web project. You may wish to route the Console.Writeline output to a text file for viewing.

To do this, place the following two routines in your WebForm1.aspx.vb code:

```
Private Sub Page_Load(ByVal sender As System.Object, ByVal e As
System.EventArgs) Handles MyBase.Load
    'Put user code to initialize the page here
    If Not Page.IsPostBack Then
```

```
            Dim fs As New System.IO.FileStream("c:\trace.txt", _
                    System.IO.FileMode.OpenOrCreate, _
                System.IO.FileAccess.Write)
            ' Create a Char writer.
            Dim w As New System.IO.StreamWriter(fs)
            Console.SetOut(w)
        End If
    End Sub
    Private Sub Page_Unload(ByVal sender As Object, _
            ByVal e As System.EventArgs) Handles MyBase.Unload
        Console.Out.Flush()
    End Sub
```

In this case, we are writing to a text file named C:\trace.txt. The code in the Page Load event routes the output of the Console object to this text file, and the Page Unload event flushes the written text to the file. This technique can be used anytime you would like to use the Console.Writeline to send output to a text file.

IMPORTANT **Depending on the configuration of your system and the operating system you are using, it may be necessary to grant appropriate access permissions to the file for ASP.NET to write to it. If access is not permitted, running the program will generate a message in Internet Explorer explaining what to do.**

The output results from running the project will be:

```
Cranking up an instance of MyBaseClass...
I'm a method
I'm a method in the base class
```

We will see a more detailed example later, after we've covered the rest of the syntax related to inheritance.

Overriding Methods and Properties

As we've seen, when a subclass inherits from a base class, it has access to all the members (properties, methods, and events) of the base class. In our previous example, the subclass used the members of the base class as is. When such a member is accessed, the code that runs is actually in the base class.

However, sometimes a subclass needs to have a different version of a property or method from the base class with its own special logic. In this case, the property or method is included in the code for the subclass. Doing this is called overriding the property or method in the base class, and it is indicated in code with the Overrides keyword.

Full overriding of properties and methods is completely supported in Visual Basic .NET. The overriding logic may be similar to that in the base class, or it may be wildly different.

In many cases, a property or method in a subclass may need to do a small amount of special work and then let the rest of the work be done by the equivalent property or method in the base class. This can be done by referring to the base class with the MyBase keyword.

Members of the base class can be overridden in subclasses only if they are declared with the keyword Overridable. However, the base class has additional control. It can require that a member be overridden in a subclass by using the MustOverride keyword.

If a base class contains a member marked as MustOverride, that class is incomplete by itself. It cannot be instantiated directly because then there would be nothing to override the member marked MustOverride. The keyword that indicates that a class must be inherited to be used is MustInherit. A class with any member marked as MustOverride must itself be set as MustInherit.

An Example to Illustrate Inheritance-Related Keywords

Now let's step through an example that shows each of these concepts in action. We'll start with our previous example, which used the classes named MySimpleClass and MyBaseClass.

To show overriding, first add this method to MyBaseClass:

```
Public Overridable Sub SomeMethod()
    Console.WriteLine("I'm a method that can be overridden.")
End Sub
```

Now add the following method to MySimpleClass:

```
Public Overrides Sub SomeMethod()
    Console.WriteLine("I have overridden the base class!")
End Sub
```

Next you need to add a line to the button event code to access the new method. Add this line at the end of the event code for Button1:

```
objX.SomeMethod
```

If you run the program now, the output now will be:

```
Cranking up an instance of MyBaseClass...
I'm a method
I'm a method in the base class
I have overridden the base class!
```

Note that the code in SomeMethod in the base class was not executed. An overriding member completely replaces the member in the base class. But we can get access to the member in the base class with the MyBase keyword. Change the SomeMethod code in MySimpleClass to look like this:

```
Public Overrides Sub SomeMethod()
    Console.WriteLine("I have overridden the base class!")
    MyBase.SomeMethod
End Sub
```

Now run the program again, and you'll get this output:

```
Cranking up an instance of MyBaseClass...
I'm a method
I'm a method in the base class
I have overridden the base class!
I'm a method that can be overridden.
```

Finally, let's demonstrate MustInherit and MustOverride. First, change the declaration of SomeMethod in MyBaseClass so that the first line looks like this:

```
Public MustOverride Sub SomeMethod()
```

As soon as you make this change, you'll get indications of two syntax errors. One is in the SomeMethod routine itself. Because it is now marked MustOverride, it cannot contain any logic. In fact, it can't even take an End Sub. So you must remove the rest of the SomeMethod code and just leave the declaration.

The second syntax error is at the top of the class. The class must now be marked MustInherit. Change the declaration of the class to look like this:

```
Public MustInherit Class MyBaseClass
```

Now the project will run again; it will give these results:

```
Cranking up an instance of MyBaseClass...
I'm a method
I'm a method in the base class
I have overridden the base class!
```

Additional Inheritance-Related Keywords

The keywords discussed previously are the ones most commonly used in classes using inheritance. There are some additional keywords that are useful for special cases.

The Shadows Keyword

We have already learned that we can override members of a base class only if those members are marked with the Overridable keyword. However, there are circumstances where a base class did not make a member overridable, but we need to override its functionality anyway. For example, if someone else wrote the base class, which has a bug in a property or method, and we don't have the source code, we need to be able to intercept calls to the property or method to correct the problem.

There is a way to do this. The Shadows keyword allows you to create a member on a subclass that has the same name as a member in the base class, regardless of whether the member can be overridden. In fact, you can even override a method and give it a different parameter list.

This technique should be used sparingly and with great care. A base class that does not mark a member overridable may assume that the member gets called at certain points, and Shadows may cause that not to happen. But for the rare cases when you absolutely must get control of a base class member, Shadows is available.

Here is an example, using the classes named MySimpleClass and MyBase-Class, that we have used for previous examples. Add this code to MyBaseClass to create a new method:

```
Public Sub TestMethod(nSize As Integer)
    Console.WriteLine("The size is " & nSize.ToString)
End Sub
```

Note that TestMethod cannot be overridden with the Overrides keyword in a base class because it is not marked Overridable. Now place this code at the end of the button click event:

```
objX.TestMethod(5)
```

The output for the program will now include the line:

```
The size is 5
```

Now use the Shadows keyword to replace this method in the subclass. The replacement TestMethod method code should look like this:

```
Public Shadows Sub TestMethod(nSize As Integer, sName As String)
    Console.WriteLine("Size is " & nSize.ToString & " and Name is " &
sName)
End Sub
```

Attempting to run the program at this point will get a syntax error because TestMethod now requires two arguments, and the button click event only supplies one. The line that invokes TestMethod must be changed to something like this to run:

```
objX.TestMethod(5, "Jack")
```

In this case, the output line will become:

```
Size is 5 and Name is Jack
```

Note that the logic in the base class version of TestMethod is not run at all after the new shadowed version is created in the subclass. However, you can run it using the MyBase keyword. To do that, this line can be inserted in the shadowed version of the method:

```
MyBase.TestMethod(nSize)
```

Protected Members

We have seen that the public interface of a base class is automatically exposed in the subclass. We have not stated it explicitly, but it should be apparent that routines marked private in a base class are not available to the subclass, either through an interface or through use of the MyBase keyword.

There are some situations in which a base class needs to provide a member to a subclass, but it is not desirable for that member to be exposed to any consumers of the subclass. The Protected keyword is used to mark such a member. Here is an example, using the classes named MySimpleClass and MyBaseClass that we have used for previous examples. Add this code to MyBaseClass to create a new method:

```
Protected Sub ProtectedMethod(nSize As Integer)
    Console.WriteLine("The protected size is " & nSize.ToString)
End Sub
```

Now place this code at the end of the button click event:

```
objX.ProtectedMethod(7)
```

This will cause a syntax error, because ProtectedMethod is only available from within the sub-class, not from calling code.

Now place the following code in the subclass:

```
Public Sub GetProtectedSize(nSize As Integer)
    MyBase.ProtectedMethod(nSize)
End Sub
```

Change the line in the button click event to:

```
ObjX.GetProtectedSize(7)
```

The output for the program will now include the line:

```
The protected size is 7
```

Inheritance Keyword Summary

Table 3.1 summarizes the keywords we've just discussed.

Table 3.1   Inheritance Keywords

KEYWORD	PURPOSE	SHORT CODE EXAMPLE
Inherits	Points to the base class for a class. Inherits SomeBaseClass	`Public Class SomeClass`
Overridable	Indicates that a member in the base class can be overridden in classes derived (inherited) from this class.	`Public Overridable Sub Clear()`
Overrides	Used in a member in a subclass to indicate that the member is overriding the member of the same name in the base class.	`Public Overrides Sub Dispose()`
MustInherit	An attribute of a class declaration for a base class. Indicates that the class cannot be instantiated directly; it must be inherited and then the subclass can be instantiated.	`Public MustInherit Class MySimpleClass`
MustOverride	Indicates that any classes that derive (inherit) from this class must supply an override for this member. Only available for classes declared as MustInherit. A member that is marked as MustOverride only supplies an interface for the member. No logic, not even an End Sub or End Function line, is allowed.	`Public MustOverride Function Name(nID as Long) As String`

KEYWORD	PURPOSE	SHORT CODE EXAMPLE
MyBase	Reference to base class for use in the subclass' code.	`StringProperty =` `MyBase.StringProperty`
Shadows	Indicates that a member in a subclass replaces the member in the base class with the same name, regardless of whether the base class member is marked overridable. A member marked with Shadows can have a different set of parameters than the equivalent base class member.	`Public Shadows Sub Name()`
Protected	Indicates that this member is only available to classes derived (inherited) from this class.	`Protected Sub Clear()`

Here's one more example to illustrate usage of inheritance-related keywords. Suppose we have a base class that represents customers. It looks like this:

```
Public Class Customer

    ' Public properties.
    Public Name As String
    Public Active As Boolean

    ' Use a constructor to initialize our public
    ' properties
    Public Sub New(ByVal Name as String, ByVal bActive as Boolean)
        Name = sName
        Active = bActive
    End Sub

    ' Use the Overridable keyword
    ' to let subclasses implement
    ' their own version.
    Public Overridable Sub CheckStatus()
        Console.WriteLine ("Name: " & Name)
        Console.WriteLine ("Active: " & Active)
    End Sub

End Class
```

Now, let's create a class for a special type of customer called a target customer. The difference is that we want a target customer to be called on a certain date. The class for TargetCustomer has the following code:

```
Public Class TargetCustomer
    Inherits Customer

    ' Declare another public property for this subclass
    Public DateToContact As Date

    ' Create a constructor for the subclass
    Public Sub New(ByVal sName As String, _
                       ByVal bActive As Boolean, _
                       ByVal datDateToContact as Date)

        ' Call the base class's constructor
        MyBase.New(sName, bActive)

        ' Initialize variables in this subclass.
        DateToContact = datDateToContact
    End Sub

    ' Override the base class's method
    Public Overrides Sub CheckStatus()
        'Call the base methods version
        MyBase.CheckStatus()

        ' Print out properties specific to subclass
        Console.WriteLine ("Call them on: " & DateToContact)
    End Sub

End Class
```

Here is code to create an instance of the TargetCustomer class. The instantiation requires passing parameters to initialize the properties for TargetCustomer (which includes the properties in the Customer base class).

```
Dim objMyTargetCustomer As New TargetCustomer_
                      ("Simple Simon, Inc.", False, #February 22,
2002#)
```

The CheckStatus method can then be called, and it will generate results from both the base class and the subclass:

```
objMyTargetCustomer.CheckStatus
```

The output would look like this:

```
Name: Simple Simon, Inc.
Active: False
Call them on: February 22, 2002
```

The first two lines are generated by the CheckStatus method in the base class (Customer), which is called within the CheckStatus method of the subclass

(TargetCustomer). Then the third line is generated by a line within that same CheckStatus method of TargetCustomer.

Everything's an Object

The last chapter mentioned that the Variant data type is replaced by the Object type and that the Object type would be discussed further in this chapter. I also mentioned in this chapter that a class that does not inherit from anything only exposes the members that are implemented in its code. At that point it was noted that that was not quite true, and now we are ready to take up both of these loose ends.

In reality, all classes and data types in .NET inherit from a base type known as Object. That includes such types as numbers and strings. Because all types descend from Object, a variable of type Object can hold any .NET type. That's why the Object type is an effective replacement for Variant.

That base Object type has a minimal interface that is then inherited by all .NET types. For example, it has a GetType method that returns the current type. That means all .NET objects have that method, too.

Perhaps the most commonly used method of the Object type is ToString, which returns a string representation of an object. This method is commonly overridden in subclasses; therefore the way the string is generated varies a lot for different types in .NET. But the reason all .NET types have a ToString method is that it is a part of the interface of the Object type.

Inheriting from the .NET Framework

One of the reasons inheritance is important in .NET is that it is common in programming to need to extend a class in the .NET Framework base classes. These classes furnish a lot of functionality, but they can't be all things to all people. For example, the ADO.NET classes for data access (covered in Chapter 8) often need to be extended. Middle-tier data objects in .NET often inherit from these data-oriented classes and then add additional functionality specific to a particular application.

More Encapsulation Features

Visual Basic .NET has some additional changes and additions that can be loosely grouped under the encapsulation banner. These include:

- Shared members on classes
- Structures as a replacement for user-defined types (UDTs)
- Nested type support

Shared Members on Classes

Most object designs completely isolate object instances from one another. That is, there is no data that is shared by different instances of a class. Setting a property in one instance has absolutely no effect in other instances. In VB6, it was required to do things this way. However, it is occasionally helpful to have information shared by all active instances in a class. In Visual Basic .NET, shared members (properties or methods) can be constructed to do this. The concept is identical to what are called static members in C++.

The Shared keyword is used to create shared members. Like regular properties, shared properties can be implemented as Public variables. Thus, to create a shared property named CommonName, you could use the following code:

```
Public Shared CommonName As String
```

If this property is set in any instance, it is set for all of them.

You can also create a shared property using a property procedure. To create such a property called CommonName, the property would be declared like this:

```
Public Shared Property CommonName() As String
```

From that point, the property is coded the way that it would normally be done, with one rather large exception. The code in the property must not refer to anything that is related to a specific instance of the class.

As a consequence, if a property needs a private, module-level variable to hold the property's value, that variable must be shared. So the full implementation of a CommonName property using a property procedure would look like this:

```
' Declaration at top of class module
Private Shared msCommonName As String

' Intervening code here...

Public Shared Property CommonName() As String
    Get
        Return msCommonName
    End Get
    Set(ByVal Value As String)
        msCommonName = Value
    End Set
End Property
```

If you place such a property in MySimpleClass (the class we used for previous examples), you could then place this code in the button click event instead of the code that we used earlier to test the shared property:

```
Dim objX As New MySimpleClass()
Dim objY As New MySimpleClass()

objX.CommonName = "Name set in instance X"
Console.WriteLine(objY.CommonName)
```

You will see that the value for CommonName that is set by objX is fetched by the last line of code, even though that line is using objY.

Shared methods can also be implemented. A shared method would be declared like this in code:

```
Public Shared Sub CommonMethod()
```

Shared methods can also be accessed with just a class name, without referencing any active instance of the class. For example, we can place the following line of code just below the preceding lines:

```
Console.WriteLine(MySimpleClass.CommonName)
```

This will return the same value for the property.

There are many constructs that you will use in your code all the time that are actually implemented as shared members. For example, the Console class has a shared method called Writeline, and that's why you can use Console.Writeline without declaring an active instance of the Console class.

Structures Replace User-Defined Types

Even before we had objects in Visual Basic, we had user-defined types. A user-defined type was declared using the Type ... End Type construct. Such a type and all of its constituent elements (members) were made publicly available.

We discussed this briefly in Chapter 2, but we're ready to go into more detail in this chapter. Let's start with a typical example done in VB6:

```
Type Employee      ' VB6 syntax for user-defined types
    EmployeeID As Integer
    EmployeePhone As String
    EmployeeStatus As Boolean
End Type
```

A variable could then be declared as type Employee like this:

```
Dim MyEmployee As Employee
```

Constituent elements were then accessed like this:

```
MyEmployee.EmployeePhone = "(615) 555-5309"
```

This looks like the syntax used to access a property. In fact user-defined types were often used in place of simple objects in VB6 and earlier for superior performance, especially if a lot of instances were needed,.

In Visual Basic .NET, the Type statement is no longer available, which means that user-defined types are not available either. In their place is something called a structure.

A structure is declared using the Structure ... End Structure syntax, similar to Type ... End Type. However, the big difference is that constituent elements of a structure must be declared with one of the following scoping qualifiers: Dim, Public, Protected, Friend, Protected Friend, or Private. Dim and Public both indicate public access, and the others give various restrictions on access.

To illustrate, if you wanted to get a structure in Visual Basic .NET that was very much like the user-defined type for preceding Employee, it could look like this, assuming that we decide to take advantage of some of the declaration modifiers:

```
Structure Employee
    Public EmployeeID As Integer        ' Must declare, even if Public.
    Dim EmployeePhone As String         ' Defaults to Public access.
    Private EmployeeStatus As Boolean   ' Can be Private inside Structure.
End Structure
```

Structures can also contain arrays as constituent elements. And structures can contain other structures nested inside of their elements, like this:

```
Structure Employee
    Public EmployeeID As Integer        ' Must declare, even if Public.
    Dim EmployeePhone As String         ' Defaults to Public access.
    Private EmployeeStatus As Boolean   ' Can be Private inside
Structure.
    Public Structure EmployeeAddress
        Public Street As String
        Public City As String
        Public State As String
        Public Zip As Integer
    End Structure
End Structure
```

The syntax for accessing a structure is object syntax, like the syntax for accessing user-defined types in VB6 and earlier. And structures can be used in that same role as lightweight objects for simple objects that require many instances.

Unlike other variables, you can't initialize any values in a structure when you declare it. You must access the elements in code to set each one individually.

Members in Structures

There is one major capability of structures that has no analog in VB6. Structures can have logic associated with them. Here is an example in which a structure has implemented its own custom constructor (New method) to ensure that an element is initialized, and has also implemented a Clear method:

```
Structure Employee
    Public EmployeeID As Integer       ' Must declare, even if Public.
    Dim EmployeePhone As String        ' Defaults to Public access.
    Private EmployeeStatus As Boolean  ' Can be Private inside
Structure.
    Public Structure EmployeeAddress
        Public Street As String
        Public City As String
        Public State As String
        Public Zip As Integer
    End Structure
    Public Sub New(ByVal nID As Integer)
        Me.EmployeeID = nID
    End Sub
    Public Sub Clear()
        Me.EmployeePhone = ""
        Me.EmployeeStatus = False
    End Sub
End Structure
```

This ability highlights the fact that everything is really an object in .NET. Because they are actually objects, structures can have these object features.

Value Types versus Reference Types

There is one big difference between structures and classes. A standard class is called a reference type. Structures, along with numeric types such as Integer, Long, Boolean, and Single, are called value types. These two different categories are processed differently by the CLR. This is done to improve the performance of .NET.

To get technical, reference types are allocated internally on the heap, which is designed for generic objects. Value types are allocated on the stack, which is optimized for more strictly defined types.

There are a number of implications of this dichotomy. Perhaps the most noticeable is that you can have two different object variables that refer to the same instance of a class. Changing a property value using one reference will cause the change to be visible through the other. This is not possible with a value type. You cannot have two different variables that refer to the same integer storage location.

Interfaces

VB5 introduced the concept of generic interfaces that could be implemented by multiple classes to the Visual Basic world. As we learned earlier in the chapter, the ability to use the same interface on different classes is key to polymorphism.

Interfaces in Visual Basic .NET share some of the features of interfaces in VB6. A class implementing an interface is required to implement all elements of the interface. And a class still indicates the interface it will implement with the Implements keyword. However, there are some key differences. These include:

- Interfaces in Visual Basic .NET are declared completely separately from classes.
- Interfaces are implemented in classes differently.
- Interfaces can now contain events.
- Interface members are accessed differently in calling code.

Let's look at the details on these.

Declaring an Interface

In VB6, an interface was declared using a class. Typically the class had no logic in the declared methods and properties (though it was possible to put logic there and instantiate the class separately from its usage as an interface).

In Visual Basic .NET, there is an Interface keyword to declare an interface. A typical example looks like this:

```
Public Interface MyInterface
    Sub MyMethod(ByVal nIntegerParameter As Integer, _
              ByVal sStringParameter As String)
    Property MyStringProperty() As String
    ReadOnly Property MyIntegerProperty() As Integer
    Event MyEvent(ByVal nEventParameter As Integer)
End Interface
```

This example also demonstrates that an event can now be a part of an interface, which was not true in VB6 and earlier versions.

Implementing Interfaces in Classes

Implementing an interface in a class is done with the Implements keyword, just as in VB6. But everything else is different.

Instead of the strange naming convention used by VB6 to declare implemented properties and methods, the syntax in Visual Basic .NET is much cleaner. Here's an example of a class that implements the interface previously declared (without any logic in the members):

```
Public Class UseInterface
    Implements MyInterface
    Public Sub MyMethod(ByVal nIntegerParameter As Integer, _
                    ByVal sStringParameter As String) _
                    Implements MyInterface.MyMethod


    End Sub
    Public Property MyStringProperty() As String _
        Implements MyInterface.MyStringProperty
      Get

      End Get
      Set(ByVal Value As String)

      End Set
    End Property
    Public ReadOnly Property MyIntegerProperty() As Integer _
        Implements MyInterface.MyIntegerProperty
      Get

      End Get
    End Property
    Public Event MyEvent(ByVal nEventParameter As Integer) _
        Implements MyInterface.MyEvent
End Class
```

As this example shows, the naming of the members is back to a more normal usage, and the tie-in to the interface is done via the Implements keyword at the end of each member declaration.

As in VB6, a class that implements an interface can also implement its own members separately from the interface. For example, the preceding class could have a method that did not implement anything in the interface, like this:

```
Public Sub NotFromInterface()

End Sub
```

Accessing Interface Members in Code

Many Visual Basic developers were confused by the way implemented interfaces had to be used in VB4 to VB6. If a class implemented an interface, its object variable had to be declared a certain way before the implemented interface was even visible. This confusing requirement is gone in Visual Basic .NET.

Figure 3.5 Available members for the UseInterface class.

Now any element of an object's interface can be accessed the usual way, whether it is from an interface or a part of the class's own members. To illustrate, Figure 3.5 is an example of Intellisense for the UseInterface class, showing the members that are available. As this example shows, all of the members of the class are available, including those from the implemented interface and those that are just part of the class's own interface.

Changes in Moving from VBScript

If you have already done some Web development in Active Server Pages, you probably used VBScript to write some of the logic needed to make these pages work. VBScript does not exist in .NET. It is replaced by Visual Basic .NET, even in scripting files where there is no explicit compilation. .NET's common language runtime performs compilation of such code automatically. That means that you can use exactly the same syntax inside ASP.NET pages as you use in Visual Basic programs. It is not necessary to learn a separate scripting language in .NET. Also, the limitations of VBScript, such as only allowing Variant data types, are gone in .NET.

Unlike Active Server Pages, ASP.NET allows any .NET-enabled language to be used for scripting in ASP.NET pages. You may see those pages using languages such as JavaScript, C#, or COBOL. Because we are focused on Visual Basic .NET, we won't be going into any more detail on that.

Wrapping Up

In this chapter, we've covered the most important changes in Visual Basic .NET that are related to objects and classes. We have by no means covered all of the changes and additions, but these are the ones you will probably need to know about right away to begin Web programming with ASP.NET and Visual Basic .NET.

As you master all the concepts and changes in this chapter, you may want to look to more advanced books on programming objects in Visual Basic .NET. Take a look at *Component Development with Visual Basic .NET*, by Nickolas Landry (John Wiley & Sons, 2002).

Now that we have covered the changes in getting from VB6 and VBScript to Visual Basic .NET, we are ready to get specifically into Web development. Chapter 4 contains an introduction to some key concepts on Web technologies such as HTTP and DHTML. This material will prepare you to learn about Web development in Visual Basic .NET, which is covered in later chapters.

Introduction to Web Application Development

With great power comes great responsibility.
Spider-Man, Amazing Fantasy Comics #15

In the last three chapters, we've discovered the new features, functions, and promise that Microsoft .NET brings us. Although the .NET platform expands the Rapid Application Model to the Web very well, you need a basic awareness of the technologies being used behind the scenes. As you learned in Chapter 3, overuse of object-oriented programming is not a good thing; neither is a lack of understanding about Web development. We need to learn how to use the powerful new features appropriately so that we can focus on making our applications more efficient and scalable.

Up to this point, we've explored the powerful new features of Microsoft .NET, ASP.NET, and Visual Basic .NET. Now it's time to learn about the fundamentals of building Web applications. These concepts are crucial for efficient and effective development. In this chapter, we will focus on the differences between traditional Visual Basic programming and Web development, the underlying technologies that make the Web work, and the new HTML controls and designer in Visual Studio .NET.

You might be tempted to ask "Why bother learning this when I can just drop a Web control on a Web form and never use this stuff?" The answer is that there will be situations in which you will need an understanding of the architecture and general Web-related technologies to build more powerful applications.

WHY YOU'VE GOT JUST 15 SECONDS...

The Web paradigm adds a whole new level of complexity to traditional application development. The phrase "You've got just 15 seconds to grab a user's attention" is fast becoming a cliché, but it really sums up the idea. You're no longer just creating an application, but a commercial or a TV show, and the user has his or her hand on the remote. It's called surfing the Web for a reason. As a developer, you need to be keenly aware of the impact of architectural and implementation decisions on application performance and scalability. With this technology, as we are discovering, we are still dealing with a client/server model.

The Importance of Protocols

Have you ever seen a diplomatic meeting on a news report? Usually these events are very formal affairs with rules that were clearly defined beforehand. For diplomats, protocol is everything. It specifies the ceremony and etiquette and generally governs every aspect of interaction between nations. In short, it's all about communication. For standards-based communication, protocols are everything as well. Internet protocols are agreed-upon standards for exchanging data between networks on diverse platforms and different environments.

Although understanding the entire network model is important, you'll spend most of your time as a Web developer using the application-level protocols, such as Hypertext Transfer Protocol.

Hypertext Transfer Protocol

HTTP is known as a stateless protocol. It's also one of the most highly used protocols in the process/application layer. Using HTTP for communication is normally divided into two parts: a *request* by the browser (or other client) to a server for information and a *response* by the server fulfilling the client request. This flow should be familiar to you because it resembles the client/server model with which we are all familiar.

HTTP uses Uniform Resource Locators (URLs) to assist in locating documents on Web servers. A URL is associated with a lower-level IP address and can be thought of as a human-readable way to access resources. We'll explore how the two identifiers are resolved later. For now, let's focus on the URL and its successive elements.

The URL Nickel Tour

Normally an HTTP URL or Web address has a form similar to:

```
http://www.gasullivan.com/ourbusiness/ourbusiness.asp
<-1-> <-    2        -> <-        4            ->
```

If you're at or near your computer while reading this, type in this URL and then we'll continue by tearing it apart. Your page should look similar to Figure 4.1.

The first part of the URL is the *protocol*. The second part is the *hostname*, which specifies the domain or server that contains the resources that we want to access. This is also known as a Fully Qualified Domain Name (FQDN). The last part specifies the *document path*, which is a similar concept to locating files on your computer's hard drive. This section is optional as well. Let's look at the next URL example for the final section, also optional, which specifies the *query string*. The query string is used to input parameters for dynamic search or information retrieval.

```
http://quote.yahoo.com/q?s=jwa&d=c
                        <-  5  ->
```

URLs may also be relative, in a similar way to DOS relative paths.

Figure 4.1   The URL (request) and Web page (response).

WHAT IS ICANN?

ICANN is the Internet's technical logistics body. Created in October 1998, ICANN manages the assignment of the following globally unique identifiers in order for the Internet to function:

◆ **Internet domain names**

◆ **IP address numbers**

◆ **Protocol parameter and port numbers**

We talked earlier about client requests and server responses in HTTP. As we begin to investigate this, let's also discover how the URL is resolved with its associated IP address along the way. When you type in a URL that is local to your network and hit Enter, the browser communicates with a server on your network that is running a domain name system service (DNS). DNS is responsible for reconciling the URL with the IP address of the server that you want to access. When you access an external URL, the URL is transmitted to the DNS service managed by interNIC, a group of organizations that have banded together to provide management and guidance for the Internet. (These responsibilities are in the process of transition to the *Internet Corporation for Assigned Names and Numbers, or ICANN.*) It is then resolved with its matching IP address in the organization's DNS registry, and then the request is transmitted to the destination Web server for a response.

The Anatomy of an HTTP Message

An HTTP message begins with a header. It lists the information that is necessary for the transport of the body, which holds the displayable content.

```
When you click Enter to submit the URL, the browser actually sends an
HTTP Request.
```

An HTTP request has two lines. The first line in an HTTP request is called a *request-line*. The request line contains an HTTP user command followed by the HTTP header entry.

HTTP user commands are used to manipulate objects on a server. Each command is associated with a URL that indicates the object's location. Let's examine four of the most relevant HTTP user commands: GET, POST, PUT, and DELETE.

GET.   Gets an object from the server. When you want to retrieve a Web page from a server, you GET it. The information is sent as parameters in the query string of the URL.

POST. Used to transfer information from the FORM tag back to the server. Remember, nothing in HTML can be seen by the server unless it's on the form. As we will see, that changes in .NET with the use of the RUNAT=SERVER.

PUT. Allows you to upload information to the server as well. It differs from POST in that the information is sent.

DELETE. The mechanism by which resources on a server are deleted.

Here's the HTTP Request header that results from our URL example:

```
GET /ourbusiness/ourbusiness.asp/ HTTP 1.1
Host: gasullivan.com
```

In this example, GET is the HTTP User command, /ourbusiness/ourbusiness.asp is the document request that the browser is making, and HTTP 1.1 signifies the version of HTTP supported by the browser.

The second line in an HTTP request is an HTTP header entry, which has the following syntax:

```
Name: parameter
```

where name is Host and parameter is gasullivan.com. The host header entry, gasullivan.com, denotes the host domain where the requested document resides.

The HTTP response header provides a lot of information. The following is the HTTP response header to our URL:

```
HTTP/1.1 200 OK
Server: Microsoft-IIS/5.0
Content-Location: http://www.gasullivan.com/Default.htm
Date: Sun, 22 Apr 2001 03:10:09 GMT
Content-Type: text/html
Accept-Ranges: bytes
Last-Modified: Wed, 07 Feb 2001 16:18:21 GMT
ETag: "5cd5c1962191c01:973"
Content-Length: 213
```

TIP If you'd like to quickly see what HTTP response header information is generated for a URL, go to networktools.com. You can type in either a URL or an IP address and get back all manner of interesting information.

Let's break down the example and investigate the elements. Note that this is not an inclusive list of HTTP headers.

HTTP/1.1 200 OK The first line in a HTTP response message is called the status line. In this example, line 1 specifies that the browser's version of HTTP is supported by the server and that the request succeeded.

The rest of the content in the header is made up of \header messages, many of which are optional.

Server: Microsoft-IIS/5.0   Line 2 specifies the Web service running on the server.

Content-Location: http://www.microsoft.com/Default.htm   Line 3 specifies the Fully Qualified Domain Name, document path, and requested document.

Date: Sun, 02 Apr 2001 02:25:37 GMT   Line 4 specifies the date of the request.

Content-Type: text/html   Line 5 specifies the content type of the document. In this example, it is text-based in an HTML format.

Accept-Ranges: bytes   Line 6 notifies the client that the server can accept byte ranges or portions of Web pages.

Last-Modified: Sat, 01 Apr 2001 00:00:37 GMT   Line 7 specifies the date that the requested document was modified.

ETag: "467d6a18f6c9c01:872"   Line 8 is an identifier that is used for specific resources. This allows the server to know the exact document location even if the server is hosting multiple sites within Web farms or the content is based on geographic location. It's simply another way to store needed state information quickly and effectively.

Content-Length: 18556   Line 9 specifies the body content length.

The last line of the header is always a blank line to separate the header from the body.

As you can see from the previous example, quite a bit of information can be passed between the client and server during the request and response. Fortunately for you, you're isolated from this lower level when using Visual Basic .NET and ASP.NET, but you can still access the information itself through the ASP.NET object model. We look at this in more detail later in the book. If you want to read more or study further about HTTP itself, check out *HTTP Essentials* by Stephen Thomas (Wiley Computer Publishing, 2001).

If you are more interested in a discussion of how lower-level Internet programming (for example, working directly with TCP/IP through sockets) relates to Visual Basic .NET, take a look at *Visual Basic .NET Internet Programming* by Carl Franklin (Wiley Computer Publishing, 2002).

One last thought before we move on. As you've probably guessed by now, there isn't a mechanism for maintaining state built into HTTP. We'll explore later some techniques that you can use to compensate for this.

Now that we have examined the header information in both the request and the response, we need to examine the body. And to do that, it's a good idea to understand how, as the body of the message is sent in HTML, dynamic HTML works and explore some examples of its use.

Dynamic HTML Support within ASP.NET (HTML 4.0)

As discussed in the introduction, I assume you have some experience with HTML. If not, check out the links page at the Web site for this book at wiley.com for some great HTML resources, or if you just like the feel of a good book, pick up a copy of *The Project COOL Guide to HTML* by Teresa A. Martin (John Wiley & Sons, 1996). That said, you might be wondering how a client-side technology such as dynamic HTML and a server-side technology such ASP.NET can interact in a way that will benefit you as developer.

HTML is very good at what it does, namely, marking up a document so that the elements will display correctly. That's all well and good, unless you want your Web site to respond to requests or user input on the fly. Every change means a round trip to the server to process and display the updated results. What a Web developer needs is a way to process some of these changes within the browser itself, thereby conserving resources and improving performance.

Dynamic HTML affords just that through the addition of the Document Object Model to HTML. Now every element in the document is an object (including the document) with properties, methods, and events. For a Visual Basic developer experienced in using objects, this should be old hat. Unfortunately, even though this is now a standard, DHTML is still implemented differently in Internet Explorer and Netscape. For an exhaustive guide to HTML 4.0 and the differences between the browsers, check out the *HTML 4.0 Sourcebook* by Ian S. Graham (John Wiley & Sons, 1998).

For our purposes, we'll focus on the extended support and resources provided by ASP.NET to client side technologies. Using it, you have programmatic access to every element in the HTML document. First, we'll explain some of the more common elements, properties, methods, and events. Then it's off to several examples to see how this all ties together.

Now it's time to take what we've learned so far in Chapter 4 and discover how it applies to .NET.

Enter ASP.NET Server Controls

You may be wondering how Web architecture and information flow fits into the overall topic of Web applications and ASP.NET. An understanding of HTML and DHTML is essential before using one of the powerful features of ASP.NET: server controls.

ASP.NET server controls are server components that render as HTML. The intrinsic HTML controls have a one-to-one mapping equivalent in the ASP.NET server controls. Notice that for each of the HTML tags in Table 4.1, there is a corresponding HTML server control. Also, the ASP.NET HTML server controls can use DHTML to accomplish their tasks. Because these are truly server side, no ActiveX, Java, or client-side script is needed to populate values from the client. As we'll see, they are simply handled in the post back. The key to the HTML server controls is that they run on the server and render themselves as HTML, as appropriate to the client. We can see the expanded list of ASP.NET server HTML controls and their associated tags in Table 4.1.

Keep in mind, that, as you think about using these, the ASP.NET HTML server controls are basically for migration and only need to be used when server-side processing, resources, or programmatic manipulation are required. Otherwise we can use the ASP.NET server controls, which are introduced in Chapter 5 and then are discussed further in Chapter 6.

Table 4.1   HTML Controls versus HTML Tags

SERVER CONTROL	ASSOCIATED HTML TAG
HtmlAnchor	<a>
HtmlButton	<button>
HtmlForm	<form>
HtmlGenericControl	Any unassociated tag, such as <div>, <span>, or <p>
HtmlImage	<img>
HtmlInputButton (Button)	<input type="button">
HtmlInputButton (Reset)	<input type="reset">
HtmlInputButton (Submit)	<input type="submit">
HtmlInputCheckBox	<input type="check">
HtmlInputFile	<input type="file">
HtmlInputHidden	<input type="hidden">
HtmlInputImage	<input type="image">
HtmlInputRadioButton	<input type="radio">
HtmlInputText (Password)	<input type="password">
HtmlInputText (Text)	<input type="text">
HtmlSelect	<select>
HtmlTable	<table>
HtmlTableCell	<td>
HtmlTableRow	<tr>
HtmlTextArea	<textarea>

Accessing the HTML elements through the ASP.NET HTML server controls is very similar to what you've used in Visual Basic.

Event Support Provided by ASP.NET HTML Server Controls

Events are raised and handled on the client by the Event object in traditional Web applications. Because of the separation of the event from its handler, the way events are raised by ASP.NET server controls is different: The events associated with server controls are raised on the client, but the ASP.NET page framework handles them on the server. During server page processing, change events are processed first, without regard for order. When the processing for the change events has occurred, the event that caused the post itself is then processed.

The Event object is crucial to the dynamic part of dynamic HTML. It ties the element to its event handlers. We can also use the Event object to tie specific events (such as those in Table 4.2) on the client to custom event handlers that run on the server.

Of course, you'll still use VBScript and JScript in Visual Studio .NET when you need to do any client-side programming in your Web page, but you'll most likely use Visual Basic .NET to take full advantage of the power of Visual Studio. NET. The control's ID parameter in the page functions just like an object name in Visual Basic. This is what ties the event procedure to the tag. Later in the chapter, we'll see how ASP.NET HTML server controls are used in Visual Basic .NET to help create Rapid Application Development to build Web Applications. Let's take a look at an example:

```
<%@ Page Language="vb" AutoEventWireup="false"
Codebehind="WebForm1.aspx.vb" Inherits="HTMLCONTROLS.WebForm1"%>
<!DOCTYPE HTML PUBLIC "-//W3C//DTD HTML 4.0 Transitional//EN">
<HTML>
  <body MS_POSITIONING="GridLayout">
<h2> NorthWind Employee Page</h2>
    <form id="Form1" method="post" runat="server">
<SELECT id=Select1 name=Select1 runat="server"
onchange="Select1Change()">
<OPTION selected></OPTION>

</SELECT>
<INPUT style="Z-INDEX: 101; LEFT: 105px; POSITION: absolute; TOP: 167px"
type=submit value=Submit id=cmdSubmit onclick="Select1Change()">
    <span id="Demo1">
    </span>
</form>
  </body>
</HTML>
```

Table 4.2   Some Common Events

EVENT	DESCRIPTION
OnClick	The OnClick event is fired when the user clicks the related element.
OnDblClick	The OnDblClick event is fired when the user double-clicks the related element.
OnBlur	The OnBlur event is fired when the object loses focus (similar to the Visual Basic LostFocus event).
OnFocus	The OnFocus event is fired when the object receives the focus (similar to the Visual Basic GotFocus event).
OnKeyDown	The OnKeyDown event is fired when any key is pressed (similar to the Visual Basic KeyDown event).
OnKeyUp	The OnKeyUp event is fired when any key is released (similar to the Visual Basic KeyUp event).
OnKeyPress	The OnKeyPress event is fired when a key with an ASCII equivalent is pressed (similar to the Visual Basic KeyPress event).
OnHelp	The OnHelp event is fired when the user clicks the related element.
OnMouseMove	The OnMouseMove event is fired when any key is pressed (similar to the Visual Basic KeyDown event).
OnMouseOver	The OnMouseOver event is fired when any key is pressed (similar to the Visual Basic KeyDown event).
OnMouseDown	The OnMouseDown event is fired when any key is pressed (similar to the Visual Basic KeyDown event).
OnMouseUp	The OnMouseUp event is fired when any key is pressed (similar to the Visual Basic KeyDown event).
OnLoad	The OnLoad event is fired immediately after the browser loads the object (similar to the Visual Basic Form_Load event).
OnUnload	The OnUnload event is fired immediately before the browser loads the object (similar to the Visual Basic Form_Unload event).
OnReadyStateChange	The OnReadyStateChange event is fired when the object's state has changed.

The following Visual Basic .NET file is associated in the preceding page by the CodeBehind directive at the top of the Web page. It's what ties the two together and enables the server control events to be defined in the Visual Basic .NET file.

In the second part of our example, we are loading the list box from within the Page_Load event. By checking the IsPostBack property of the page, we are assured of only loading the list box when the form is posted. We normally use this to initialize, much like the Form_Load event in Visual Basic 6.

The second thing that this example shows is the Select1Change Event. This server-side event fires when the list box selection is changed on the client. The two in this case are tied together through the OnClick = attribute of the tag in the page example. Although the preceding HTML sample shows the one-to-one relationship between ASP.NET HTML server controls and their corresponding tags, this one shows the functionality that the controls provide:

```
    Private Sub Page_Load(ByVal sender As System.Object, ByVal e As
System.EventArgs) Handles MyBase.Load
        'Put user code to initialize the page here
        Dim addList As ArrayList = New ArrayList()
        If Not IsPostBack Then
            addList.Add("Nancy Davolio")
            addList.Add("Andrew Fuller")
            addList.Add("Janet Leverling")
            addList.Add("Linda Peacock")
            addList.Add("Steven Buchanan")
            addList.Add("Linda Peacock")
            addList.Add("Linda Peacock")

            Select1.DataSource = addList
            Select1.DataBind()
        End If
    End Sub
    Public Sub Select1Change()

        Demo1.InnerText = "You chose: " & Select1.Value
    End Sub
```

Event Bubbling

Remember event bubbling in DHTML? Well, now you really don't need to use it nearly as much as in the past because it's used in a more limited way. Event bubbling is used by nested controls (such as buttons within template columns in a data grid row), as opposed to each one raising an event itself. This raises a single generic event called ItemCommand that passes parameters (CommandArgument) that indicate the control that raised the original event. You can set the CommandArgument property to unique values and then use the event handler to capture and act on them accordingly in a single event and avoid having to write an event handler for each control.

Creating a Web Project Using the HTML Designer

For the remainder of the chapter, let's explore the HTML designer and build a user interface. We'll also jump to the associated Visual Basic file and add a bit of code to show the power and one-to-one mapping of the HTML server controls.

Our first step is to create a new Visual Basic project within Visual Studio .NET. This project will familiarize you with the HTML designer, the code-behind files, and how the HTML server tags relate to Visual Basic .NET. First, we want to set it up as follows:

1. Create a Visual Basic ASP.NET Web application on server http://local-host. Name the application HTMLApp1.

2. Right-click on HTMLApp1 in the Solution Explorer window.

The Web form is the object that reflects the HTML document in the browser. Let's think of it, conceptually, as a Visual Basic form. The next step is to set and verify some properties.

Now that we have the Web form page open, we'll want to specify the Page-Layout property to make us feel even more at home. We'll also change the targetSchema property to handle older browsers:

1. Select DOCUMENT item in the Properties window drop-down list.

2. Set the PageLayout property to GridLayout. This allows HTML elements to be positioned on the document in a similar fashion to a Visual Basic form.

3. Verify that the targetSchema property is set to Internet Explorer 3.02/Navigator 3.0.

A bland Web page is pretty boring. Let's add some buttons on the page that will show how easy formatting is. Then we'll start to add functionality.

1. Drag two Button elements and the Text Field element from the HTML tab of the toolbox to the HTML page. These are the HTML server controls. Arrange the buttons in a column, with the Text Field next to the first button.

2. Left-click on the topmost button to select it.

3. Hold down the Shift key, and left-click on the other button to it.

4. From the Format menu select Align, then Lefts from the popup menu

5. Press the Escape key on the keyboard to deselect all buttons.

Now that we have added our buttons, let's begin to change some properties. This should seem like old hat. We're going to demonstrate that Web development model is consistent with what we've used before.

1. Select the topmost button. Verify that Button1<INPUT> appears in the drop-down list of the Properties window.

2. In the Properties window set the value attribute to Script and press Enter. Note that the caption on the button changed from Button to Script.

3. Set the ID property to btnScript.

4. Select the bottom button. Verify that Button2 <INPUT> appears in the Properties window drop-down list.

5. In the Properties window set the value attribute to Code and press Enter. Note that the caption on the button changed from Button to Code.

6. Set the ID property to btnCode.

Let's pause for a moment and investigate the HTML source. If we want to ensure that our application can be used in the widest variety of browsers, we need to use HTML 3.2. The table that we'll examine is used to position the buttons for older browsers supporting the HTML 3.2 standard. This allows for consistent formatting and proper placement of our controls when using HTML 3.2.

1. Click the HTML tab at the bottom of HTMLPage1.htm to switch to HTML Source view.

2. Examine the HTML. Note that it contains an HTML <table>.

If our browsers can support a richer level of functionality, we'll use HTML 4.0 instead. Let's make the change now:

1. Click the Design tab at the bottom of HTMLPage1.htm to switch to HTML Design view.

2. In the Properties window drop-down list, make sure that DOCU-MENT is selected. In the Properties window, set the targetSchema to HTML 4.0.

We're still being consistent with the Visual Basic Rapid Application Model so that we can place our code in the associated Visual Basic .NET file even though we are programming for the Web. Just as we did in the past, we've got a form with Visual Basic behind it. Let's continue by converting our HTML server controls to run on the server. Then we'll add some code to change some document properties when the button is clicked. The browser still gets the HTML, but we are manipulating it now with Visual Basic .NET. For the first button, we'll change the code in a script tag and use a span tag to show our change, and in the second one, we'll do it in the code window.

1. Left-click on the topmost button to select it.
2. Hold down the Shift key, and left-click on the other button to select it.
3. Right-click and select Run as server control.
4. Press the Escape key on the keyboard to deselect all the buttons.
5. Left-click on the text field to select it.
6. Right-click and select Run as server control.
7. Click the HTML tab at the bottom of the Web form to switch to HTML view.
8. Locate the </HEAD> tag.
9. Just before it add the following code:

```
<script language="VB" runat="server">

Sub btnScript_Click(source As Object, e As EventArgs)

    Message.InnerHtml = "Hi From Script Block"


End Sub
```

10. Locate the INPUT id=btnScript tag.
11. Scroll to just before runat=server and type the following:

```
onserverclick="btnScript_Click"
```

12. Locate the FORM tag.
13. Just after it, add the following code:

```
<H1><span ID="Message" runat="server"> </span></HI>
    </script>
```

Now, let's do the same for the second button. Only this time we'll change the property from the code-behind file.

1. Click the Design tab to return to form view.
2. Double-click btnCode to access the code window and the button control's click event handler.
3. In the ServerClick event procedure, add the following code:

```
txtHello.Value = "Hi from CodeBehind"
```

One of the added benefits of HTML 4.0 is dynamic positioning of controls and text within a page. ASP.NET supports this directly. We can use a panel to see how this works:

1. Double-click on the Panel (Linear Layout) control in the HTML tab of the toolbox. A new panel will appear selected in the middle of the document.

2. Drag a Text Field element from the toolbox and drop it in the center of the panel. The Text Field will appear at the top of the panel because of the panel's flow layout rule.

3. Drag and drop two more Text Field elements into the Panel element.

4. Click on an empty part of the panel and drag it to the left side of the HTML page.

5. Resize the panel to the right by dragging the center selection box on the right side of the panel to the size you want. Note that the Text Fields will rearrange (flow) themselves as needed to fill the panel from left to right, top to bottom.

The document outline enables us to keep track of all the elements contained within the document, allowing for efficient movement within. Let's examine the document structure and see how all the elements within our page are laid out in a hierarchical format. We drop the controls on our Web form, which is consistent with how we've programmed in the past, but they're implemented on the client side as HTML.

1. Show the Document Outline by pressing Ctrl-Alt-T.

2. Use the Document Outline to explore the structure of the HTML document (when you click on an item in the Document Outline panel, the corresponding item is highlighted in the Designer).

3. Notice how the panel is implemented using an HTML <div> object and that the three text items are logically contained within the <div>.

Finally, let's see the page we created. We'll save and then view our page in the browser and test the resulting functionality.

1. Save the HTML page using the File menu.

2. Right-click on the HTML and choose View in Browser. Note that the Preview is integrated into Visual Basic. You also have the option to preview in one or more external browsers.

3. Click the buttons and observe that the code is functional.

We've explored basic HTML functionality within Visual Basic .NET. Now for a quick review and then on to Chapter 5.

Wrapping Up

In this chapter, you have learned about Web development fundamentals. We investigated Web architecture and the underlying technologies within the network communication model. Next, we focused on the HTML server controls that ASP.NET provides and saw how each tag can now be manipulated as an object, complete with server-side event handling.

We rounded out this chapter with a focus on how DHTML fits within both Visual Basic .NET and ASP.NET and worked through some exercises that illustrated how closely the Visual Basic Rapid Application Development model has been ported to Web development. We've learned about the fundamentals of Web Application Development specifically as it relates to ASP.NET and its basic technologies. Now it's time to move into the parts and pieces of ASP.NET, starting with the Page Framework in Chapter 5.

ASP.NET Pages and Web Forms

Somewhere, something incredible is waiting to be known.
Carl Sagan

When you first began working with previous versions of Active Server Pages, you had to leave a lot of your expertise behind. Rather than dropping controls on a form in an IDE, you wrote HTML tags that, when parsed on the client browser, would result in some sort of user interface elements appearing on the user's screen. For anything but the simplest pages, you wrote server-side script to generate the HTML tags. This server-side code did not implement the user interface, however. The actual UI was run on the client. You had to deal with the difficult paradigm of sending the UI down to the client and then receiving data posted back to the server. To provide the user with the illusion of a stateful application, you had to manage state manually, through the use of session variables, hidden form fields, query string variables, or other mechanisms.

Writing code in the old model is a bit like solving the puzzle involving two nails twisted together. If you manipulate and twist it just right, eventually the nails can be separated. Although this can be amusing, it isn't a very productive use of your time. In this chapter, we'll examine ASP.NET Web forms. Web forms allow you to write Web pages much in the same way you do Visual Basic form-based application development. Much of the complexity of Web development is hidden. It's like having the solution to the puzzle before you start. You still have to actually perform the work to get your project done, but you don't have to spend as much time dealing with mind-twisting contortions.

ASP.NET Web Forms

Web forms are a Web-based implementation of the Visual Basic form paradigm. Visual Basic 6 did offer a partial implementation of this functionality through WebClasses, with which a few of you may be familiar. Although Web-Classes weren't widely adopted, Web forms are the primary means for Web development in Visual Basic .NET. With ASP.NET Web forms, you can make use of the skills and expertise you have gained as a Visual Basic developer. Web forms allow you to write Web pages in much the same way you wrote Visual Basic applications in the past. You don't need to think about the details of whether the code runs on the client or the server, the differing capabilities of HTML objects on various browsers, management of state, and the like. You work in the IDE in the manner to which you are accustomed: dropping controls on a page, setting properties at design time, writing event handlers, and so on.

The .NET platform manages much of the complexity that you were forced to deal with in the past with ASP, freeing you to focus on the welcome complexity of the problem you're really trying to solve. If you're a seasoned Visual Basic developer who has never worked with the old versions of ASP, you've been spared a learning experience and can look forward to a much easier transition into the world of Web development.

Visual Basic .NET provides a much richer object model for Web development than Visual Basic 6 or ASP did. The .NET Framework Class Library is a comprehensive object model that covers every aspect of .NET, from the C# compiler to XML parser. A substantial portion of the object model is slanted toward Web development. The Web development objects are included in the System.Web namespace.

System.Web.UI

Within System.Web, the System.Web.UI namespace is the root of all of the user interface objects that you will work with when creating Web pages with .NET. For the discussion at hand, the most important classes under System.Web.UI are the Control and Page classes.

System.Web.UI.Control

You are already familiar with the concept of controls, such as the TextBox and Timer controls in Visual Basic. ASP.NET allows you to create Web forms server controls to encapsulate functionality just as did Visual Basic. Also like Visual Basic controls, Web forms server controls, or Web controls, can implement a portion of the user interface or may just provide a handy set of functionality to the Web page developer. Most Web controls are involved in generating the user interface in one way or another. Microsoft provides a set of Web controls to generate common HTML UI elements such as input tags, selection lists, labels, tables, and the like. You can create your own Web controls, called user controls, to abstract and reuse the functionality you require.

We will explore a few of the most frequently used Web controls in this chapter. More details about Web controls in general are in Chapter 6.

System.Web.UI.Control is the base class of every Web control that you will use on a Web form, whether it is an intrinsic Web control, a third-party control, or your own user control. Because it is the base class of all Web controls, the events, methods, and properties it exposes are available in every Web control.

Three of the most important methods exposed by the Control class are responsible for producing HTML for the end user's browser application and allowing Web controls to save and load (persist) their state.

Rendering HTML: The Render() Method

The primary channel for communication from a Web application to a user is HTML. As mentioned previously, most Web controls are involved in the user interface. *Rendering* is the process of producing a string of HTML that will result in the user seeing a visual representation of a Web control. For example, the TextBox control will render itself into an HTML <input type='text'> tag, which will display on the end user's Web browser as a text box into which the user may type data.

The generic Control class exposes a Render method. Every Web control that produces output to the user must override the base class Render method with its own Render method. Each Web control's Render method contains the code and logic necessary to generate the appropriate HTML, based on the control's internal state, and the type of browser being used to view the Web site.

One of the intrinsic Web controls is the TextBox control. This control includes a Text property, which stores the value the user has entered. If the Text property has been set, the Render method of this control will include a value attribute in the HTML input tag it produces. For example, if the Text property has been set to xyz, this control's Render method will produce output like <input type='text' value='xyz'>.

Persisting State: SaveViewState() / LoadViewState()

As you learned in the previous chapter, Web pages run on HTTP, a stateless protocol. Each time the user clicks a link to view a new Web page, that page displays independently, with no knowledge of what came before or after. One of the challenges for a Web developer is to provide users with the illusion that they are working with a stateful application that just happens to run inside their browser window.

Imagine that you are purchasing CDs online. You want to finalize your order, and you must enter all of your shipping and billing information, but you forget to fill in the street address field. When you attempt to submit your order, the commerce application will probably take you back to the shipping information page, with an error message indicating that you must enter a street address. Even though you have been returned to the page that you just left, the Web server and your Web browser consider this an entirely different request. By default, the form is going to appear just as it did when you first saw it—all of the fields will be blank. As a customer, you will probably be less likely to complete your order if you have to reenter all of the fields too many times. You would much prefer to have all of the other information (your name, zip code, credit card information, etc.) reappear, allowing you to just enter the missing information (street address) and continue. As a developer, you could accomplish this with ASP. But you had to write the code yourself.

In ASP.NET, each of the input fields in your Web browser was probably rendered by its own instance of the TextBox Web control. When you completed the form the first time, all of the data you entered was sent to the server, and each TextBox control set its own Text property based on the value from the corresponding HTML input field. When the code realized that some data was missing, it had to rerender the same page. When each TextBox rendered the second time around, it was able to render value tags to cause your Web browser to show the same values that you entered.

This works well for data that can be communicated from server to client and from client to server using standard HTTP. This is certainly the case for the Text property of a TextBox; the server sends data in the value tag, and the client sends data back in an HTTP POST message. Other properties may not be so straightforward. The TextBox control also includes an Enabled property that determines whether or not the user may edit the data in the input field. When the control is rendered, this property determines whether or not a disabled attribute is included in the HTML input tag. However, there is no way built into HTTP for the client to communicate this setting back to the server. In addition, other Web controls may not even be able to send their value data to the client. For example, they might render into static text with no HTML at all.

Controls can still persist all of the data the developer needs. They do so by overriding the SaveViewState and LoadViewState methods. The SaveView-State method is responsible for serializing the state of a control into a character string. When the page is rendered to the client browser, this serialized data string is stored in an automatically generated, hidden form field. The hidden view state field is not displayed to the end-user. The hidden form field is posted back to the server when a round-trip occurs. The LoadViewState method must be capable of parsing the resulting string and restoring the control to its original state.

System.Web.UI.Page

The Page class is the base class of every ASP.NET Web page. When you create a Web page with Visual Studio .NET, you are in fact creating a derived class from System.Web.UI.Page. When users view your Web page, the server creates an instance of your Page class and allows it to render itself to HTML for the user's viewing pleasure.

The Page class is in fact derived from System.Web.UI.Control and thus has all of the functionality of the Control class. Just as with a control, a Page object must expose a Render method that produces the HTML for the page. The Render method of an instance of the Page class will automatically call the Render method of every Web control that appears on that page. Similarly, the Page class exposes SaveViewState and LoadViewState methods, which are smart enough to call the corresponding methods of every Web control on the page.

The Page class, like most derived classes, adds additional functionality beyond that provided by its base class. Some of the features we will be discussing in this chapter include methods to control tracing, communicate state information among different Web pages, and add and remove controls from a Web form at runtime.

We'll cover the Page class in more detail later in this chapter.

The Model You Already Know— Now for the Web (Almost)

If you're like most readers of this book, when you write Visual Basic code, you don't refer to MSDN for every other line of code. You don't spend time searching through the UI to find out how to set a breakpoint. You focus on writing code, and the IDE becomes transparent to your thought processes.

As mentioned at the beginning of this chapter, you can create Web applications using the Visual Studio .NET IDE in much the same way you created Visual Basic applications using Visual Basic. The Web form designer allows you to drag and drop Web controls on a form, move and resize the controls, set their design-time properties, and write event handlers and other code associated with the form and controls.

Important Differences

Of course, Web applications really aren't Windows applications. Microsoft has done a great job of allowing you to leverage your Visual Basic skills with

ASP.NET. However, there are fundamental differences in the underlying technologies between Visual Basic and ASP.NET. Some things simply will not work as expected until you learn some of what's happening behind the scenes.

State, State, State, State

The stateless nature of the HTTP protocol has a large impact on how you must code your Web application. Previous chapters began to discuss state management in relation to the view state of Web controls. We showed examples of the kinds of state data that might need to be persisted for a Web control, such as the Text and Enabled properties of the TextBox control.

As a Visual Basic developer, you've never had to consider just how stateful your application is. Visual Basic applications retain state while they are running. If you made changes to the properties of objects, the properties retained their values as long as the program ran. If necessary, you wrote the code to persist state to data files, a database server, the registry, or some other back up store.

Page LifeTime

When you run a Visual Basic application, the executable code is loaded into memory. A process and one or more threads are created to execute that code. The process continues to execute until the user quits the application or some other event such as system shutdown occurs. The user may exit the program after only a few seconds or may leave it running on the system for many months or longer.

When a user views your ASP.NET Web page, the Web server instantiates a Page object for that user. The instance of the Page object exists solely to fulfill a single request from a single user's Web browser. Once the page has been fully rendered into HTML, that instance of the Page object is destroyed. The lifetime of the object may be measured in milliseconds or in extraordinary cases such as a database connection timeout, in tens of seconds.

Even if the same user immediately rerequests the same page, a new instance of the Page object must be created. Properties of any objects that were set in the previous instance of the object are *not* retained in the new instance unless some mechanism has been implemented to persist the state of these objects. Fortunately, .NET will persist quite a significant amount of state information for you. We discussed the SaveViewState and LoadViewState methods of the Control class, which is the base class for every Web page and every Web control. In general, your Web form (because it is derived from Control) and all of the Web controls you use (because they are derived from Control) will automatically persist almost all of their state information.

What Is Persisted and What Isn't

Although most state information is automatically persisted for you, there are cases where you must write the code to persist state.

I mentioned earlier that the Page object knows how to persist its own state and the state of any controls you have placed on the page. However, your specific ASPX page implements a class derived from the Page class. The implementation of the view state methods in the base class know how to persist the state of all the properties in the base class, but they do not know how to persist the state of any new properties that you have added to your derived class. Therefore, you must persist the values of any variables or properties you have added to your derived Page class.

The same is true if you create a derived class that extends another Web control by adding new properties; you must remember to extend your derived class's view state methods to persist the new properties. The view state methods in the base class only know about properties of the base class.

Your derived Page class is a compiled object. During execution, you may programmatically make changes to an instance of the Page class. You can add and remove controls to and from your Web page. The next time the page loads, the new instance of the class will not know about these additions or deletions unless you persist information about any such changes. Similarly, you can programmatically assign event handler functions to objects at runtime. You must write the code to redo any such assignments each time your Page object is instantiated.

The intrinsic Web control, Table, is provided to work with HTML tables. It is possible to add rows and cells to a Table Web control at runtime. The Table control implements this by allowing you to create new instances of the TableCell and TableRow controls and adding them to the existing Table control. However, in doing so, you are programmatically adding new controls to your page. The next time your Page object is instantiated, it will not know about the added controls. Again, you must write the code to save this state information and later reperform the creation and addition of table cells and/or rows.

Finally, you should be aware that when your Page object is executed, saving state is *not* the last thing that happens. Specifically, your objects' Render methods and your objects' destructors are called after state is saved. Be careful that the code that executes during rendering and object clean up does not make any changes to any properties that need to be persisted.

You can use the ViewState object to manually persist state information about your Page object. The section, *ViewState Object*, later in this chapter has more information about this.

Transferring Information between Pages

The fact that your Page object is instantiated by the Web server service and only exists long enough to render a page of HTML for the user complicates multipage applications. Each Web page in your application has its own distinct Page class. Instances of these Page classes are created only by the Web server. It is not possible for your code within one of your Page classes to directly create an instance of another one of your Page classes. You can't get a reference to another instance of a Page class. The Page classes for any pair of Web pages within your application will probably never both be instantiated at the same time for the same user. So how do you pass information between pages? Furthermore, if the only way to instantiate one of your Page classes is by getting the user to request a Web page from the server, how do you control the flow of execution between pages?

First, let's look at navigation. There are four ways to get a user from one page to another within a multipage application:

1. Your page can display standard HTML hyperlinks. Each hyperlink includes the URL of another page within your application. When users click a hyperlink, their browser will send a request to the server for the corresponding URL. The user controls the flow of the application, but you decide which hyperlinks to display on a particular page.

2. Your page can include HTML forms. When users click a Submit button enclosed in the form, their Web browser sends a request to the Web server for the ASPX page specified in the form tag. This request also includes all of the values of the input tags within the form. You can also write client-side script to programmatically cause the form to be submitted. This option was frequently used in ASP. Since ASP.NET focuses on server-side processing, this option won't be used as frequently in .NET applications.

3. While processing a user's request for a given Web page, your server-side code can use the Redirect method of the standard Response object (Response.Redirect). This stops the processing of the Page class for the page that the user originally requested and sends a redirect message to the client browser, causing the browser to request a different Web page. The browser sends the request for the new page to the server, which begins execution of the Page class for the Web page specified by the URL you passed. This technique allows you to programmatically control the flow of your application. It is not necessary for you to instantiate the Response object. An instance is automatically provided for you. Note that Response.Redirect results in a round-trip between the server and client. The same task can also be accomplished in ASP.NET, without a roundtrip, using the Transfer method of the standard Server object (Server.Transfer). As with the Response object, it is not necessary for you to instantiate the Server object.

4. Your Page object may download client-side script that includes code to navigate the user to a different page. For example, your client-side script can use the Navigate method of the IE DOM Window object. Window.Navigate accepts a URL as a parameter. When called, this

method stops processing of client-side script and sends a request to the server for the specified Web page, just as if the user had clicked on a hyperlink to the URL you specified. Like a server-side redirection, you programmatically control the flow of your application. Navigating the user from client-side script is more efficient because it does not require that one Page object be instantiated on the server only to terminate and redirect the user to a different Page.

Next, let's examine passing information from one page to another. Obviously, just moving the user from one page to another isn't enough to create a cohesive application. You must be able to communicate parameters and data among the various Web pages. There are a number of techniques for doing so.

Query string parameters can be specified as part of a URL. Each query string parameter is simply a name/value pair, separated by an equals sign. Query string parameters are added to the end of a URL. The first parameter is introduced with a question mark. Additional parameters, if used, are introduced with ampersands.

For example, say we have the URL http://myserver/myapp/pageone.aspx. We need to specify three parameters. The userid parameter has a value of 23, the mode parameter has a value of search, and the country parameter has a value of us. The resulting URL would be:

```
http://myserver/myapp/pageone.aspx?userid=23&mode=search&country=us
```

The user can be navigated to the resulting URL using any of the four methods described previously. If Response.Redirect is used, the user's Web browser is involved in redirecting the user to a different URL. The user is not able to modify the parameters passed on the URL string. Of course, a knowledgeable user could simply enter the same URL with different parameters into the Address field of their browser.

To retrieve the parameters on the destination page, the code in your Page object uses the QueryString method of the standard Request object. This method accepts the name of a parameter and returns its value. It is not necessary for you to instantiate the Request object. An instance is automatically provided for you.

Query string parameters work best for simple data types. If necessary, you can pass an array of a simple data type using a query string parameter, although there is a limit on the amount of data that can be included in a URL. It is not possible to pass objects using query string parameters.

There are two drawbacks to using query string parameters. They are visible to, and can be changed by, the user. In the previous example, we specified a userid parameter. Presumably, the value of this parameter controls the user's level of access to the functionality on the destination page. There is nothing to prevent users from copying the URL, modifying the query string parameters' values, and pasting the new URL into the Address bar of their Web browser.

Users can save copies of URLs by setting a bookmark, adding the page to their favorites, or through other mechanisms. The query string parameters and values will be saved with the URL. The values of query string parameters are part of the state of your application. Your application may have other methods of storing state. If a user saves an URL with parameters and later attempts to access it in another session, the state stored in the query string parameters may not be consistent with other state stored internally in your application. This may cause your application to produce errors or to fail to work the way the user expected.

Hidden form fields are simply HTML input tags with their type attribute set to hidden. They can be created by placing an HTMLInputHidden control on your Web form. Hidden form fields are not displayed to users in their browser window. When the form that encloses the input tags is posted to the server, the values of the hidden fields are also sent, along with the values of any ordinary fields. Like any other Web control, the value sent by the user will be automatically retrieved by the HTMLInputHidden object during the initialization of your Page object.

Like query string parameters, hidden form fields can only pass simple data types. You can't pass objects from one page to another using them.

Users do not have the opportunity to change the values of a hidden form field. Sophisticated users can view the values of hidden form fields by using the View Source option in their Web browser.

When using this technique to send data from one page to another, you can only navigate the user from one page to another by submitting the appropriate form. You can't use a standard hyperlink or Response.Redirect or Window.Navigate. Because the user's Web browser must submit a form, data can't be passed directly from one ASPX page to another without involving the client browser.

NOTE If you want to create a hidden input field, use the HTMLInputHidden control. This will cause a hidden input field to be sent to the user's browser. If you create a TextBox control and set its Visible property to false, you won't get what you expected. When you set the Visible property of a Web control to false, the control does not render hidden content. Instead, the control renders no HTML at all. Not only are non-Visible controls hidden from the user, but they are hidden from the user's browser as well.

The *Session object* allows you to maintain a list of name/value pairs that can be accessed by any Web page in your application. You can store a value in the Session object by using it as an lvalue. An example is:

```
Session("UserID") = 23
```

You can retrieve the value stored by using the Session object later as an rvalue:

```
lUserID = CLng(Session("UserID"))
```

The code that reads and writes values from the Session object may be in different Page objects, in different instances of the same Page object, or in the same instance of the same Page object. Users of your application have their own Session object, which lasts for the duration of their session with your application. If users return to your Web application after their session has expired, the data you stored earlier in the Session object will no longer be available.

It is not necessary for you to instantiate the Session object. An instance is automatically provided for you. A user's session data is maintained even if the Web service is stopped and restarted on the server. ASP.NET maintains the same session data for a given user's session even if the Web application is distributed across multiple servers in a Web farm.

Session variables cannot be viewed or edited by end users. Unlike query strings and hidden form fields, it *is* possible to store instances of objects in the session—assuming the objects can be serialized as XML. It is not possible to communicate state from one user's session to another user's session using the Session object.

Session data can be stored in memory or in a SQL Server database. If you require a great deal of data to be stored for each user's session, you should store the session data in SQL.

The Application object is used just like the Session object. However, only one Application object exists for all users of your Web application. Code executing in your Page objects on behalf of one user can read and write values in the Application object, which will be accessible by code running in your Page objects on behalf of any other user of your application.

It is not necessary for you to instantiate the Application object. An instance is automatically provided for you. There are some important limitations on the Application object:

The Application object exists as long as your application is active.   If your application is stopped and restarted, all data stored in the Application object is lost. If the Web service is stopped and restarted, the Application object is lost. The Application object is always stored in memory. If you require a great deal of data to be stored on the application level, consider using some other mechanism, such as a SQL Server database. ASP.NET does not maintain the same application object across multiple servers in a Web farm.

Data stored in the application object is shared by all instances of all Page objects in your application.   When one Page instance writes data to the Application object, the application state must be locked. Other

Page instances must wait until the application state is unlocked before they can use it. If you have many concurrent users, and your code frequently uses the Application object, this contention may result in slow performance.

Cookies are lists of name-value pairs that are stored on the end-user's machine by their browser. Multiple pages within a single web application may share the same set of cookies, and use them to communicate parameters. The client browser associates cookies with the Web site that generated them. Most browsers will keep each Web applications' cookies independent of cookies associated with any other Web applications the user visits. Cookies can be created, accessed, and modified directly by script running on the client. Cookies are sent from the client to the server, and back again, on each round-trip. This allows code running on the server-side to create, access, and modify cookies as well. Cookies are normally neither displayed to, nor modifiable by, users. When your code creates a cookie, it can specify an expiration date and time. The client browser can delete expired cookies. You should be aware that users are able to delete any and all cookies. Furthermore, some users may configure their browser to reject all cookies, to enhance security and privacy. If your Web site relies on cookies, these users may not be able to take full advantage of the functionality you provide.

Data Binding

So far our discussion of differences between Visual Basic forms and Web forms has been limited to the myriad implications of the statelessness of the HTTP protocol. Another important difference exists in the realm of data binding.

The most important difference between data binding in Visual Basic and Visual Basic .NET is that in Visual Basic .NET, data binding simply works better than it did before. It is actually a usable, and useful, technology.

Data binding in .NET is limited in scope as compared to data binding in Visual Basic 6. It is intended to easily get data from the database into Web controls. It does not update data in your database based on user actions. You must write the code to send the data back to the database, because in almost every case you will want to perform verification and validation.

In Visual Basic, you implemented data binding by creating controls and setting properties. In .NET, you implement data binding by creating controls, setting properties, *and* explicitly calling the DataBind method of your control. This gives you a higher degree of control over the process.

Finally, data binding in .NET works the same way whether you are binding to data in a database or binding to data in in-memory objects. The section *A Simple Data Binding Example* later in this chapter has more information about this.

Using the Code-Behind Method

In Visual Basic, there is a clear separation between objects such as forms and text boxes and the code associated with them such as event handlers. In previous versions of ASP, there was no clear distinction. A single ASP file might contain hundreds of transitions between source code and HTML content. Like the puzzle referenced at the beginning of this chapter, extricating the code from the HTML tags was difficult and time consuming. If the developer who wrote the ASP page did not implement coding standards to separate HTML from script code, it could be nearly impossible for other developers to maintain the page.

ASP.NET introduces the concept of code behind. This simply means that you can put the code and the HTML tags in separate files. The code behind a button click, for example, is no longer mixed in with the HTML that renders the button. This results in a tremendous improvement in the readability and maintainability of your ASP code.

An additional benefit of keeping the HTML in a separate file is that it is much easier for a less-technical UI expert to apply styles, themes, and layouts to a Web site without breaking functionality.

Example: Multiplication Application

We've spent quite a bit of time discussing Web forms. At this point, let's create a form that allows the user to enter two numbers, click a button, and see the result of multiplying the numbers.

With a few simple steps, we'll create a very simple application. No big deal, right? That's exactly the point. If there's one thing you'll hear over and over regarding .NET, it is that .NET does for Web development what Visual Basic did for Windows development. Just as Visual Basic did a good job of hiding low-level details from the developer, Web forms allow the developer to see past the messy details of the Web and get busy writing code to solve business problems.

First, we'll create an empty Web application project:

1. Fire up Visual Studio .NET. Select File, New Project. In the New Project dialog box, do the following:

    ■   Leave Visual Basic Projects as the selected Project Type. Click ASP.NET Web Application under Templates.

    ■   Enter http://localhost/Ch5-Ex1 in the Location field. Click OK to create the project. A new, empty Web application will be created for you.

    Just as with Visual Basic 6, our next step is to add some controls to the form. The IDE will come up with the grid layout mode of

WebForm1.aspx. You'll be familiar with the appearance of the grid from the Visual Basic IDE.

2. A list of Web controls appears in the toolbox on the left side of the screen. Locate TextBox in the list. Double-click TextBox, and the IDE will drop a new TextBox1 on your form in the upper-left corner.

3. Drag and drop a second text box onto your form. The IDE creates a new TextBox2. Drag it so that it is placed underneath the first text box.

4. Drag and drop a button onto the form. Place it underneath the second text box.

5. Drag and drop a third text box (TextBox3), and place it underneath the buttons.

6. To make everything line up nicely, select all three text boxes and the button. On the Format menu, select Align, Centers. On the Format menu, select Vertical Spacing, Make Equal.

   Now that we've added controls to the form, the next step is to set properties of the controls. Just as with Visual Basic 6, we set properties of the controls at design time to get just the behavior we want.

7. Because you selected all four controls in the last step, click on a blank area of the form to unselect the controls. Then click to select TextBox1, the first text box at the top of the page. Set its ID property to txtNumberA. Leave its other properties unchanged.

8. Select TextBox2, and set its ID to txtNumberB.

9. Select the button, and set its ID to btnMultiply. Set its Text property to Multiply.

10. Select TextBox3, and set its ID to txtResult. Because we plan to use this field to display the result of a calculation, we don't want the user entering numbers directly. Set its Enabled property to false.

    Although the controls' built-in functionality goes a long way toward what we want to accomplish in our example application, the controls don't do everything. At this point, we need to write some actual code. We'll define an event handler to perform the multiplication when the user clicks the Multiply button.

11. Double-click the Multiply button on your form. Just as in Visual Basic, the system will throw down a blank sub, btnMultiply_Click, for you.

12. In the On Click handler for the Multiply button, enter the following line of code. Remember that you don't get default properties in Visual Basic .NET.

```
txtResult.Text = txtNumberA.Text * txtNumberB.Text
```

At this point, we're ready to run the program.

13. Select Start from the Debug menu, or press F5. Note that your program compiles before it runs. After a brief wait, you should see your form in a browser window.

14. Enter an integer in each of the first two text boxes, and then click Multiply. You should see the result of the multiplication in the third text box. Note that you can't enter text directly in the result box.

When you created this example application, you actually created two source files: WebForm1.aspx and WebForm1.aspx.vb. The WebForm1.aspx file contains the descriptions of the controls you dropped on the form. The WebForm1.aspx.vb file contains the Visual Basic .NET code behind the controls.

Page Processing Sequence

You've learned a few of the many operations that automatically take place when your Page class is instantiated and executes, such as state management and rendering. Let's take a more detailed look at exactly what is done, and in what order:

1. A request is sent to the Web service for an ASPX page. This request may be generated explicitly by the user (such as manually entering a URL or clicking a hyperlink), or it may be generated through code (such as Response.Redirect in server-side code or Window.Navigate in client-side code).

2. If this is the first time this page has been requested, or if the page has been modified since its last request, the ASPX file is compiled to create a DLL.

3. Your Page class is instantiated. Any objects associated with your page, such as controls, are instantiated. The Init event is fired, causing each object's OnInit method to be invoked.

4. If this is a post back from an earlier instance of the page, each control's LoadViewState method is called. The controls load their view state from the ViewState object.

5. If form data was posted to the page, the LoadPostBack method of each input control is called. The controls load their value properties from the Form method of the Request object. The LoadPostBack method returns true if it changed the value properties of its control; it returns false otherwise.

6. If data was posted to the page, and you are using validator Web controls, validation occurs at this point.

7. The Load event fires. The Page object's OnLoad method is called.

8. Post-back change notifications are sent. When each control's LoadPost-Back method was called in step 5, the system kept track of which controls indicated that their values changed. The RaisePostDataChangedEvent method of each such control is now called. Depending on the control type, an appropriate event will fire. For example, a text box would fire its TextChanged event.

9. Post-back events are handled. If data was posted to the page for a Web control, its RaisePostBackEvent method is called. Depending on the control type, an appropriate event will fire. For example, a button would fire its Click event.

10. The PreRender event is raised. Each control's OnPreRender method is called. This is the last event that fires before rendering. This is the last opportunity for your code to make changes to state, if such changes need to be persisted.

11. The view state is saved. Each control's SaveViewState method is called. Any changes to state made after this step will *not* be persisted.

12. The Render event is raised. Each control's Render method is called. Each control must respond by outputting to the client browser the HTML that represents the visual representation of the control, if any.

13. The Dispose method of your Page object is called. It calls the Dispose method of each control on the page. This is your last opportunity to deallocate and release any resources you have allocated. The instance of your Page object is destroyed.

14. Users perform actions in their client browser based on the information that is displayed as a result of the render operation. The user's action will most likely result in another page request (to the same page or a different page). The entire process starts over.

As you can see, even this simple Web application has a lot of moving parts. In previous versions of ASP or Visual Basic, you would have had to either live with less functionality or expend the effort to write everything yourself. With Visual Basic .NET Web forms, it's all done for you.

The Web Form Designer

The Web form designer is part of the IDE for creating ASP.NET Web pages, whether you use Visual Basic .NET or some other language (such as C#). If you worked the example above, you've already seen the IDE. If not, it should be very familiar to any Visual Basic developer.

The Web form designer is a form layout tool, which defaults to Design mode (grid view). A toolbox is available, from which you can drag and drop controls onto your form. If you select a control, form, class, or any other component of your solution, you can view and edit its properties in the properties window. Properties are organized in a tree view structure into conceptual groupings, such as Appearance, Behavior, and Layout. All of the other windows with which you are familiar (class view, object browser, etc.) are available.

ASP.NET form layout information is stored in HTML format. As you work with the Design view in the Web form designer, the IDE is creating and maintaining HTML for you. If you want to work with the HTML directly, you can switch between Design mode and HTML mode at the click of a button.

HTML Templates

The HTML created by the Web form designer can be thought of as a template for the user interface. Although it is not strictly the HTML that will be sent to the client browser, there is a high degree of correspondence between this server-side template HTML and the HTML that will be rendered on the client-side.

When you created the ASPX file for the multiplication application example, you did so by dragging and dropping controls from the toolbox onto a grid-layout form. Behind the scenes, the IDE was creating an HTML template to describe the form you designed. If you return to the IDE and click on the HTML button (rather than the Design button) at the bottom of the Web-Form1.aspx window, you can see the following HTML. For brevity, I have eliminated some elements (such as style attributes).

```
<%@ Page Language="vb" AutoEventWireup="false"
Codebehind="WebForm1.aspx.vb" Inherits="Ch5_Ex1.WebForm1"%>
<!DOCTYPE HTML PUBLIC "-//W3C//DTD HTML 4.0 Transitional//EN">
<HTML>
  <HEAD>
    <title></title>
    <meta name="GENERATOR" content="Microsoft Visual Studio.NET 7.0">
    <meta name="CODE_LANGUAGE" content="Visual Basic 7.0">
    <meta name="vs_defaultClientScript" content="JavaScript">
    <meta name="vs_targetSchema"
content="http://schemas.microsoft.com/intellisense/ie5">
  </HEAD>
  <body MS_POSITIONING="GridLayout">
    <form id="Form1" method="post" runat="server">
      <asp:TextBox id="txtNumberA runat="server"></asp:TextBox>
      <asp:TextBox id="txtNumberB" runat="server"></asp:TextBox>
      <asp:Button id="btnMultiply" runat="server"
```

```
Text="Multiply"></asp:Button>
      <asp:TextBox id="txtResult" runat="server"
Enabled="False"></asp:TextBox>
    </form>
  </body>
</HTML>
```

We'll examine this code in some detail in the following sections. For now, you might want to compare the code to what you see in the Web form designer in the IDE. This HTML code and the UI you see on the screen are simply two different representations of the same object.

Rendering versus Declaration

Some of the HTML we just showed is standard HTML and will be downloaded to the client browser as is, without any changes. The rest of the HTML requires further processing, or rendering, before it will be usable by the client.

<% %>

Anything appearing within the ASP delimiters <% and %> will get processed on the server. Content appearing inside these delimiters is not HTML, but it may result in HTML being rendered. Two ASP delimiters are used: <%@ Directive Attributes %> and <% Code %>.

<%@ Directive Attributes %>

As with ASP pages, every ASP.NET page begins with a directive. The directive tag is identified by the opening ASP delimiter (<%), followed by an at sign, a directive name, a set of attributes, and the closing ASP delimiter (%>). In the HTML code from the previous section, we can see several Page attributes. The Language=vb attribute specifies that this page is implemented in Visual Basic .NET, as opposed to some other language. The Codebehind attribute specifies the source file that contains the actual code.

If no directive name is specified, as in <%@ Attributes %>, the system assumes we are specifying Page attributes, as in <%@ Page Attributes%>. Other directives allowed are Control, Import, Register, Assembly, and Output-Cache. The attributes that can be specified vary with each directive type.

<% Code %>

For compatibility with previous versions of ASP, you can place source code within the ASPX file, mixed with the HTML. All source code must be enclosed within the <% and %> delimiters. It is possible to have many such blocks of code. Any output produced by the code is sent directly to the client browser. The Language attribute in the Page attribute tag (discussed previously) specifies the language in which this code is written.

> **NOTE** To realize the benefits of the code-behind model, you should *not* place source code in your ASPX file. Keep it in your ASPX.VB file where it belongs. If you do choose to include code in your HTML template, you should know that this code is executed during the Render phase of page processing, as discussed earlier in this chapter.

Server-Side Controls

Some of the tags in the HTML template correspond to the controls you placed on your form in the Web form designer. These special tags can be recognized by the fact that they use the asp: namespace and include the runat attribute.

asp: Namespace

As mentioned earlier, not all of the HTML tags in the ASPX file are intended to be seen by the client browser. A number of tags are specific to the .NET platform. These tags are preceded with the asp: namespace identifier. Examples include asp:TextBox and asp:Button. These tags represent the Web controls you placed on your Web form. Note that if you wrote your own server-side controls, or installed third-party controls, the namespace identifier user by those controls would be something other than asp:.

runat Attribute

The client browser doesn't know how to process the tags in the asp: namespace. These tags represent server controls that must be instantiated as part of page processing. The server controls then render themselves to standard HTML before they are sent to the client. You know from the earlier discussion that .NET Framework objects get instantiated for your server-side code. The runat=server attribute makes this happen. The tags that begin with asp: and include the runat=server attribute are directives to the ASP engine to create server-side objects such as a text box (System.Web.UI.WebControls.TextBox).

All of the HTML you see in WebForm1.aspx was automatically created for you by the IDE as you dropped controls onto your form and set their properties. You can return to design view and continue to maintain this file through the graphic UI. Alternatively, you can make changes directly to this text file, and the changes will be reflected in design mode.

Client HTML for Multiplication Example

Let's look at what the client browser received when we ran the multiplication application. Switch back to Visual Studio .NET and run the program again (Debug, Start, or F5). When the application pops up in your browser window, right-click the page, and select View Source. Internet Explorer will display the HTML that was downloaded from IIS. You'll see something like the following code. For brevity, I've again eliminated some of the attributes of certain tags, such as the style attributes of the input tags.

```
<!DOCTYPE HTML PUBLIC "-//W3C//DTD HTML 4.0 Transitional//EN">
<HTML>
  <HEAD>
    <title></title>
    <meta name="GENERATOR" content="Microsoft Visual Studio.NET 7.0">
    <meta name="CODE_LANGUAGE" content="Visual Basic 7.0">
    <meta name="vs_defaultClientScript" content="JavaScript">
    <meta name="vs_targetSchema"
content="http://schemas.microsoft.com/intellisense/ie5">
  </HEAD>
  <body MS_POSITIONING="GridLayout">
    <form name="Form1" method="post" action="WebForm1.aspx" id="Form1">
<input type="hidden" name="__VIEWSTATE" value="dDwyNjY4NzY3NzE7Oz4=" />

      <input name="txtNumberA" type="text" id="txtNumberA"/>
      <input name="txtNumberB" type="text" id="txtNumberB"/>
      <input type="submit" name="btnMultiply" value="Multiply"/>
      <input name="txtResult" type="text" id="txtResult"
disabled="disabled"/>
    </form>
  </body>
</HTML>
```

HTML Rendering

When you created your form for the multiplication example, you added three text boxes and one button. Looking at the HTML source, you'll find there are four input tags, three of type text and one of type submit. You didn't write these HTML tags. Here, the .NET Framework has handled the mapping, or rendering, of the button and text box semantics to the necessary HTML syntax.

Browser Capabilities

Before ASP.NET, the process of rendering HTML was greatly complicated for any application that had to support multiple browser applications or even multiple versions of a single browser. If you were lucky, you were developing for a captive audience such as a corporate intranet and had the freedom to target a minimum version of a specific browser. However, if you were writing an Internet application, the people paying the bills wouldn't have been too happy if you had told them you planned to exclude all customers who aren't running Internet Explorer 5.5 or later.

I used Internet Explorer 6.0 to view this page. If you are using a browser with fewer (or more) capabilities, the HTML source you get may be very different than that shown here. However, it's no longer up to you to figure out how to render HTML for all the various browsers that might be out on the Internet. All of the standard Web controls (including the TextBox and Button controls you used here) are intelligent enough to determine the capabilities of the client browser and render the appropriate HTML.

State Management

If you haven't done so already, close the window that shows the HTML source for the example application. Return to the browser, and enter 5 in the first text field and 10 in the second text field. Click the Multiply button. As expected, the number 50 appears in the third text field. However, it wasn't as simple as it looks.

Recall that the UI is running inside your client browser. It doesn't know that you intended to multiply the two numbers. When you viewed the HTML source of the page, you certainly didn't see any event handler code. When you clicked the Multiply button, the data you entered in the first two text fields got sent (posted) back to your server-side ASPX file. There, your code multiplied the two numbers and stored the result in the Text property of the txtResult object. The server-side code then downloaded an entirely new set of HTML source to the client, which caused the client browser to display the two numbers you entered, as well as the result of the multiplication.

A very important distinction needs to be made at this point. The objects (such as txtResult) referenced in your server-side code (such as the btnMultiply_Click event handler) are server-side instantiations of Visual Studio .NET Framework objects. Specifically, txtResult is System.Web.UI.WebControls.TextBox. Although the txtResult object referenced in the HTML source shares the same name, it is an entirely separate object. It is an IE DOM Input object, and it knows nothing about your server-side code.

The server- and client-based objects are not only different instances, but they are not even of the same class. How does the server-side txtNumberA TextBox object know that the user entered 5 in the client-side txtNumberA Input object? How does the client-side txtResult object know that it needs to display the value (50) of the server-side txtResult object? Finally, because the client-side page got re-created after the user clicked Multiply, how do the *new* instances of the client-side txtNumberA and txtNumberB objects retain their values of 5 and 10?

In lower versions of ASP, it was your responsibility to know the answers to these questions because you had to write the code to make these things happen. As we've seen, the Web controls you dropped onto your ASP.NET Web form encapsulate all of this logic for you. All of the complexity is handled in the controls' Render, LoadPostBack, SaveViewState, and LoadViewState methods.

Intrinsic Web Controls—The Ones You'll Use the Most

Microsoft provides a set of useful Web controls with Visual Studio .NET, just as it provided a standard set of UI controls with Visual Basic. In this section, we'll examine a few of the built-in, or intrinsic, Web controls. I'll describe a few of the most important properties, methods, and events of each control.

> **NOTE** The controls described in this section are Web controls. Microsoft also provides a set of HTML controls. Both Web and HTML controls are Web forms server controls. However, the HTML controls have a high degree of correspondence to standard HTML and do not provide much functionality beyond HTML. The Web controls provide a greater degree of abstraction and provide additional functionality beyond the HTML controls. This can be confusing because both sets of controls produce HTML when rendered for the client browser. All HTML controls are derived from the HTMLControl class. All Web controls are derived form the WebControl class. For more information, consult the product documentation and compare the feature sets provided by controls in the System.Web.UI.WebControls namespace to those in the System.Web.UI.HtmlControls namespace.

Button

In the multiplication example application, we used a Button control to create a button that submits the user's inputs on a form to the Web server. Two types of buttons can be created with the Button control.

By default, the Button control creates a Submit button, which simply submits the user's inputs (as in our example) and may have an OnClick event handler.

If you set the CommandName property of a Button object, the object creates a Command button. Like a Submit button, a Command button submits the user's inputs on a form to the server. However, a Command button also passes the values of its CommandName property (and if specified, CommandArgument property) to its event handler. Command buttons have OnCommand events rather than OnClick events. The primary advantage to using a Command button is that a single event handler can process the user's interaction with many Command buttons.

The text displayed on the face of a button is stored in the button object's Text property.

Label

The Label control is used to display text on a Web page. From the client browser's standpoint, the text is static. The user cannot change the text. Of course, your ASPX code can do so. The text displayed by this control is stored in its Text property.

Example: Adding a Label Control

Let's examine how the addition of a control to a Web form changes the HTML that gets sent to the client's browser. We'll add a Label control to the multiplication example:

1. Return to the Visual Studio IDE, and open the multiplication application we created earlier. In the Web form designer, view the grid layout of your form.

2. Select the three TextBox controls and the Button control. Drag them down the form to make room for a label at the top.

3. Drag and drop a Label control from the toolbox onto your form. Position the label at the top of the form.

4. Set the label's ID property to lblWelcome. Set its Text property to Welcome, followed by your name. Although we are setting the property statically at design time, in a real application we might be required to query the user's name from a database.

5. Run the application by pressing the F5 key. Note that your welcome message now appears above the first input field.

When the server-side Label control renders HTML for the client, it produces an HTML span tag that contains the text of the label. If you view the HTML source in the browser, you can see the span tag:

```
<span id="lblWelcome">Welcome, Brian Wendt</span>
```

TextBox

A TextBox creates an input field in the user's Web browser. This control has three modes of operations, selected by setting its TextMode property.

In *SingleLine* mode, the TextBox creates an HTML input tag with a type attribute of text. The user may enter a single line of text. This is the default mode for the control.

In *Password* mode, the TextBox creates an HTML input tag with a type attribute of password. Just as in SingleLine mode, the user can enter a single line of text. However, the data entered by the user in the input field is not displayed on the user's screen.

In both SingleLine and Password modes, the MaxLength property can be set to control the maximum number of characters the user may enter in the field.

In *MultiLine* mode, the TextBox creates an HTML textarea tag. The user can enter multiple lines of text. The user's input is visible on the screen. The Rows and Columns properties can be set to control the size of the text area in characters. If the user enters additional data, the text area will scroll. These properties do not prevent the user from entering a large amount of data.

If the user enters a value or changes the value in a TextBox, the control's TextChanged event will fire. You can prevent the user from entering data (or changing existing data) in an input field by setting the Enabled property of the TextBox object to false.

Table

The Table control creates an HTML table. An instance of the Table control usually contains many instances of the TableRow and TableCell controls.

In previous versions of ASP, tables were very frequently used to control the layout of the content on a page, for example, to make the fields on a form line up. In ASP.NET, the Web form designer takes care of ensuring that the user's browser positions controls as you originally laid out the form. The primary use of the Table control on a Web form is just what you might expect: to display static data to the user in a tabular format. If your UI design requires the user to work with the data, consider using the DataList or DataGrid controls.

The Height and Width properties control the size of the table. If these properties are not set, the table will be sized to fit its contents. The GridLines property controls whether grid lines will be displayed around and between the cells in the table. This property can be set to None, Horizontal, Vertical, or Both.

The Rows property is the collection of rows in the table. Each member of this collection is a TableRow.

TableRow

TableRow objects are members of the Rows collection of a Table object. They define the rows in the table.

The Height and Width properties control the size of the row. If these properties are not set, the row will be sized to fit its contents or to fit the space occupied by the enclosing Table object. The HorizontalAlign property controls the horizontal alignment of cells within the row. This property can be set to NotSet, Left, Center, Right, or Justify. The VerticalAlign property controls the vertical alignment of cells within the row. It can be set to NotSet, Top, Middle, or Bottom.

The Cells property is a collection of cells in the row. Each member of this collection is a TableCell.

TableCell

TableCell objects are members of the Cells collection of a TableRow object. They define the cells in the row. Like TableRow objects, instances of this class have Height, Width, HorizontalAlign, and VerticalAlign properties.

If you want a cell to span multiple columns within a table, you can set its ColumnSpan property to the number of columns to span. If you want a cell to span multiple rows, you can set its RowSpan property.

The Text property stores the value displayed in the table cell. The Wrap property controls whether or not the value wraps if it is too large to fit within the width of the cell.

Page Class

When you create an ASP.NET Web page, you are creating a Page class. Your Page class is derived from System.Web.UI.Page and includes properties and methods that correspond to the controls and other functionality that you implement on the Web page.

System.Web.UI.Page is itself derived from System.Web.UI.Control. Every derived Page class that you create has many properties and methods exposed from its base classes.

In the discussion of state, I mentioned that the system provides Request, Response, Session, and Application objects for you. In reality, these objects are properties of the base class of your Page class. If you have used previous versions of ASP, you will recognize these objects. The Server object from ASP is also provided as a property of the base Page class.

The ErrorPage property stores the URL to which the user will be redirected if your code raises an unhandled exception. The Trace property returns a reference to a TraceContext object, which can be used for debugging. Tracing and the TraceEnabled and TraceModeValue properties of the Page object are covered in more detail later in this chapter.

The IsPostBack property is false if the user is visiting this page for the first time or has linked to this page from a different page. This property is true if the page has posted data back to itself.

The User property returns information about the user who requested the Web page.

Example

Let's examine the derived Page class that we defined when we created the multiplication application example earlier in this chapter.

The ASPX.VB file contains the Visual Basic .NET code behind the user interface objects defined in the ASPX file. Here are the contents of the ASPX.VB file for the multiplication application, WebForm1.aspx.vb:

```
Public Class WebForm1s
    Inherits System.Web.UI.Page
    Protected WithEvents txtNumberA As System.Web.UI.WebControls.TextBox
    Protected WithEvents txtNumberB As System.Web.UI.WebControls.TextBox
    Protected WithEvents btnMultiply As System.Web.UI.WebControls.Button
    Protected WithEvents lblWelcome As System.Web.UI.WebControls.Label
    Protected WithEvents txtResult As System.Web.UI.WebControls.TextBox

    Private Sub Page_Load(ByVal sender As System.Object, ByVal e As
System.EventArgs) Handles MyBase.Load
        'Put user code to initialize the page here
    End Sub

    Private Sub btnMultiply_Click(ByVal sender As System.Object, ByVal e
As System.EventArgs) Handles btnMultiply.Click
        txtResult.Text = txtNumberA.Text * txtNumberB.Text
    End Sub
End Class
```

With the exception of the line of code that actually performs the multiplication, all of the code shown here was generated by the IDE for you, as you created your form in design mode or when you created the project.

Class WebForm1

Earlier we worked with instances of the TextBox, Button, and Label classes. You created these instances by dropping them onto a form. Your ASPX page, itself, is an object. It is an instance of a class that we were defining as we edited the form in Design mode. In this case, the name of the class is WebForm1. The class was initially created from a template when you created the project.

Inherits System.Web.UI.Page

Because it uses the Inherits keyword, class WebForm1 is a derived class. It is derived from the public base class System.Web.UI.Page. A derived class has all of the properties and methods of its base class *plus* whatever additional properties and methods you choose to define. The derived class does not contain a copy of the base class. It *is* the base class, along with additional functionality. Any code that works with the base class will also work with the derived class.

You are familiar with the Me keyword in Visual Basic, which provides a reference to the instance of the class on which a method was invoked. (It corresponds to the This keyword in other languages.) Visual Basic .NET adds a MyBase keyword. Because the derived class literally is an instance of the base class (plus some added properties and/or methods), it is possible to coerce an instance of the derived class to be of the type of the base class. The MyBase keyword simply provides a reference to the base class of the class on which a method was invoked. Both Me and MyBase return a reference to the *same object*. The only difference is that Me is of the type of the derived class, and MyBase is of the type of the base class.

Fields

The code generated for our example contains five fields. Fields are also known as member variables. Each of these fields is an instance of a Web control: TextBox, Button, or Label. These fields correspond directly to the five controls we placed on the form. Note that WebClass1 is *not* derived from the TextBox, Button, or Label classes. Rather, WebClass1 contains fields that are references to instances of these classes.

The IDE automatically added these fields to the class as you added the corresponding controls to the form in Design mode. If you delete a control from the form, the IDE will delete the corresponding field from the definition of class WebClass1. Just as in previous versions of Visual Basic, if you delete a control, the IDE will not delete any of the other code that is associated with the control, such as event handlers.

Methods

This code contains two methods. The Page_Load method is an event handler. Because it is specified as Handles MyBase.Load, this event handler is called when a Load event is raised to the base class of WebClass1. (See the discussion of MyBase earlier in the chapter.) To clarify, this event handler fires when the page is loaded. An empty event handler was created by the IDE when you created the project.

The btnMultiply_Click method is also an event handler. Because it is specified as Handles btnMultiply.Click, this method is called when the user clicks the Multiply button. (As you've seen, this event actually fires on the server when the client browser posts back data indicating that the user clicked the button on the client.) The IDE created an empty event handler when you double-clicked the Multiply button in Design mode; you then manually entered the single line of code that performs the multiplication.

ViewState Object

Your Page object, as well as every Web control, is derived from the Control base class. This class exposes a ViewState property, which is a reference to an instance of the StateBag class. This class is a Dictionary object, which allows you to store name/value pairs.

You can use the ViewState object to store any state information by using the object as an lvalue. For example, to create an element named arg1 with a value of 23, you would use the following:

```
ViewState("arg1") = 23
```

When your page saves its view state, this new element will automatically get persisted. If the client browser posts back to the page, arg1 will automatically get loaded back from the saved view state, along with all of the other elements. You can retrieve the value of arg1 with the following code:

```
lArg1 = CLng(ViewState("arg1"))
```

Each object derived from the base Control class, including your Page object, has its own instance of the StateBag class. You don't need to worry about naming conflicts among the various controls on your page.

Events

Your Page object receives the following events in the following order:

The *Init* event occurs when the Page object is instantiated.   This is your first opportunity to execute code on the page. After this event completes, the view state and post back data are loaded into the page, and validation is performed.

The *Load* event is then raised for your Page.   After the Load event completes, data-changed events are fired for Web controls on your page, if necessary. If any post-back events occurred, the appropriate events are raised for the relevant Web controls.

Your Page object next receives the *PreRender* event.   This is your last opportunity to make persistent changes to view state. Once this event completes, the view state is saved.

The *Render* event is sent to your Page object.   This event causes all page content to render itself to HTML.

The *UnLoad* event is then raised.   Once this event completes, the *Disposed* event is raised. Once your Page object's disposed event handler completes, the instance of your Page object is destroyed.

More Examples

The examples we've worked with so far introduced you to the fundamentals of ASP.NET Web forms. Now that you're more familiar with the underlying technology, let's try a few more examples and gain some hands-on experience with ASP.NET. The examples in this section will introduce some more advanced techniques and bring together several of the concepts we've introduced.

A Simple Data Binding Example

In this example, we'll create a form that lets you select your favorite color from a drop-down list. In a real application, we might want to let users select a choice for a product they are ordering. In that case, we would almost certainly obtain the list of available colors from a database. To keep this example simple, we'll bind the drop-down list to an in-memory array of strings. As before, our first step is to create an empty Web application:

1. Run the Visual Studio IDE. Close any project you have open. Select File, New Project. In the New Project dialog box, leave Visual Basic Projects as the selected Project Type. Click ASP.NET Web Application under Templates.

2. Enter http://localhost/Ch5-Ex5.9.1 in the Location field. Click OK to create the project. A new, empty Web application will be created for you.

Next, we'll add controls to the form, and set the controls' design-time properties.

3. Add a Label control to the upper-left corner of your form. Set the Label ID property to lblColorPrompt and its Text property to Please select your favorite color. The IDE will automatically resize the label to be large enough to display the message you enter in the Text property.

4. Add a DropDownList control to the form, beneath the first label. Set the DropDownList ID property to selColors. Set the AutoPostBack property to true.

5. Add a second Label beneath the drop-down list. Set this label's ID to lblSelectedColor. Clear this label's Text property.

   We need to build the array of colors for the drop-down list. We don't want to go to the work of obtaining the list of colors every time the page posts back to itself. Although in this example the colors come from an array, an actual application would probably need to query a database. To avoid the overhead of building the array after the initial load of the page, we only do so if the page's IsPostBack property is false. If this is the first visit to the page, we build the array (using a new Visual Basic .NET language feature to initialize it at declaration) and then set a reference to the array in the DataSource property of the selColor control. On subsequent post backs to the page, the list of colors will be reloaded into the drop-down list as part of its view state data. The next step implements this.

6. Double-click the new Web form to display the Page_Load event handler. Add the following code to the page on load subroutine:

```
If Not IsPostBack Then
    Dim astrColors As String() = {"Red", "Orange", "Yellow",
"Green", "Blue", "Indigo", "Violet"}

    selColors.DataSource = astrColors
End If


DataBind()
```

We must call the Page's DataBind() method to data bind all bound controls. If we wanted to, we could bind just selColors by calling selColors.DataBind(). If we do neither of these, the list box will not get populated.

When the user makes a selection from the drop-down list, we want the Web page to display the name of the color. We'll use lblSelectedColor to do so. We must write an event handler for the change event of the drop down list.

7. In the Web form designer, double-click the drop-down list. The IDE will create an empty event handler for the list's SelectedIndexChange event. Add the following code to the event handler:

```
lblSelectedColor.Text = "Selected Color: " &
selColors.SelectedItem.Text
```

The program is now ready to be tested.

8. Select Debug, Start, or press F5. You Web form will compile and run in a browser window.

9. Select a color in the drop-down list. The page will post back to the server. When it is rerendered, the second label will display the color you selected.

This example isn't very impressive when you run it. However, it does illustrate data binding. We did not manually set the collection of color options in the drop-down list control. Instead, we built an array of colors and bound the array to the drop-down list. The distinction is important. In a real application, we would use data binding, as we did here. However, instead of explicitly building an array of colors in the page's load event, we would retrieve the list of options from the database. We would bind the drop-down list control to the result set returned from the database. Presumably, the list of options returned from the database would depend on business rules or relational data, such as the set of available colors for a selected product.

Adding Controls at Runtime

In this example, we'll add a text box to a form at runtime. We'll illustrate, and then correct, the problem of .NET not tracking the addition of controls after a post-back operation.

Once again, our first step is to create an empty Web application:

1. Run the Visual Studio IDE. Close any project you have open. Select File, New Project. In the New Project dialog box, leave Visual Basic Projects as the selected Project Type. Click ASP.NET Web Application under Templates.

2. Enter http://localhost/Ch5-Ex5.9.2 in the Location field. Click OK to create the project. A new, empty Web application will be created for you.

3. Next, we add controls to the form, and set design-time properties of the controls. Add a Label control to the upper-left corner of your form. Set the Label ID property to lblFieldA and its Text property to Field A. The IDE will automatically resize the label to be large enough to display the text you enter.

4. Add a TextBox control to the form, to the right of the first label. Set the ID property to txtFieldA.

5. Add a second Label beneath the first one. Set this label's ID to lblFieldB and its Text property to Field B.

   Don't create a second text box at this time.

6. Add a Button control to the form. Place it below the second label. Set the ID to btnShow and the Text to Show Values.

7. Add a second button to the form, to the right of the first. Set its ID to btnCreate and its Text to Create Field.

8. So far, you have been working with the Web forms controls in the tool-box. Locate the HTML group of controls. Add a Horizontal Rule control to your form, beneath the Show Values button.

9. Return to the Web controls group in the toolbox. Add a new Label control. Place the new label beneath the horizontal rule. Set the label's ID property to lblValueA. The IDE automatically sets the Text property of a new label control to Label. Clear this entry in the Text property.

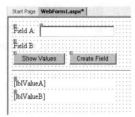

Figure 5.1   Web form designer, form view.

10. Add a final new Label control beneath the most recent one. Set its ID to lblValueB. Clear its Text property.

11. Use the Align and Spacing commands on the Format menu to clean up the layout of your form.

    Your form should now look something like Figure 5.1.

    Before we continue with this example, we'll write the click event handler for the Show Values button.

12. Double-click the Show Values button in the Web form designer. The IDE will display the button's Click event handler. Add the following code:

```
lblValueA.Text = "A = " & txtFieldA.Text
```

Do not add any other code at this time.

Now run the program. We haven't written any code for the Create Field button, so clicking it will do nothing but cause a round trip to the server. Enter a few words in field A, and click the Show Values button. The first label beneath the horizontal rule will display A = *value*, where *value* is whatever you entered in the text box.

Now that we've seen how the show values function works, we'll implement the create field function. This function is the point of the example: It does the actual work of adding a control at runtime. I don't like to perform too much work within event handlers, so I've put the code to add the control in a separate subroutine:

1. Return to Visual Studio and view WebForm1.aspx.vb. Add the following subroutine:

```
Private Sub AddFieldB()
    Dim txtFieldB As New TextBox()
    txtFieldB.ID = "txtFieldB"
    txtFieldB.Width = txtFieldA.Width
    txtFieldB.Height = txtFieldA.Height
```

```
            txtFieldB.Style("LEFT") = txtFieldA.Style("LEFT")
            txtFieldB.Style("TOP") = 49
            txtFieldB.Style("POSITION") = "absolute"

            Dim objForm As HtmlForm
            objForm = Page.FindControl("Form1")
            objForm.Controls.Add(txtFieldB)

            btnCreate.Enabled = False
        End Sub
```

In this subroutine, we create a new text box control and set its properties. We set most of its position and style properties to be identical to the first text box. We then add the text box as a child control of our Page object's Form control.

Let's try calling the subroutine from the click event handler of the Create Field button.

2. Return to the Web form designer and double-click the Create Field button on your Web form. Visual Studio will display an empty btnCreate_Click subroutine. Add a call to the new AddFieldB() subroutine to the body of this event handler.

3. Do not add any code to display the value of Field B at this time.

    Run the program again at this point. Click the Create Field button. A new text box will appear on the form. So far, we have been successful. However, in our earlier discussion of state management, I identified the problem of .NET not persisting the fact that new controls have been added at runtime. We can force a post-back operation by clicking the Show Values button at this time. Note that the new field we just added disappears. This is because the post-back operation caused a new instance of our Page object to be created from our derived Page class. Our derived Page class does not include the text box for Field B.

    To fix this problem, when we add the new text box at runtime, we must also add some information to our view state to remember that we created the control. Then, we must check for this flag when we reload the page. If we find the flag, we have to add the control again.

    We'll modify the code to persist this change (the addition of the control at runtime) through multiple round trips from client to server.

4. Add the following line of code to the btnCreate_Click event handler:
    ```
    ViewState("blnCreatedFieldB") = True
    ```

5. Add the following lines of code to Page_Load:
    ```
    Dim blnCreatedFieldB As Boolean
    blnCreatedFieldB = CBool(ViewState("blnCreatedFieldB"))
    ```

```
If blnCreatedFieldB Then
AddFieldB()
End If
```

6. Add the following lines of code to btnShow_Click:

```
Dim txtFieldB As TextBox
txtFieldB = Page.FindControl("txtFieldB")
If Not txtFieldB Is Nothing Then
    lblValueB.Text = "B = " & txtFieldB.Text
End If
```

The Web page should now work as expected. Experiment with entering values and clicking the buttons.

A Multipage Example

All of the examples we've seen so far consist of single-page Web sites. In practice, most Web applications you write will contain dozens or perhaps even hundreds of Web pages. This example demonstrates how information can be passed from code executing in one Web page's Page class to code executing in another page's Page class.

We'll build on the earlier data-binding example. We'll implement two Web pages. The Color Selection page will allow users to select the color of car they are interested in purchasing. The user will then be redirected to the Car Inventory page. The Car Inventory page will provide a list of cars that are available in the selected color. The purpose of this example is to demonstrate maintenance of state information about a user's selection. To simplify this example, we'll give the user the same list of cars for every color. In a real application, we would query the database to retrieve the list of cars actually on hand in the selected color.

For the Color Selection page, we'll start with the code from the data-binding example and make a few changes:

1. You can start by opening the solution you created for the data-binding example. If you wish to keep the earlier code, you can either create a copy of the solution and Web application, or you can repeat the steps for the data-binding example, specifying Ch5-Ex5.9.3 as the project name.

    Presumably, the user's color selection will be useful on many other pages. The Session object allows us to retrieve the information from any Web page within the application, for the duration of the user's session. If we only needed the color selection on the Car Inventory page, and nowhere else in the application, we would probably use a different mechanism to pass the user's selection. A good choice in that case would be to send the color selection using an HTTP form POST. Because we expect to use the color selection on many pages, we'll use the Session object to store the selected color.

2. Add the following line of code to the existing selColors_SelectedIndex-Changed:

```
Session("strColor") = selColors.SelectedItem.Text
```

The user needs to be able to get from the Color Selection page to the Car Inventory page easily. We'll place a hyperlink on the Color Selection page that allows users to navigate to the Car Inventory page with a single click. We won't allow users to use the hyperlink until they've selected a color.

3. Add a Hyperlink control from the toolbox to your Web form. Position the control below the lblSelectedColor label. Set the Hyperlink ID property to objCarsLink, Text to Click Here to View Inventory, NavigateUrl to Cars.aspx, and Enabled to False.

4. Add the following line of code to the existing selColors_SelectedIndex-Changed:

```
objCarsLink.Enabled = True
```

We've now completed the modifications necessary to change the data-binding example into the Color Selection page. Next, we'll create the Car Inventory page. Because we already have a project, we *don't* need to create an empty Web application. Instead, we'll add an additional Web page to the existing project.

5. In the Visual Studio IDE, locate the Solution Explorer window. If the window is not visible, you can select it from the View menu. Right-click the Web site (Ch5-Ex5.9.3 or Ch5-Ex5.9.1) and select Add, Add Web Form...

6. The Add New Item dialog box appears. Leave Web Form selected in the Templates window. Enter Cars.aspx in the Name field, and click Open. A new, blank Web form will be added to your application.

7. In the Solution Explorer window in the IDE, right-click WebForm1.aspx, and select Set as Start Page.

Our Web application now consists of two Web pages. WebForm1.aspx is the Color Selection page, and Cars.aspx is the Car Inventory page. We've added the Car Inventory page to the Web application, but currently the form is blank. We'll now add controls to the form and set the design-time properties of the controls.

8. On the new Cars Web form, add a Label control in the upper-left corner of the form. Make the control about 25 pixels tall and 300 pixels wide. Set the label's ID property to lblTop. Clear its Text property.

9. Add a ListBox control beneath the label on the new form. Make the list box the same width as the label control and about 150 pixels tall. Set the list box's ID property to selCars.

10. Locate the Items property in the ListBox properties window. Click the value field for this property. Click the ellipsis button that appears. The List Item Collection Editor dialog box will display.

11. In the List Item Collection Editor, click the Add button. Set the Text property of the new ListItem to Acura RSX Type-S. Click the Add button again and create an item with a Text property of Toyota MR-2 Spyder. Repeat this process to create items for Nissan 2003 Z-Concept and Chevy SSR/S10 Roadster. Once all four items have been added, click OK to close the collection editor.

When users visit the Car Inventory page, we need to retrieve their selected color from the Session object. In this example, we'll just show the selected color on the Inventory page to prove we actually did pass the information from the Color Selection page.

12. Double-click the new Cars.aspx Web form. The Code-Behind file, Cars.aspx.vb, will display. Add the following code to Page_Load:

```
Dim strColor As String
strColor = Session("strColor")
lblTop.Text = "We have the following " & strColor & " cars in stock."
```

13. Select File, Save All to save all changes. Select Debug, Start, or hit F5. WebForm1.aspx displays in your browser. Select a color. The server-side code stores your color selection in the Session object, sets the text of the label property to display your selection, and enables the hyperlink at the bottom of the page.

Click the view inventory hyperlink. Cars.aspx displays in your browser. It retrieves your selected color from the Session object and displays it in the Label control. It then displays the static list of cars that you created at design time. Of course, in an actual application, you would query a database for the stock on hand.

A Peek behind the Curtain: Tracing

Debugging Web applications can be difficult. Your code is actually executing on the Web server, but the user interface is displayed in a Web browser. Usually these processes are running on different machines. A large number of copies of your code may be running in parallel if many people are using the

Web site. You may not have full control of the Web server. There are many collections of information involved: session and application variables, HTTP post data, cookies, and HTTP headers, for example.

In previous versions of ASP, the easiest solution was to add debugging code in the form of calls to the Write method of the Response object. This method accepts a string and outputs it literally to the client browser. The debugging information was probably mixed in with the HTML for the page content, because it would be difficult to separate the two streams of data. Frequently, adding or removing the code to produce diagnostic output introduced new errors.

ASP.NET introduces the Trace object. Trace is actually a property of the base Page class and is a reference to a TraceContext object. This object provides properties and methods to write diagnostic messages to a separate output stream. You can control tracing on an application or Web page level. Tracing can be disabled or enabled. If enabled, trace messages can either be appended to the end of the rendered Web page, or they can be stored in memory and retrieved using the trace.axd utility.

When Not to Use Tracing

Tracing is great for quickly debugging applications in development or to provide additional data for developers to watch for bugs that might not be readily apparent in the UI. When an application is deployed to the production server, tracing should be disabled because it adds additional processing and memory overhead to the Web service. If an application is being beta tested or otherwise made available to the public, you should be wary of leaving tracing enabled. Depending on the design of your application, trace messages could expose application data that would create a security risk or violate privacy or confidentiality. Finally, if you are debugging a complex problem, you may be better off using a debugger.

TraceContext Class

The TraceContext class is the main programmatic interface to the tracing facilities in ASP.NET. Each Page inherits from its base Page class a Trace property, which is a reference to an instance of this class. This following methods and properties are exposed.

Methods

The Write method adds an entry to the trace log. It exposes three overloads. The first variation accepts a single string parameter and adds it to the log as a trace message. The second variation accepts two string parameters. The first parameter is a category; the second is the message. The final variation accepts two string parameters and a reference to an exception object. The first two parameters are the category and message, and the third parameter is the error information to be logged.

The Warn method is identical to the Write method in all ways except that any trace log entries created with the Warn method are displayed in red.

Properties

IsEnabled returns a boolean value that indicates whether or not tracing is enabled for the current page.

TraceMode is a read/write property that indicates the order in which trace messages are displayed. It can take the values SortByCategory and SortBy-Time.

Implementing Page-Level Tracing

You can turn tracing on or off for individual Web pages by specifying a Trace attribute in the Page directive. As you recall from earlier in this chapter, every ASPX page begins with a list of page attributes enclosed in a <%@ %> tag. The ASPX file for our multiplication application began with the following page directive:

```
<%@ Page Language="vb" AutoEventWireup="false"
Codebehind="WebForm1.aspx.vb" Inherits="Ch5_Ex1.WebForm1"%>
```

To enable tracing for this page, we would add the Trace attribute with a value of true:

```
<%@ Page Trace="true" Language="vb" AutoEventWireup="false"
Codebehind="WebForm1.aspx.vb" Inherits="Ch5_Ex1.WebForm1"%>
```

If we view the page after adding this attribute, we can see that a great deal of diagnostic information is now provided, even though we haven't added any explicit trace messages.

Implementing Application-Level Tracing

Web.config is an XML file that specifies a number of application-level settings in ASP.NET. This file can be found in the root directory of the application's Web site. Tracing can be controlled for an entire application by setting attributes of the trace tag in the application's Web.config file.

NOTE If tracing is specified at both the application and page level, the setting in the page's directive tag overrides the setting in the Web.config file. To make it easier to disable tracing when your application is ready for deployment, it would be best to control tracing at the application level, in Web.config.

Modifying Web.Config for Tracing

Visual Studio automatically created the following entry in our Web.config file when we created the multiplication application:

```
    <trace enabled="false" requestLimit="10" pageOutput="false"
traceMode="SortByTime" localOnly="true" />
```

This tag includes the following attributes:

■ The enabled attribute enables or disables tracing for the application.

■ The pageOutput attribute controls where messages are displayed. If this attribute is set to true, trace messages are appended to the end of each Web page. If this attribute is set to false, trace messages are kept in memory, and you must use the trace.axd tool to view the messages.

■ If pageOutput is set to false, the requestLimit attribute controls how many sets of trace data are kept in memory. Each request for a page with tracing enabled creates a new set of trace data.

■ The traceMode attribute sets the default value of the TraceMode property of the all pages' Trace objects. This attribute's value can be either SortByTime or SortByCategory.

■ The localOnly attribute specifies that trace.axd is only available locally, on the machine on which the Web server is running.

If we want to enable tracing for this example application, we need only change the value of the enabled attribute from false to true. It is not necessary to recompile the application after changing Web.config.

Using Trace.axd

If tracing is enabled and the pageOutput option is set to false, the Web server will record trace log data in memory. This data can be viewed using trace.axd. This tool is an HTTP handler that appears to your Web browser to be located in the root directory of each application on your Web server. For example, if the URL for the multiplication application is http://localhost/Ch5-Ex1/WebForm1.aspx, the trace data can be viewed by accessing the URL http://localhost/Ch5-Ex1/trace.axd.

You can also disable trace.axd for an application by editing the application's Web.config file. You might want to disable this tool to avoid placing temptation in the path of hackers. To disable trace.axd, locate the <httpHandlers> tag. Add the following tag just before the </httpHandlers> tag:

```
<remove verb="*" path="trace.axd" />
```

You can disable trace.axd for an entire Web server by editing the server's machine.config file. This file is located in the directory:

```
%SystemDrive%\WINNT\Microsoft.NET\Framework\Version\CONFIG
```

Open the machine.config file and locate the <httpHandlers> tag. Within this tag, find the <add> tag for trace.axd. Place a begin comment tag (<!—) at the beginning of the line and an end comment tag (—>) at the end of the line. The <add> tag should look similar to the following:

```
<!—<add verb="*" path="trace.axd"
type="System.Web.Handlers.TraceHandler, System.Web, Version=1.0.2411.0,
Culture=neutral, PublicKeyToken=b03f5f7f11d50a3a" />—>
```

Once you changed either the Web.config or machine.config file, you will receive a resource not found error if you try to view the trace data, even if tracing is enabled for an application or Web page.

Trace Output

When you enable tracing, you get more information than the trace log entries you created with Trace.Write. We'll examine each section of the trace data individually. The sample trace output sections are from our multiplication application.

When you request trace.axd for a Web application, the first thing you'll see is a list of the trace logs that exist in memory for that application, as shown in Figure 5.2. You can click the View Details link to see all of the information for the selected log.

Requests to this Application					Remaining: 8
No.	Time of Request	File	Status Code	Verb	
1	7/29/2001 2:56:01 PM	/WebForm1.aspx	200	GET	**View Details**
2	7/29/2001 2:56:08 PM	/WebForm1.aspx	200	POST	**View Details**

Figure 5.2 List of trace logs.

Request Details			
Session Id:	okx1n3554gfgspyzvrbpib55	**Request Type:**	GET
Time of Request:	7/29/2001 2:41:01 PM	**Status Code:**	200
Request Encoding:	Unicode (UTF-8)	**Response Encoding:**	Unicode (UTF-8)

Figure 5.3 Summary of the selected trace.

Request Details

The View Details link displays multiple sections of detailed information about the selected trace. The summary section, shown in Figure 5.3, includes general information about the Web page request that created the trace log. This section includes information such as the session ID, time of request, type of request, and HTTP status code.

Trace Information

The next section, shown in Figure 5.4, lists the trace log entries. The .NET Framework automatically created the log entries. If you added any additional trace logs with the Write or Warn methods of Trace, they would appear in this section. Each row in the table is a trace log entry. Each entry includes the category and message, the number of elapsed seconds from the first log message to the current entry, and the number of elapsed seconds from the previous log message to the current entry.

Control Tree

The control tree, shown in Figure 5.5, contains truncated information about each control on your page. Controls exist in a tree structure, with your derived

Trace Information			
Category	**Message**	**From First(s)**	**From Last(s)**
aspx.page	Begin Init		
aspx.page	End Init	0.002520	0.002520
aspx.page	Begin PreRender	0.004672	0.002152
aspx.page	End PreRender	0.004931	0.000259
aspx.page	Begin SaveViewState	0.075388	0.070457
aspx.page	End SaveViewState	0.111786	0.036398
aspx.page	Begin Render	0.112045	0.000259
aspx.page	End Render	0.240440	0.128395

Figure 5.4 List of events for the selected trace.

Control Tree

Control Id	Type	Render Size Bytes (including children)	Viewstate Size Bytes (excluding children)
__PAGE	ASP.WebForm1_aspx	1258	20
ctrl0	System.Web.UI.ResourceBasedLiteralControl	428	0
Form1	System.Web.UI.HtmlControls.HtmlForm	809	0
ctrl1	System.Web.UI.LiteralControl	5	0
txtNumberA	System.Web.UI.WebControls.TextBox	118	0
ctrl2	System.Web.UI.LiteralControl	5	0
txtNumberB	System.Web.UI.WebControls.TextBox	118	0
ctrl3	System.Web.UI.LiteralControl	5	0

Figure 5.5   Control tree for the selected trace.

Page object at the root. (Recall that your Page object is derived from the base Page class, which is, itself, derived from the Control class).

The size columns in this table are useful for determining the amount of overhead for each control. All of the render and view state data must be downloaded to the client browser on each round trip. The view state data must also be posted back to the server on every post-back operation.

Cookies Collection

The Cookies Collection, shown in Figure 5.6, displays information about each cookie used by your page. Information includes the name, value(s), and size in bytes of each cookie. In the multiplication application, we aren't using any cookies explicitly. ASP.NET does use a cookie, as shown in Figure 5.6, to maintain session state.

Headers Collection

The Headers Collection, shown in Figure 5.7, includes the list of name/value pairs of HTTP headers. Headers are sent from the client to the server as part of each request.

Cookies Collection

Name	Value	Size
ASP.NET_SessionId	okx1n3554gfgspyzvrbpib55	42

Figure 5.6   Cookies for the selected trace.

Headers Collection	
Name	**Value**
Connection	Keep-Alive
Accept	*/*
Accept-Encoding	gzip, deflate
Accept-Language	en-us
Host	localhost
User-Agent	Mozilla/4.0 (compatible; MSIE 6.0b; Windows NT 5.0; .NET CLR 1.0.2914)

Figure 5.7   HTTP headers for the selected trace.

Form Collection

If the selected request included a form post, the posted data will be displayed. The Form Collection, shown in Figure 5.8, consists of a simple list of name/value pairs. The VIEWSTATE form variable is used internally by ASP.NET to maintain view state across page post backs.

Server Variables

The final section is the list of name/value pairs of all server variables. Due to the large size of this table, I have included only a subset of the rows in Figure 5.9. You can access server variables in your ASP.NET code through the Server-Variables collection of the Request object.

Form Collection	
Name	**Value**
__VIEWSTATE	dDwxNTU0NTc0OTTE0OOzs+
txtNumberA	10
txtNumberB	20
txtResult	
btnMultiply	Multiply

Figure 5.8   Form variables for the selected trace.

Server Variables	
Name	**Value**
INSTANCE_ID	1
INSTANCE_META_PATH	/LM/W3SVC/1
LOCAL_ADDR	127.0.0.1
PATH_INFO	/Ch5-Ex1/WebForm1.aspx
PATH_TRANSLATED	h:\inetpub\wwwroot\Ch5-Ex1\WebForm1.aspx
QUERY_STRING	
REMOTE_ADDR	127.0.0.1
REMOTE_HOST	127.0.0.1
REQUEST_METHOD	POST
SCRIPT_NAME	/Ch5-Ex1/WebForm1.aspx

Figure 5.9   Server variables for the selected trace.

Tracing in Deployed Applications

One of the big advantages of the new tracing facility in ASP.NET is that it is no longer necessary to go through the code and remove all of the diagnostic logging messages prior to deployment. The calls to the Trace object's methods can be left in place. Once tracing is disabled for the application, the calls will simply be ignored.

Unfortunately, disabling tracing turns off *all* trace log entries. There may be a few log messages that you want to generate regardless of whether tracing is enabled or disabled.

System.Diagnostics

The System.Diagnostics namespace includes classes that can be used for application logging and debugging. You can use members of the EventLog class to write events to the NT event log from your Page object. Compare this to the Write or Warn methods of the Trace class. Both classes allow you to write logging information. The methods of the Trace class are intended for use during active development and QA of your application. You'll probably disable most or all tracing when you deploy to production. The EventLog class, on the other hand, might be used to log more important exceptions. The information you log to the event log might be relevant to the network administrator. Alternatively, you might use the event log to log critical information, such as suspected data integrity issues. Because you'll probably only use the event log when the most serious exceptions are detected, you can leave the event log code enabled in the production application.

Writing to the Event Log

Before you can write events to the event log, you must register an event source. An event source is simply a name under which all of your log entries are listed. Its purpose is to add a level of organization to the event log. You can use the CreateEventSource method to register an event source in your code. If you want to avoid reregistering the source each time your code executes, use the SourceExists method to check for prior registration. Both of these methods are shared members of the EventLog class, so it is not necessary to create an instance of EventLog to use them. You do need to add the following line to the top of your file:

```
Imports System.Diagnostics
```

You can the use the following code to add the event source MultExample to the NT application log:

```
If Not EventLog.SourceExists("MultExample") Then
     EventLog.CreateEventSource("MultExample ", "Application")
End If
```

Once you have registered your event source, you can log events using the WriteEntry method of the EventLog class. This method is also shared, so again no object instance is required.

```
EventLog.WriteEntry("MultExample", "This is a test log entry.")
```

To view the application log, right-click My Computer on your desktop and select Manage. The application log is located under Computer Management, System Tools, Event Viewer, Application.

Wrapping Up

As you've seen, creating Web pages with ASP.NET can be as easy as creating windows applications with the Visual Basic IDE.

In this chapter, we've discussed Web forms and taken a look at many of the complex details beneath the surface. We've delved into HTML rendering, basic state management, server and client HTML, and the code behind the Web form. We've worked with a few of the intrinsic Web controls that Microsoft provides for rendering HTML to the client. In the next chapter, we'll learn how you can write your own Web controls.

Using ASP.NET Web Controls

A man's mind stretched to a new idea can never go back to its original dimension.
Oliver Wendell Holmes

One of the exciting new features of ASP.NET is the ability to use and customize server-side controls. Control use is natural to every Microsoft Visual Basic Developer; now we can use our knowledge of these and apply them to ASP.NET. Building on the discussion in Chapter 4 about HTML controls, in this chapter we will shift focus to the Web controls. I will illustrate how to use them and how they function with practical examples. Because many of the Web controls will be familiar to the Visual Basic developer from the start, we're going to see essential use scenarios such as the difference between HTML, ActiveX, and Web server controls, how to build a Web server control, how to persist a control, state maintenance within the control, and Web server controls versus Web user controls. Once you see how powerful Web server controls are compared to their predecessors, you'll always want to find a way to leverage them in your Web applications.

Web Server Controls versus HTML Controls

Traditional Web Controls came in two well-known varieties. First, the HTML Control was controlled by the browser. The browser was responsible for the graphical representation of the control, as well as responsible for handling the events of the HTML on the client-side. A second type of control was the ActiveX Control. This control had to be approved by the client, and then had to be downloaded for use. The Web page then referenced the CLSID of the control and all processing was still handled on the client-side. The IIS Server would receive the ASP request for an ASP page, parse and process server-side logic, and handle information entered for the control. Anytime an update for the control was introduced, the CLSID changed, forcing the user to download the new ActiveX Control before the correct functionality could resume. Both HTML and ActiveX Controls still exist and operate today, as well as a new type of control, the Web Server Control, that works exclusively with Web forms and has the special ability to abridge convoluted processing logic, concealing the code and processing intricacy from the user and the developer.

The client-side logic behind HTML Controls is interpreted and rendered in the client's browser. The events that occur for HTML Controls are generally supported in the same HTML Web page or an include file, creating the potential for exposing the source code to a user. Even if the ASP page is encrypted, viewing the source can still expose lengthy pages of unsightly rubbish to a user. A huge issue with HTML Controls is infirmity. For instance, you cannot make API calls using HTML Controls, and all client-side logic must either be embedded in the HTML page or exist in include files that are included in the ASP page.

Conversely, ActiveX Controls are more robust controls, offering a developer greater client-side dexterity because the control consists of compiled Microsoft Visual Basic Code, as well as offers a more appealing GUI to the user. The real downfall to the ActiveX control is the fact that its fate depends on some presumptuous and somewhat risky factors.

First, the end-user is given the ability to determine whether or not an ActiveX Control can be downloaded to their PC. If options on the Browser are not explicitly set, then the ActiveX Control will not be downloaded to the client's PC. Also, only certain Web browsers support the use of ActiveX Controls, and a number of COM interfaces are required in order for a Web browser to run ActiveX Controls. If a call is made to an ActiveX Control that does not exist on the client's PC, then obviously the Web application will fail.

Second, if the application uses custom components, and the code within a custom ActiveX Control is modified to the extent that it requires recompilation, then the CLSID will change, forcing the user to download the component and run a Setup Application each time this occurs. Also, a modification must be made to the ASP Page so that it references the correct CLSID of the newer component being published. If the proper ActiveX Control is not present on the client's PC, then the call to reference the component in the browser will once again fail.

The Web Server Control can be thought of as a hybrid between the HTML Control and the ActiveX Control, offering all of the positive aspects of these types of controls, and at the same time overcoming the negative traits of each as well.

Web Server Controls, much like ActiveX Controls, allow you to separate the processing layer from the presentation layer of the component. The code is compiled, again like the ActiveX Control, but the components are not downloaded and referenced on the client's PC. Instead, Web Server Controls reside and respond to client events on the Server.

When certain events are fired on the ASPX Page, page information relating to the event is sent to the IIS Web Server for processing. The IIS Server determines which ASCX file is responsible for handling the events associated with the events invoked by the user, and references the file.

User Controls

In addition to the conveniences offered by Web Server Controls, Web user controls exist to allow users to create custom controls. Also known as pagelets, user controls can be thought of as ASP.NET pages encapsulated within an ASP.NET Web form, allowing you to save your Web page as a user control without having to write any additional lines of code or use any server-side includes.

User controls are created using the same programming model as ASP.NET pages, which allows you to create custom controls using the same methods that are required to create a Web forms page.

Each individual user control requires that you use a single language to author it; however, multiple controls that are written in different Microsoft-supported languages can work together peacefully on a single Web form. The user control is not initially compiled. However, it does automatically compile when initially called by the Web form and preserved in the memory of the server to prevent diminishing response times that can occur by ongoing requests of interpreted code. The syntax for calling a control in to memory within the ASPX Page looks like this:

```
<%@ Register TagPrefix="YourPrefixHere" TagName="YourTagHere"
Src="RelativePathToTheSourceFile" %>
```

Remember this line of code because we implement it later in the chapter when we create our own custom Web user control.

Templates

Templates allow you to separate the data layer and the presentation layer of the control. We will provide an example of a template when we create our own custom User Web Control later in this chapter. The template portion of the Web user control allows you to create a Web interface that is isolated from any of the manipulative code that takes place behind the scenes. Although client-side script can exist in the template, the primary purpose of a template is to provide a standard look and feel interface for the user. The template portion of the control is housed in the .ascx* file, and the associated code that manipulates the content resides in the .ascx.vb portion of the .ascx control.

Control Class

As briefly discussed in Chapter 5, ASP.NET Web server controls originate from the System.Web.UI.Control Class. Two classes are considered to be base classes of ASP.NET server controls: System.Web.UI.Control and System.Web.UI.WebControls.WebControl. Let's take a look at both of these.

System.Web.UI.Control

The *properties*, *methods*, and *events* that are common to all ASP.NET server controls are defined in the System.Web.UI.Control base class. Some of the most commonly used properties of System.Web.UI.Control are:

ID.   The unique identifier of the control that is assigned by the developer and offers the developer a simple way to differentiate between two like controls and respond to events initiated by each distinctive control on the client-side.

UniqueID.   A unique identifier that is assigned to the control by ASP.NET when a page first loads. It is different from the ID, because it is automatically generated and is read-only.

Page.   The Web form containing the Web server control. It is responsible for the presentation layer of the application.

Controls.   A collection of control classes child controls. Controls that are placed on a Form class fit this description.

ViewState.   Used for persisting data on the Web form. As Web server control events force communication between the client and the server, the ViewState is responsible for persisting state between page views.

Visible.   Determines the visibility of a control during runtime. This property read/write, so it can also be modified at runtime.

The following is a list of the most common methods for this class:

LoadViewState.   Defines how persisted data is returned between page views.

SaveViewState.   Defines how data is persisted during the transition between page views.

CreateChildControls.   Used by composite controls for child control creation.

Render.   Initiates the rendering of a control in a Web browser.

Dispose.   Provides for the unloading and cleanup of a control.

The most commonly occurring events in a System.Web.UI.Control base class are:

Init.   Fires during the initialization stage of the control.

Load.   Fires during the loading of the control.

Data Binding.   Fires during data binding.

PreRender.   Fires prior to the output being rendered.

Unload.   Fires just prior to unloading the control.

System.Web.UI.WebControls. WebControl

The System.Web.UI.WebControls.WebControl is responsible for offering additional properties and methods for managing the functionality of the user interface. The most commonly used properties in a System.Web.UI.WebControls. WebControl are:

Forecolor.   Controls the Forecolor of the Web control. You can choose from the Web Palette, Named Colors, System Colors, and Custom Colors.

Backcolor.   Controls the Backcolor of the Web control. You can choose from the Web Palette, Named Colors, System Colors, and Custom Colors.

BorderStyle.   Controls the BorderStyle of the Web control. You can choose from notset, none, dotted, dashed, solid, double, groove, ridge, inset, and outset.

Height.   Controls the Height of the Web control. You can choose pixel-Height or posHeight.

Width.   Controls the Width of the Web control. You can choose pixel-Height or posHeight.

Declaring a Control

Controls offer the user an attractive presentation layer to insert and examine data and offer developers a component oriented way to layout a page, as well as capture and manipulate the data.

As covered in the previous chapter, Microsoft offers a foundation of Web server controls that provide support for inserting, examining, and capturing user data and allow a developer to create custom Web server controls to meet the needs of unique software solutions.

Let's create a new form that displays a server control:

1. Make sure you either create or already have at hand an IIS recognized virtual directory established to store your test code.

2. Open up a text-based editor of your choice. Microsoft Notepad will be fine for these very small examples that are simply used to familiarize you with declaring .NET Web server controls.

3. Now try declaring a simple Web server control in the editor by copying in the following line of code. We are using the TextBox control, listed in Table 6.1, and we are manipulating the text property and telling IIS to run the code server side.

```
<HTML>
    <HEAD>
    </HEAD>
    <body MS_POSITIONING="GridLayout">
        <form id="Form1" method="post" runat="server">
            <asp:TextBox id="TextBox1" style="Z-INDEX: 101; LEFT:
203px; POSITION: absolute; TOP: 84px" runat="server">Nothin' but
.NET!!!</asp:TextBox>
        </form>
    </body>
</HTML>
ox runat="Server" Text="Nothin' but .NET!!!"></asp:textbox>
```

> **NOTE** In the code example above, we created a textbox, supplying it with an ID, the unique identifier of the control defined earlier in this chapter. Normally, the id attribute would allow a developer to access the properties and methods of this specific textbox in client-side script. But, the "runat=server" attribute forces the server to handle events that are invoked by the ASP.NET Web forms page, using the UniqueID of the Web server control's naming container when the page request is handled on the server.

4. Now Save this line of code to a file in the virtual directory identified in step 1. Remember to save it with an .aspx file extension or it will not work.

Figure 6.1   Textbox control example.

5. From the Microsoft IE browser, navigate to the virtual directory that contains the .aspx file that you just created and press the Enter key. The contents should look like Figure 6.1.

   There you have it, a .NET Web server control in action.

6. Now let's try an example using the DropDownList control. Copy the following lines of code into your text-based editor and save it. Render the page in your browser, and it should resemble Figure 6.2.

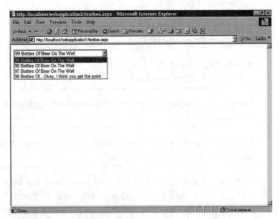

Figure 6.2   DropDownList control example.

```
<HTML>
     <body MS_POSITIONING="GridLayout">
          <form id="Form1" method="post" runat="server">
               <asp:DropDownList id="DropDownList1" runat="server">
                    <asp:ListItem Value="0" Selected="True">99 Bottles
Of Beer On The Wall</asp:ListItem>
                    <asp:ListItem Value="1" Selected="False">99 Bottles
Of Beer On The Wall</asp:ListItem>
                    <asp:ListItem Value="2" Selected="False">99 Bottles
Of Beer On The Wall</asp:ListItem>
                    <asp:ListItem Value="3" Selected="False">99 Bottles
Of Beer On The Wall</asp:ListItem>
               </asp:DropDownList>
          </form>
     </body>
</HTML>
```

Table 6.1   Commonly Used Default Web Forms Server Controls

WEB SERVER	DESCRIPTION
Label	Provides a standard and programmatically editable manner of presenting text on a Web form.
Button	Allows a user to submit a command from a Web form or perform some other internal action. The three visually distinctive valid button controls that essentially offer the same type of functionality are: • Standard Command Button (Button control) • Hyperlink Button (LinkButton control) • Graphical Button (ImageButton control)
Image	Programmatically displays graphical images on a Web form.
TextBox	Captures or displays single and multiline user text-based input on a Web Form
DropDownList	Displays a group of data in a drop-down list box. A default item will be listed initially, and all items within the list box will be displayed once a user clicks the control.
Table/TableCell/ TableRow	Provides the ability to create a common table on a Web form.

WEB SERVER	DESCRIPTION
Calendar	Provides the ability to create a common calendar, display dates by month, and captures user date selections.
CheckBox/CheckBoxList	A Boolean-based control that allows users to select one or more items from a generally inclusive list.
RadioButton/ RadioButtonList	Allows users to quickly select a single item from mutually exclusive lists of items.
ListBox	Allows a user to choose one or more items displayed in the list box. The list box, by default, will show all pieces of data available.
Panel	A container used to encapsulate the control of all other user controls placed within its boundaries, allowing for a single point of control through the panel. This is usually used to group mutually inclusive controls together.
HyperLink	Allows a developer to create navigational to links on a Web page.
Repeater	Displays a list in a user-defined manner.
Ad Rotator	Displays semi-random graphic images. Allows the developer to dictate the odds of which graphics display more often.

Persisting Your Control

The control object contains a ViewState property that allows you to easily persist and manage state. It supports name/value pairs in a string data type and is passed back and forth between the client and server in the form of a hidden variable. When used on property data, the property value will continue to be persisted. Because of its nonencrypted, simple-text form, I don't advise you to store sensitive information, such as passwords or the equivalent in terms of confidentiality, in a ViewState property. However, for all non-sensitive data, the ViewState property is an appropriate means for persisting data.

```
Public Property Car() As String
    Get
        Return CStr(Viewstate("Car"))
```

```
        End Get
        Set(ByVal Value As String)
            ViewState("Car") = Value
        End Set
    End Property
```

ViewState allows information to persist by taking advantage of the *state bag*, whereby the page and all its values are cached during processing and returned on the next return trip. The state bag is a location where all property name/value pairs are stored in memory. The ViewState property applies primarily to controls. For typical .aspx Web processing, the Session and Application objects continue to live on and will most likely meet your persistence needs.

Because of the overhead associated with persisting state, minimize the amount of information that is being persisted to crucial elements.

NOTE .NET state bags are very similar to the property bags that were used heavily in client-side ActiveX controls. If you are familiar with the property bag, the state bag probably will not present much of a challenge to you. They are much easier to deal with because most of the overhead has been taken care of for you by .NET. The state bag is used to maintain a data structure and house values on the server in a name/value pair and can be resurrected to the client calls that are made to it during processing on the server. We will discuss ViewState further in Chapter 9.

Building a Simple Control

Now let's build a simple Web form user control that we can call from an .aspx file. The following steps will walk you through creating a Web user control and displaying it in a Web form. Before we begin, make sure you create, or already have at hand, a virtual directory in which to store your test code.

1. Open up the VisualStudio.NET IDE, and click on File, New, Project. You should now see the New Project dialog box as shown in Figure 6.3.

2. Choose the ASP.NET Web Application as the template to use, and name it MyWebControlProject. Follow along by looking at Figure 6.4.

3. Now add a Web user control to the project by clicking on File, Add New Item as shown in Figure 6.5. The Add New Item dialog box will appear. Choose the Web user control as the template and name the file MyWebUserControl.ascx. An example of this is shown in Figure 6.6.

   You are now returned to the .NET IDE, and the MyWebUserControl.ascx file should be highlighted in the Solution Explorer pane of the IDE.

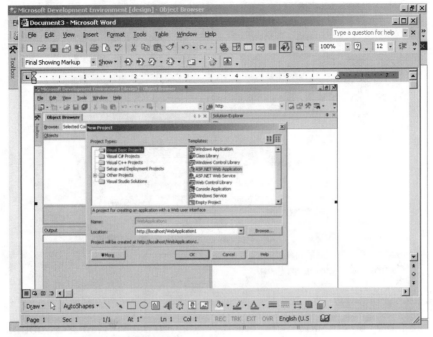

Figure 6.3   The New Project dialog box.

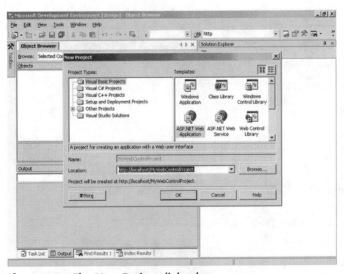

Figure 6.4   The New Project dialog box.

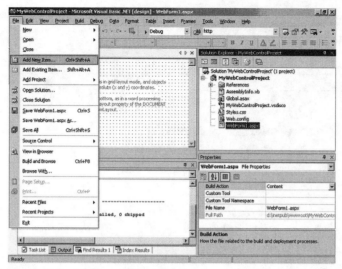

Figure 6.5 Adding an Item.

4. Now copy the following lines of code into the MyWebUserControl.ascx file HTML Editor pane. The destination file for this code is the template file that we talked about earlier in this chapter. After doing this, click on the Design Editor pane, and you will see the control that you just created in HTML (see Figure 6.7 for a visual display of what your screen should look like at this point).

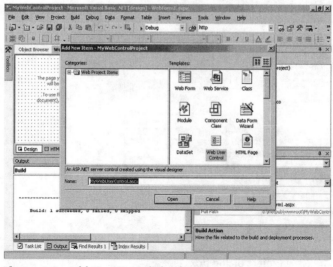

Figure 6.6 Add New Item dialog box.

```
<%@ Control Language="vb" AutoEventWireup="false"
Codebehind="MyWebUserControl.ascx.vb"
Inherits="MyWebControlProject.WebUserControl1" %>
<HTML>
<body>
  <div id="ServerCode">
        <table>
                <tr>
                        <td>
                                <b>User ID: </b>
                        </td>
                        <td>
<ASP:TEXTBOX id="UserID" runat="server"></ASP:TEXTBOX>
                        </td>
                </tr>
                <tr>
                </tr>
                <tr>
                        <td>
                                <b>User Password: </b>
                        </td>
                        <td>
<ASP:TEXTBOX id="Password" runat="server"
TextMode="Password"></ASP:TEXTBOX>
                        </td>
                </tr>
                <tr>
                </tr>
                <tr>
                        <td>
                        </td>
                        <td>
<ASP:BUTTON id="cmdSend" accessKey="S" runat="server"
Text="Submit"></ASP:BUTTON>
                        </td>
                </tr>
        </table>
  </div>
<asp:TextBox id="txtArea1" runat="server" TextMode="MultiLine"
Width="274px" Height="95px"></asp:TextBox>
</body>
</HTML>
```

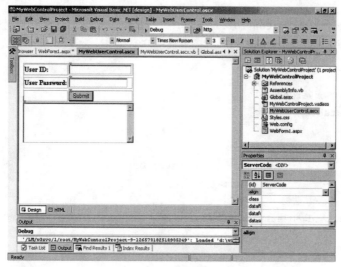

Figure 6.7   Web user control.

5. Double-click on the Submit button that you created. It will appear in the Design pane. You will then be taken to the MyWebUserControl.ascx. vb code window as shown in Figure 6.8. Copy the following lines of code into this window:

```
Public MustInherit Class WebUserControl1
    'Web Server Controls Declaration Area.
    Inherits System.Web.UI.UserControl
    Protected WithEvents UserID As System.Web.UI.WebControls.TextBox
    Protected WithEvents Password As
System.Web.UI.WebControls.TextBox
    Protected WithEvents txtArea1 As
System.Web.UI.WebControls.TextBox
    Protected WithEvents cmdSend As System.Web.UI.WebControls.Button

#Region " Web Form Designer Generated Code "
    Dim strStartRoot As String
    Dim strEndRoot As String
    'This call is required by the Web Form Designer.
    <System.Diagnostics.DebuggerStepThrough()> Private Sub
InitializeComponent()

    End Sub

    Private Sub Page_Init(ByVal sender As System.Object, ByVal e As
System.EventArgs) Handles MyBase.Init
        'CODEGEN: This method call is required by the Web form
designer
```

```
            'Do not modify it using the code editor.
            InitializeComponent()
            strStartRoot = CStr(Session("StartRootTag"))
            strEndRoot = CStr(Session("EndRootTag"))
        End Sub

#End Region

    'This is the UserID Textbox property.
    Public Property strUsrId() As String
        Get
            Return ViewState(UserID.Text).ToString
        End Get
        Set(ByVal Value As String)
            ViewState(UserID.Text) = Value
            txtArea1.Text = txtArea1.Text & "UserID='" & UserID.Text
& "' />" & vbCrLf
        End Set
    End Property

    'This is the Password property.
    Public Property strPsswrd() As String
        Get
            Return ViewState(Password.Text).ToString
        End Get
        Set(ByVal Value As String)
            ViewState(Password.Text) = Value
            txtArea1.Text = txtArea1.Text & "Pswrd='" & Password.Text
& "' />" & vbCrLf
            txtArea1.Text = txtArea1.Text & strEndRoot
        End Set
    End Property

    'Called on the Load of the page.
    Private Sub Page_Load(ByVal sender As System.Object, ByVal e As
System.EventArgs) Handles MyBase.Load
        txtArea1.Text = "XML will appear here." & vbCrLf
    End Sub

    'Called when the Send Command Button is clicked.
    Public Sub cmdSend_Click(ByVal sender As System.Object, ByVal e
As System.EventArgs) Handles cmdSend.Click
        txtArea1.Text = strStartRoot & vbCrLf & "  <User "
        strUsrId = UserID.Text
        txtArea1.Text = txtArea1.Text & "  <Pass "
        strPsswrd = Password.Text
    End Sub
End Class
```

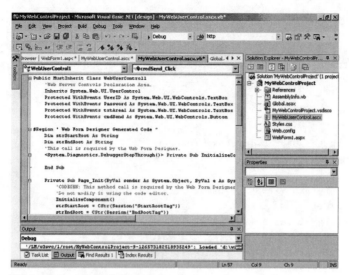

Figure 6.8   My Web User Control.

6. Now copy the following two lines of code into the Sub sub Application_Start subprocedure of the Global.asax file. Look at Figure 6.9 to see the actual location within the Global.asax file into which we will copy these lines. We are creating a small application that will display our UserID and Password information in an XML format so that these will be our global root tags. You will learn more about XML in Chapter 7 and more about the Global.asax file in Chapter 9.

```
    Sub Session_Start(ByVal Sender As Object, ByVal e As
EventArgs)
        Application("StartRootTag") = "<root>"
        Application("EndRootTag") = "</root>"
End Sub
```

7. Change the sessionState mode in the Web.config file to InProc, which will now allow us to save session state within our Web application and change the authentication mode to Windows. These entries should look like the following ones:

```
<authentication mode="Windows" />
<sessionstate mode="InProc"
stateConnectionString="tcpip=127.0.0.1:42424
sqlConnectionString="data source=127.0.0.1;user id=sa;password="
cookieless="false" timeout="20" />
```

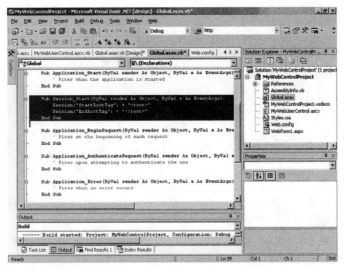

Figure 6.9   The Global.asax file.

8. Compile the code by clicking on Build on the menu bar, and then click Build once again on the dropdown menu. The Output pane should now appear as shown in Figure 6.10. This will allow you to see the outcome of your build.

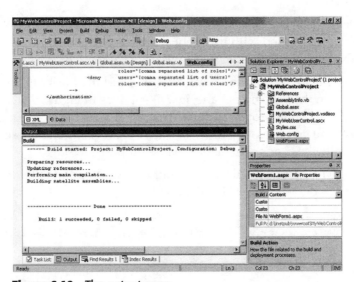

Figure 6.10   The output pane.

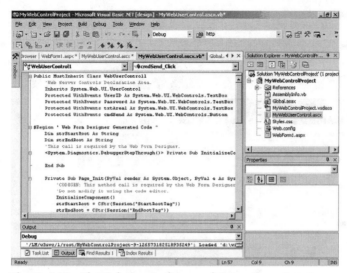

Figure 6.11   The Solution Explorer and Properties panes.

As you can see, our build succeeded, and a data link library was automatically created in the virtual directory that was automatically created when we initially began this project. Because our data link library is scoped to our virtual directory, we no longer need to worry about registering our DLL. I will talk about this more in the next few paragraphs.

9. For now, let's finish implementing our Web user control in our Web form, which is identified with the WebForm1.aspx extension in the Solution Explorer pane, located within the .NET IDE.

10. Click on this file in the Solution Explorer Pane, and the file's properties will show up in the Properties Pane, just like it does in Figure 6.11. Change the File Name property of the WebForm1.aspx file to MyLogin. aspx. Make sure you press the Enter key after making the change so that it commits the change to the File Name property.

11. Click on the MyLogin.aspx file in the Solution Explorer and enter the following lines of code in the HTML pane:

```
<%@ Page Language="vb" AutoEventWireup="false"
Codebehind="MyLogin.aspx.vb" Inherits="MyWebControlProject.WebForm1"
EnableSessionState="True"%>
<%@ Register Tagprefix="MyLogin" Tagname="UserInfo"
```

```
Src="MyWebUserControl.ascx" %>
<HTML>
  <HEAD>
          <meta name="GENERATOR" content="Microsoft Visual Studio.NET
7.0">
          <meta name="CODE_LANGUAGE" content="Visual Basic 7.0">
          <meta name="vs_defaultClientScript" content="JScript">
          <meta name="vs_targetSchema" content="Internet Explorer
5.0">
  </HEAD>
  <BODY MS_POSITIONING="GridLayout">
          <FORM id="WebForm1" method="post" runat="server">
                  <MyLogin:UserInfo runat="server" ID="objLogon"
autopostback="true" />
          </FORM>
  </BODY>
</HTML>
```

Save all the files, using the Save All icon on the .NET IDE toolbar. We have now created a very simple interactive Web control. To display the new Web form user control, click the Start icon on the .NET IDE toolbar. It should look like the example show in Figures 6.12 and 6.13. Note that in the last code example, ViewState is used to persist data on the server.

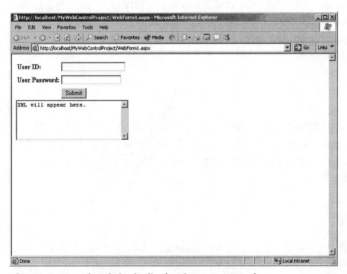

Figure 6.12   The default display for our control.

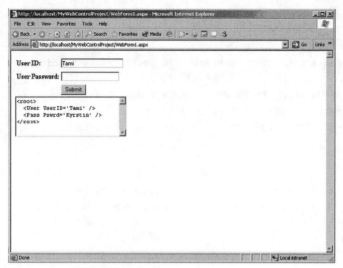

Figure 6.13   Test driving our control.

Managing State

Managing state can be an extremely tricky thing. There are so many things that can affect the behavior of processes that simultaneously execute that it can sometimes become an overburdening challenge. Luckily for us, .NET has made this challenge less stressful for developers by integrating *Application* and *Session* State management services into APIs that are compatible with the complete .NET Framework.

Session State

Session State is capable of raising reliable management events, storing data on the server for use across multiple browser request, and releasing data that has not been revisited within a specified timeout period. We will discuss Session State further in Chapter 9.

Application State

The Application object exposes the HTTPApplicationState class. This class in turn exposes a dictionary of objects that support state management with .NET Framework objects, thereby sustaining an insightful approach and orchestrating access to global variables stored in application state objects, including those that even support earlier adaptations of ASP.

We will discuss Application State further in Chapter 9.

Composite Controls

Composite controls are simply two or more unlike controls that are coupled together to make a single control. Each unique control still exists and operates independently, but composite appear to be spawned as a single control.

Composite controls are compiled and stored in the assembly as a data link library and called from the client using the control Namespace and Assembly. It also uses the Create Child Controls Method to instance controls.

A Composite Control can be added to the toolbox in the .NET IDE.

WebServer Controls versus Web User Controls

The biggest difference between Web server controls and Web user controls is that Web server controls are compiled controls and user controls are programmatically declared controls. Often, Web user controls incorporate preexisting Web server controls and extend their capabilities by providing additional properties and methods that will help a user accomplish a specific task.

A good example of this is the Web User control we created in Figure 6.7, earlier in this chapter. It took advantage of some existing Web Server Controls that Microsoft provides in .NET, specifically the Textbox and Button controls that are declared programmatically and offer common language support. The example also extended them by allowing you to declare additional methods and properties. In addition to the subsequent differences, Table 6.2 shows additional dissimilarities between Web server controls and Web user Controls.

Table 6.2 Differences between Web Server Controls and Web User Controls

WEB SERVER CONTROLS	WEB USER CONTROLS
Web server controls are declared programmatically in a Web form.	Are created by a developer and then programmatically declared.
Web server controls are compiled precompiled DLL's and persist in the assembly.	Can be created by a developer in a text-based editor and saved as an .ascx file.
Can be stored in the toolbox.	Cannot be stored in the toolbox.

Wrapping Up

In closing, we discussed the differences between HTML, ActiveX, and Web Server Controls. We briefly discussed the differences between Web Server Controls, Composite Controls, and User Controls. We talked about persisting control information, and worked through an example on how to build a Composite control.

Web Server Controls offer a presentation layer that intuitively allows you to enter data. But, what if a presentation layer wasn't necessary? What if all you needed to do was to call a method to obtain information? In the next chapter, we will explore XML and SOAP-based Web Services, a W3C Standard protocol that will allow you all of the functionality possessed by the Web Server Control we discussed in Chapter 6 but without the unnecessary overhead of the presentation layer for HTTP Calls that don't require a user interface.

Web Services: Family Fun with XML, SOAP, and WSDL

Any sufficiently advanced technology is indistinguishable from magic.
Arthur C. Clarke

In some respects, the way that Web Services allow for the sharing of resources across the Web seems indistinguishable from magic. This technology is just in its infancy, but the promise of true interoperability moves ever closer to full realization through the programmaticization of the Web. The majority of industry analysts and players in the industry are emphasizing the importance of Web Services. Let's begin with tying this subject to what you already know as a Visual Basic programmer.

Web services can be thought of as COM components for the Internet. In .NET they allow you to encapsulate code, publish interfaces, discover services, and communicate between the publisher and consumer of services using vendor-independent, standards-based technologies.

You are familiar with the Microsoft COM model, which allows developers to encapsulate code into objects and publish interface(s) to those objects. The COM model is the standard on Windows platforms and has been extended to support distributed applications in its later incarnations as DCOM, MTS, and COM+.

Perhaps you have code that implements business logic that can be reused in multiple applications. As an example, consider the complex business logic of credit decisions for consumer loan applications. It's easy to create a COM+ object that encapsulates this code. Once the object is installed on server in your network, any of your applications can call upon that code to obtain at least a preliminary decision for a loan application. Using the term *service* in the generic sense, you could say that the object provides a loan approval service to the multiple applications that use it.

The familiar COM model is easy to implement within the scope of well-connected Windows servers. Throw in the complications of non-Windows operating systems, non-Intel platforms, and interconnected networks, and you'll find yourself fighting an uphill battle.

Web services allow you to solve the same problems but are based on vendor-independent Internet technologies and protocols such as HTTP, XML, and TCP/IP. The Web services stack implements standard protocols such as SOAP and UDDI. Web services allow business logic to be shared across boundaries, such as platform, programming language, and organization.

The Windows 2000 platform provided all of the building blocks required for implementing Web services, even before ASP.NET. You could write a Web service using a combination of ASP/IIS, MSXML, and COM. To do so, you would have had to become intimately familiar with XML, SOAP, and UDDI.

With ASP.NET, support for Web service authoring is built into the development platform. As you'll see, writing a Web service is now as easy as writing an MTS or COM+ component. In this chapter, we'll examine the DCOM-like functionality of Web services and the supporting technologies.

Understanding the Underlying Technologies

If you want to get right down to business and implement a Web service, you could skip to the *Implementing Web Services* section later in this chapter. However, it is important to understand the underlying technologies on which Web services are built, namely, HTTP, XML, SOAP, WSDL, and UDDI. We covered HTTP in Chapter 4. Let's take a look at the others.

XML

XML is the medium of communication for all data and requests that go in or out of your Web service. You don't need to know XML to implement and use Web services. The .NET platform will do the work for you. If you are interested in seeing what goes on behind the scenes, read on. Most of the other technologies we'll discuss in this chapter are based on XML.

By now, you should have at least a passing familiarity with HTML, a text-based format for describing page formatting information to client browsers. It is a specific language that solves a specific problem. You might use HTML to present a table of customers' information to a user of a Web application. The technology wouldn't work as well to communicate a table of customers' information from one DBMS to another.

XML, or eXtensible Markup Language, is similar in structure to HTML. Although HTML is a tool that was built to solve a specific problem, XML is a general-purpose tool that can be applied to many problems. XML is a way to encode just the data, without any of the visual rendering info provided by HTML. XML is just data. HTML defines tags that have specific meanings, such as table, hr, and input. In XML, you define your own tags with the meanings your applications require.

XML can be considered a superset of HTML. For the most part, HTML follows the rules of XML—most HTML would be accepted by an XML parser. XML should appear quite familiar to anyone who has worked with HTML.

Benefits of XML

At its core, XML is a way of communicating structured data between applications and computer systems, even where multiple architectures, languages, and standards are involved.

One mechanism for exchange of structured data with which you are already familiar is the ADO Recordset object. For example, you might build a recordset on the database server, return it to an MTS or COM+ component running on the middle-tier server, and possibly even download it to the client browser using RDS. Some of the drawbacks of recordsets are:

- They may be unusable in non-Microsoft environments (such as a competitor's Web browser, even if it is running on a Windows system).

- They include a great deal of information that you might not actually require.

- The data is stored in a binary format. While binary data is more compact, it is not directly human-readable. XML is a text-based format.

- A recordset has a fixed structure, consisting of zero or more rows of zero or more fields that have specific properties. ADO is based on the relational model, which is not as good at handling complex data as XML.

Another mechanism with which you are familiar is HTML. HTML is primarily created by ASP code or CGI or directly by a developer or Web site designer. HTML is primarily consumed by Web browsers running on client computers. Some of the drawbacks of HTML for data interchange include:

- HTML is designed for communication of data and formatting information about the data.

- It is not a general-purpose tool and is not extensible.

- It is not designed to allow further processing of the data by the recipient.

XML is designed to encode both data and information about the data (metadata). Both the data and the metadata can be anything your application requires. In the case of HTML, the only information the Web browser needs to know is related to formatting the data on the user's screen. In XML, you could include information about a product's dimensions, weight, and electrical requirements; about a state's population or average, low, and high temperatures; about a customer's demographic and purchasing habits; or about anything else you can imagine. You could store this information in HTML, but it would be very hard to programmatically match up which piece of data is which.

When your code generates HTML, you expect it to be consumed by a Web browser. XML might be consumed by other code within your application, by code in a separate application, by a database management system, or even displayed to user, formatted using XSL.

XML is an open standard and is supported by many vendors on many platforms. It opens up the barriers between different applications, databases, operating systems, and computer architectures. It allows data to be processed by the recipient application rather than simply being displayed to the user. XML data is self-describing—it includes both the data and information about the data. XML is the Esperanto of computer systems on the Internet. As long as both the sender and the recipient follow the XML standards, and agree on how the data is to be used, any two systems can communicate.

XML Structure

As mentioned earlier, if you have used HTML, XML should be very familiar to you. Let's first examine some HTML that presents a customer table to the user:

```
<TABLE BORDER=1>
  <TR>
    <TH>Name</TH>
    <TH>Customer ID</TH>
    <TH>Current Due</TH>
    <TH>Balance</TH>
  </TR>
  <TR>
    <TD>Doe, John</TD>
    <TD>0089153</TD>
    <TD ALIGN='Right'>$118.00</TD>
    <TD ALIGN='Right'>$2,095.00</TD>
  </TR>
  <TR>
    <TD>Doe, John</TD>
    <TD>0089153</TD>
```

```
      <TD ALIGN='Right'>$57.20</TD>
      <TD ALIGN='Right'>$887.00</TD>
   </TR>
   <TR>
      <TD>Smith, Lydia</TD>
      <TD>9583651</TD>
      <TD ALIGN='Right'>$295.00</TD>
      <TD ALIGN='Right'>$4,899.00</TD>
   </TR>
   <TR>
      <TD>Xyzzy, Fred</TD>
      <TD>1234556</TD>
      <TD ALIGN='Right'> </TD>
      <TD ALIGN='Right'> </TD>
   </TR>
 </TABLE>
```

If you viewed this HTML in a Web browser, you might see output that looks something like Figure 7.1.

What if you wanted to do something more with this data than just put it on the user's screen? If you had to write code to read the preceding HTML and build data structures in memory about customers, you might have a hard time. For example, the fact that the third table column represents the amount currently due is not really made clear unless you refer to the header row and match up column positions. Fred Xyzzy has no loan outstanding at this time. If we tried to retrieve his loan information from the HTML, we'd get — the HTML nonbreaking space. If we found this string, we could assume there was no loan, but how often is it safe to make assumptions about our customers' business information? John Doe has two loans, but we'd have to match on customer number to figure this out from the HTML. HTML just isn't the right tool for the job of data interchange between systems.

Now let's examine one possible XML string that includes the same data. Depending on your requirements, you might define a completely different set of XML to represent this data:

```
<CustomerList>
  <Customer ID='0089153' FirstName='John'  LastName='Doe'>
    <Loan CurrentDue='118.00' Balance='2095.00'/>
    <Loan CurrentDue='57.20'  Balance='887.00'/>
  </Customer>
  <Customer ID='9583651' FirstName='Lydia' LastName='Smith'>
    <Loan CurrentDue='295.00' Balance='4899.00'/>
  </Customer>
  <Customer ID='1234556' FirstName='Fred'  LastName='Xyzzy'/>
</CustomerList>
```

Name	Customer ID	Current Due	Balance
Doe, John	0089153	$118.00	$2,095.00
Doe, John	0089153	$57.20	$887.00
Smith, Lydia	9583651	$295.00	$4,899.00
Xyzzy, Phred	1234556		

Figure 7.1   Table output from HTML.

The XML includes all of the same data as the HTML. The difference is in the structure and the additional information sent. In the XML, the structure makes it clear which data is associated with which customer. Without even knowing how I've defined the XML schema, you can see that there is a one-to-many relationship between customer and loan. You can see that names go with customers and balances go with loans.

XML consists of tags, elements, and attributes. We'll examine each in the following sections.

Tags

Each related set of data in XML is surrounded by a *begin tag* and an *end tag*. Begin tags start with the left angle bracket. In the previous example <CustomerList> is the first begin tag. End tags start with a left angle bracket and a forward slash. In the example, </CustomerList> is the last end tag and matches the <CustomerList> begin tag. Tags introduce the data they surround and define what that data means. For example, when you see the <Customer> begin tag, you know that the information that follows is related to a customer. When you see the </Customer> end tag, you know that all available information has been provided on that particular customer, and the data that follows will be about another customer or some other type of information altogether.

Unlike HTML, tag names in XML are case sensitive. A <CUSTOMER> is not the same thing as a <Customer>.

Elements

An element consists of an opening tag, any information it contains, and the closing tag. Elements may have child elements. In the previous example, the root element is CustomerList. It contains three Customer child elements. Each of these Customer elements contains zero or more Loan child elements. The Loan elements do not have child elements.

At first glance, it may appear that some of the elements in the example are missing their end tags. None of the Loan elements has a closing tag, nor does the final Customer element. In fact, we are using a shortcut. Note that the begin tags for some elements contain a slash prior to their closing right angle bracket. This trailing slash indicates that the begin tag has completely defined the element and no closing tag is necessary. This shortcut is commonly used for elements that do not contain child elements. In general, the syntax:

```
<MyTag ...></MyTag>
```

is interchangeable with:

```
<MyTag ... />
```

A properly formatted XML document can contain only a single root element. After that, you can use any level of nesting you require. Additionally, you can place different types of elements at the same level. For example, we could include a certificate of deposit as a child element of a Customer. The same customer element may have any combination of zero or more loan elements and zero or more certificate of deposit elements.

An element may contain data between its begin and end tag. For example, we could define a Notes element that might appear as a child element of Customer or Loan:

```
<Customer ID='9583651' FirstName='Lydia' LastName='Smith'>
  <Loan CurrentDue='295.00' Balance='9.00' />
  <Notes>One of our best customers, Ms. Smith has been doing business
with us for many years, and always greets our tellers with a
smile.</Notes>
</Customer>
```

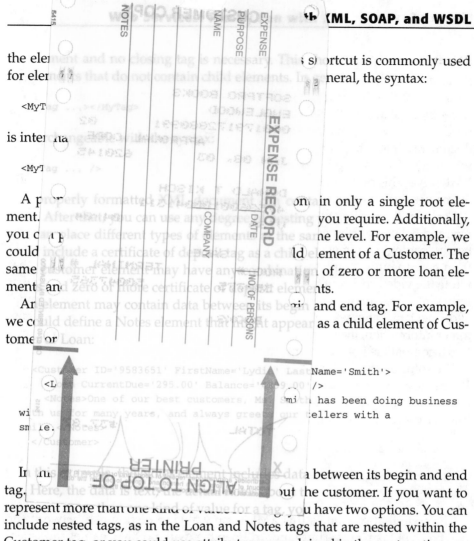

In this example, the Notes element includes data between its begin and end tag. Here, the data is text about the customer. If you want to represent more than one kind of value for a tag, you have two options. You can include nested tags, as in the Loan and Notes tags that are nested within the Customer tag, or you could use attributes, as explained in the next section.

Attributes

Attributes are name/value pairs that appear with the begin tag of an element. In the previous example, the Customer element contains attributes of ID, First-Name and LastName. The Loan element contains attributes of CurrentDue and Balance. The CustomerList and Notes elements contain no attributes. It's up to you to define how attributes will be used in your XML. You may decide to require certain attributes on certain tags, such as the ID attribute of the Customer tag. Other attributes may be optional, such as a MiddleName attribute on a Customer tag.

Unlike HTML, XML requires that the values of attributes be enclosed in quotes. Both HTML and XML allow you to use either single or double quotes when specifying attributes. In HTML, the quotes aren't necessary unless the value contains a space or other special characters.

Namespaces

Because XML does not define any tags, every development team must agree on the schema—the structure, elements, tags, and attributes of the XML messages that the application will use to communicate. What happens when we need to include information from two different schemas within a single XML document? If any tag name was used in both schemas, it's impossible to tell which set of rules applies. This situation is referred to as a *namespace clash*. XML solves this problem by allowing you to define a namespace and to prefix tag names with the name of the namespace in which they reside.

Consider the earlier example, which included a Loan element with Current-Due and Balance attributes. Let's say that the organization that uses this schema begins loaning consumer education videos to its customers, with topics ranging from how to buy a home to avoiding bankruptcy. The development team that wrote the video checkout software might decide to define a Loan element that represents the loan of a video tape and include attributes such as TapeNumber and DueDate. Later, we wish to build an XML document that includes all customer information, including monetary loans and loans of videotapes. We have two incompatible Loan elements that need to be included in the same message.

The solution is to define a separate namespace for the video checkout data. We create a prefix that identifies the video checkout namespace such as VC in our document. We then prefix the video checkout tag names with VC, followed by a colon. We could then write XML like the following:

```
<Customer ID='9583651' FirstName='Lydia' LastName='Smith'>
  <Loan CurrentDue='295.00' Balance='4899.00'/>
  <VC:Loan TapeNumber='11832' DueDate='1/1/2002'/>
</Customer>
```

The code that consumes this XML is now able to distinguish between the two types of Loan tags. The standard Loan tag, with no XML namespace specified, refers to a bank loan. The VC:Loan tag refers to the loan of a videotape.

Using XML within Web Services

Before using .NET, I wrote a lot of client-side JavaScript that used RDS to obtain ADO recordsets from MTS and COM+ components. I could do this because my customers' environments were Microsoft from end to end—database server to Web browser and everything in between.

When my JavaScript code needed to call a method of COM+ object, I didn't need to worry about any of the details of remote procedure calls, marshalling, and interfaces. RDS and ADO hid these details from me.

Correspondingly, when code in any section of your application needs to use a Web service, the .NET platform will hide the details of how the method calls are made and how the data is transmitted and received. All of the technologies used are built on XML.

SOAP

SOAP is a standard for sending data back and forth between a client and a server. It is based on XML and is a simple, lightweight protocol. SOAP is a developing standard and is not owned by one particular vendor.

SOAP implements the remote procedure call functionality for Web services. When you call a subroutine that is defined within your Visual Basic project, the calling sequence is simple and machine dependent. The compiler probably generated machine code to save machine registers, push parameters on the stack, and jump to the address of the subroutine. When you call a method of a COM+ component, the calling sequence is much more complex because the component code may live in a separate address space (or even a different computer) from your code. When you make a call to a Web service, another level of complexity is added. The code that implements the Web service not only might be on a distant node of the Internet but it also might be running on an incompatible processor and operating system. To make this work, the client and server must both implement a common protocol. SOAP is the standard protocol designed to solve this problem. Using XML, SOAP handles the encoding and decoding of the structured data that is sent and received between the client and server of a Web service.

PROTOCOLS CURRENTLY SUPPORTED

SOAP is the protocol of choice for access to Web services. SOAP messages are designed for RPC-like functionality and are the most feature-rich method of access. SOAP is transport protocol independent. It can travel on HTTP, SMTP, or raw sockets (known as Direct Internet Messaging or DIME).

Web services may also be accessed through the HTTP protocol with GET and POST messages. GET and POST are discussed in Chapter 4. As a quick review, both types of requests include a collection of name/value pairs. In a POST message, the name/value pairs are sent as form variables, which are not displayed directly to or are editable by the user. In a GET message, the name/value pairs are included as query string variables on the URL itself, are viewable by the user, and potentially could be tampered with by the user.

When GET and POST messages are used to access Web services, the collection of name/value pairs are in fact the parameters to the method of the Web service that is being called. Because the GET or POST message is sent by your application code, rather than directly from a user's Web browser, the exposure of the query string variables in a GET message is not as important.

If you use .NET to create a Web service, your Web service will automatically support SOAP, HTTP GET, and HTTP POST. In fact, the .NET platform will automatically generate a Web UI to allow you to test your Web service without writing any code. More details are in the section *Consuming Web Services*.

Structure of a SOAP Document

Earlier, we discussed XML namespaces. We looked at a short example in which we needed to merge two different XML schemas into a single XML message. In the example, there was a name conflict because both schemas defined a Loan tag. An XML namespace can also be used to refer to a standard schema. w3c.org defines standard schemas for SOAP messages, and SOAP documents refer to these schemas using XML namespaces. So, a SOAP document is really an XML document that uses a SOAP namespace.

The elements of a SOAP message are the Envelope, Header, and Body. Let's take a look at each of these parts.

Envelope

The Envelope is the root element of every SOAP message and is required. Much like an envelope you receive in the mail, the main purpose of this element is to contain the message.

We'll use the following SOAP message as an example. You can see that we are using the soap-envelope XML schema and referring to it as the env namespace.

```
<env:Envelope xmlns:env="http://www.w3.org/2001/09/soap-envelope">
 <env:Header>
  <n:boguscontrol xmlns:n="http://bogus.org/boguscontrol">
   <n:registerno>897582352</n:registerno >
  </n:boguscontrol>
 </env:Header>
 <env:Body>
  <m:mymethod xmlns:m="http://bogus.org/mymethod">
   <m:param1>33</m:param1>
   <m:param2>99</m:param2>
  </m:mymethod>
 </env:Body>
</env:Envelope>
```

The first and last lines of this example are the Envelope. Everything between the <env:Envelope> start tag and the </env:Envelope> end tag is the contents of the Envelope.

Header

The Header element contains information related to the message. The header is SOAP's extensibility mechanism. The actual information sent within the header is not defined by the SOAP standard. It is up to the person who designs the Web service to decide what, if any, information may be specified in the header. The Header element in a SOAP document is optional. If it is used, it must be the first child element of the Envelope. The Header element does not directly contain the header information. Instead, it is a container for header blocks. All child elements of the Header element are header blocks. Header blocks provide a mechanism to specify information that is relevant to the entire message.

In this example, a single header block is included. The header block is the registerno tag. Perhaps this Web service uses a shareware model and requires that a registration number be sent to call its methods.

Body

Every SOAP message includes a Body element. The Body element is the second child element of the Envelope and appears after the Header. If no Header element appears in a particular message, the Body element will be the first child of the Envelope. Just as the Header element serves as a container for header blocks, the Body element serves as a container for body blocks.

Body blocks contain the actual content of the message. In the case of a method call to a Web service, the body block would contain the name of the method to be called, along with the values of its input parameters. The structure and type of data sent in a body block are not defined by the SOAP standard. However, the ways that data is encoded for inclusion in the body are specified. The only case in which the structure and type of data sent is defined by the standard is the SOAP Fault.

A SOAP Fault is a body block defined by the SOAP standard and is used to communicate error information. Much like the Visual Basic Error object, a Fault element includes the error number (faultcode), description (faultstring), and source (faultactor). A SOAP Fault may also include additional detail information about the error. Note that a SOAP message can contain at most one Fault element.

The body of our example is a method call to the mymethod method. Two parameters are being passed: param1 with a value of 33 and param2 with a value of 99.

SOAP Namespace

SOAP is built on XML, which doesn't define any tags—it is up to the developer whose applications need to communicate to define which tags, attributes, and elements will be used. SOAP is a standard built on XML. Ideally, the code that sends and receives SOAP messages should know the SOAP standard. How do we define a standard built on a completely open model like XML? We use XML namespaces and refer to schemas published on the Internet by the World Wide Web Consortium.

Using SOAP within Web Services

SOAP is used to implement remote procedure calls and exchange data between code that uses a Web service (the client) and the Web service itself (the server). SOAP and XML are the media for communication between Web services and clients of Web services. You may have used the SOAP Toolkit to implement Web services in Visual Basic 6. In .NET, SOAP is still used for method calls to Web services. However, all of the SOAPy details are hidden behind the scenes. You could implement and/or use a Web service in .NET without knowing anything about SOAP or even XML.

WSDL

WSDL, or Web Services Description Language, is an emerging vendor-independent standard for the definition of interfaces to Web services. A WSDL document defines all of the methods exposed by the Web services; the names, data types, and order of parameters; and the types of data returned. It has been described as the contract between a Web service and the clients of that Web service.

WSDL is built on XML and can be used to define the interface to a Web service that communicates via SOAP. WSDL can also be used to define the interface to a Web service that uses mechanisms other than SOAP, such as HTTP GET/POST or MIME.

WSDL Document Structure

A WSDL document is a complete description of the interface to a Web service and includes types, message, PortType, Binding, Port, and Service. Let's look at each of these in more detail.

Types

WSDL can use any XML schema to define the data types for parameters and return values. The WSDL standard recommends the XSD schema to define a set of standard data types. If your Web service requires inclusion of any user-defined types in the interface, the WSDL Types element defines these UDTs.

Many standard data types are included. Some examples of simple data types are boolean, which can accept a value of 1 or 0; string, which stores a sequence of alphanumeric characters; dateTime, which stores a date and time; integer, which stores an integer number; and float and double, which store floating point values. Complex types are also supported. An array stores multiple values of a simple data type, which are accessed by index. Struct stores multiple values of different simple data types, which are accessed by name.

For the actual XML definition of all data types supported, refer to http://schemas.xmlsoap.org/soap/encoding/.

Message

In WSDL, a method is referred to as a message. Each Message element defines a single method of a Web service. The Message element defines the method name. Each input parameter to the method is defined by a Part element, which includes attributes for the parameter name and data type. All of the Part elements for a given method are direct child elements of the corresponding Message element.

If a method has a return value, a second Message element is defined to represent the data type of the return value. This special Message element has the same name attribute as the method's primary Message element, with the word *Response* appended. This response Message element has a single Part element that describes the return value of the method.

PortType

A Message element might describe either the input parameters to a method or the return value from a method. To make the interface definition explicit, the PortType element is used. This element is a container for operation tags. Each operation tag specifies the name of the input Message and output (response) Message for a single method of the Web service.

Binding

Binding elements specify the protocol and encoding that is to be used for each method of a Web service. Each Binding element might be considered an entry point into the Web service. Every method exposed by the Web service has its own Binding element. If a method name is overloaded, each overload has a separate Binding element.

Port

Each Port element defines an entire interface to the Web service. It specifies the ASP file that is to be used to process requests and the name of the Binding element that defines the protocol and encoding for method calls. Web services in .NET expose a single interface and will therefore have a single Port element.

Service

The Service tag defines the name of the Web service and includes child Port tags for each interface exposed by the Web service. Just like Visual Basic objects, Web services can expose multiple interfaces. Because an interface is defined by a Port tag in WSDL, a Web service with multiple interfaces would have multiple Port tags. The Service tag is simply the owner, or parent tag, of the collection of Port tags.

How SOAP Relates to WSDL (Binding)

WSDL defines the interface to the methods of the Web service that may be invoked using SOAP. In WSDL documents created by the .NET Framework, there will be a single Binding element for each PortType element. All of the

Binding elements will specify that SOAP is to be used. In other words, SOAP is always the RPC mechanism for .NET Web services. If you implement your Web service and client using .NET, all of the work of creating and consuming SOAP messages will be handled for you behind the scenes.

Disco/UDDI

DISCO is a Microsoft technology for publishing the interfaces of Web services. DISCO uses files (with the unsurprising extension .disco) to describe the interface. The .disco files are published on the Web server that provides the Web Server.

UDDI, or Universal Description, Discovery, and Integration, is a standard for a distributed Internet database of business and its Web services. UDDI itself can be considered a Web service—applications access UDDI through SOAP messages. UDDI is a joint venture of IBM, Microsoft, and Ariba.

UDDI allows services to advertise, and applications to discover, Web services on the Internet. DISCO allows a Web server to be queried to discover what services it provides. UDDI is a more comprehensive service because it is a distributed database. DISCO, although simpler, requires you to know the URL of the Web server before you can discover its services and their interfaces.

In Visual Basic terms, using UDDI or DISCO to download the WSDL document for a Web service could be described as a form of early binding—the developer queries the WSDL document for interface information during coding and caches this information for use by their application at runtime.

NOTE UDDI is also the name of the organization that develops and publishes the UDDI standard. You can visit its Web site at http://UDDI.org. UDDI.org is a large cooperative group of businesses that have joined forces to create the UDDI standard.

Structure

UDDI stores information about Web services in an XML schema. This schema includes the following types of information:

Business Information.   The businessEntity element stores the name of the business that provides the Web services. It can also contain address, contact, and description information about the business. All of this information is referred to as white pages data. This element can also store category information about a business. Category information is referred to as yellow pages data. This element is the root element of the XML document and has Service Information child element(s).

Service Information.   businessService element(s) are used to categorize Web services into functional groupings. For example, you may wish to group all Web services related to your organization's bid approval process together. Each businessService element represents a group of Web services. This element is a direct child of the businessEntity element. The businessService element has Service Specification child element(s), described soon. The Service Information, along with the Binding Information, is referred to as green pages data.

Binding Information.   The bindingTemplate element contains technical information about the actual Web services, including the services' Web addresses and routing information. Information on the standards and specifications supported by the Web service is also included here. This element is a child of a businessService element. The binding information is referred to as green pages data. This element contains references to Service Specification element(s), described next.

Service Specifications.   The tModel element is a pointer to an interface specification for a Web service. This element does not describe the interface directly. Instead, it includes the URL of the interface specification. This allows multiple services and organizations to share a published interface and write Web services that adhere to that interface.

As you can see, the UDDI schema goes beyond simply describing an interface. UDDI provides information about what servers provide the Web service, allows services to be grouped together, and allows the publisher of the Web service to provide its contact information.

Registering Your Service

If you are writing a Web service that is only intended for use within your organization, you probably won't bother to register it with UDDI — unless you want to publish it internally to your organization, using an internal UDDI server. However, if you want to make your Web service easily accessible to other organizations and individuals on the Internet, you can use UDDI to publish it. Publishing your Web service using UDDI makes it easy for developers to find the service and to write code to interface with the service. Keep in mind that UDDI only publishes information about your service (and your business). You would still have to publish the Web service itself by placing it on a Web server that is accessible from the Internet at large.

The Internet servers that host the UDDI database are referred to as Operator Nodes. Authorized users of an Operator Node can make UDDI registrations. All Operator Nodes replicate registration information, so you can add, edit, or delete your registrations in one place. To be authorized, you must register with the organization that maintains the Operator Node. The requirements to establish an account with an organization that maintains an Operator Node are defined by that organization. At a minimum, you must provide your contact information and a verifiable email address, agree to adhere to the operator's policies, and obtain a user ID and password.

UDDI registrations can only be changed or deleted by the person who created the registration in the first place. If that person is no longer available, ownership, or custody, of the registration can be transferred to another person or organization.

Changes or deletions must be requested through the Operator Node on which the registration was originally made.

Implementing Web Services

Creating a Web service with Visual Basic .NET is as easy as creating a Web page—perhaps easier because you don't need to worry about page layout. In this section, we'll create a sample Web service and a Web page that uses the Web service and provides a user interface for testing the service. We'll be running both a Web service and the code that uses the service on the same machine. In practice, the Web service may not even belong to the same organization as the code that uses it. All Web service servers and clients agree to use the SOAP standard for communication between client and server. This makes Web services completely independent of computer architecture, operating system, server, and computer language. In the final example in this chapter, you'll actually write code that calls a Web service implemented on an Apache server.

Your First Web Service

Let's begin by creating a Web service project. The first thing we'll need to do is to create an empty Web service project:

1. Fire up Visual Studio .NET. Select File, New Project. In the New Project dialog box, do the following:

   ■ Leave Visual Basic Projects as the selected Project Type. Click ASP.NET Web Service under Templates.

   ■ Enter http://localhost/Ch7-Ex1 in the Location field. Click OK to create the project. A new, empty Web application will be created for you.

   In the Solution Explorer window, you'll see five files that were created automatically by the New Web Service wizard.

Figure 7.2   Solution Explorer window with five new files.

The files, shown in Figure 7.2, are as follows:

AssemblyInfo.vb   A standard ASP.NET assembly file. This file contains information about the project that is used by the compiler, such as the GUID of the class for use from COM, and the version of the project.

ProjectName.vsdisco   A DISCO file that allows clients to find your Web service and discover its functionality. As discussed in the earlier section on DISCO/UDDI, this file contains XML describing the interface(s) supported by your Web service.

Global.asax   The standard ASP.NET application file. Contains event handlers for application-level events, such as AuthenticateRequest or Error.

Service1.asmx   This file is the entry point for the Web service. Clients that need to use the Web service will connect to this file's URL. To view the code-behind file (Service1.asmx.vb) that contains the actual source code for the Web service, right-click Service1.asmx, and select View Code.

Web.config   The standard ASP.NET application configuration file. This file is used to control runtime options like tracing and security.

At this point, we've created a skeleton of a Web service. Our new Web service does not implement any methods yet. Let's create a simple Web service that provides methods to multiply or divide two floating-point numbers. All we need to do is actually add some methods to the skeleton of the Web service and write the code to implement the methods.

2. Return to the Web service project you created previously.

3. Right-click Service1.asmx and select View Code.

4. Delete the Hello World Sample comments and commented-out Web Method. These lines were added by the New Web Service wizard.

5. Create Multiply and Divide methods. Your Service1.asmx.vb should look like the following:

```
Imports System.Web.Services

Public Class Service1
    Inherits System.Web.Services.WebService

    <WebMethod()> Public Function Multiply(ByVal dblA As Double,
ByVal dblB As Double) As Double
        Multiply = dblA * dblB
    End Function

    <WebMethod()> Public Function Divide(ByVal dblA As Double, ByVal
dblB As Double) As Double
        Divide = dblA / dblB
    End Function

End Class
```

Everything in this code should look pretty familiar to you, with the possible exception of <WebMethod()>. This is referred to as an *attribute*. An attribute instructs the compiler to take special action. In this case, we are using the Web method attribute to specify that the Multiply and Divide methods are to be exposed as methods of a Web service. The attribute tells ASP.NET to generate the code to support a SOAP interface to these methods.

Congratulations, you've created your first Web service. We can test the service, even though we haven't written any client application to use the code. Visual Studio .NET automatically provides test user interfaces for Web services. Let's use the automatically generated test UI to run our new service:

1. Right-click Service1.asmx and select Set As Start Page.

2. Select Start from the Debug menu or just press F5.

3. Visual Studio will compile your Web service and launch a Web browser window to display a list of methods supported by your Web service. You should see a page similar to the one shown in Figure 7.3.

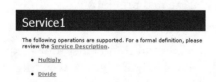

Figure 7.3 Public methods of example Web service.

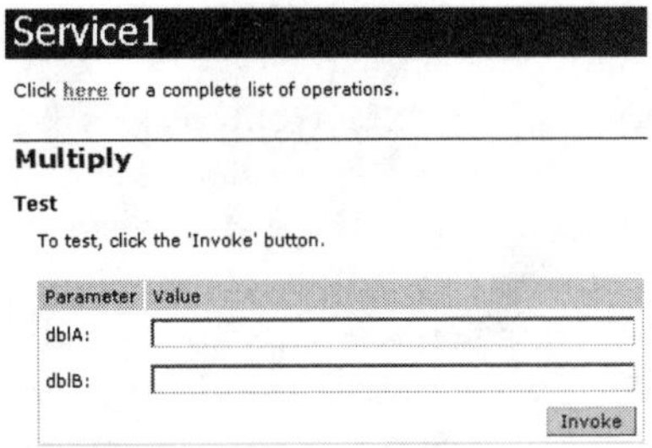

Service1

Click here for a complete list of operations.

Multiply

Test

To test, click the 'Invoke' button.

Parameter	Value
dblA:	
dblB:	
	Invoke

Figure 7.4   Test page for the multiply method.

The Service Description link will display the WSDL document for your service. As we mentioned, this is an XML-based standard for publication of interfaces to Web services. Visual Studio .NET automatically creates a WSDL document when you click on this link.

Let's continue to explore our new Web service using the UI that was generated for us by Visual Studio .NET.

4. Click on the Multiply link. Your browser will display a test Web page for the Multiply method, which should be similar to Figure 7.4.

   This page also displays the format of the SOAP and HTTP messages that you could use to invoke the Multiply method programmatically.

5. Enter numeric values in the dblA and dblB text boxes, and click the Invoke button. An HTTP GET message will be sent to your Web service to invoke the Multiply method. Your code within the method will multiply the values and return the result. Your browser window will display an XML message containing the return value.

```
<?xml version="1.0" encoding="utf-8" ?>
<double xmlns="http://tempuri.org/">200</double>
```

This XML message contains a single tag, the double tag. This tag is used to represent an extended precision floating point value. In this example, the value contained within the tag is 200. I entered the values 10 and 20 when I tested this method call; 200 is the value that resulted when the Web service multiplied 10 by 20.

Experiment with the test UI that the Visual Studio .NET platform provides. Be sure to close your browser when you are done, or Visual Studio will think you are still debugging your Web service. If Visual Studio gets confused and remains in debug mode even after all browser windows are closed, just select Stop Debugging from the Debug menu.

IDENTIFYING EXISTING CANDIDATES FOR CONVERSION

So far, we've seen Web services as a replacement for COM+ components, built on Internet standards, providing vendor, platform, and programming language independence. With all these advantages, you may be ready to start rewriting all of your COM+ components as Web services. As a colleague of mine is fond of saying, "When you've got a hammer, everything starts looking like a nail."

You shouldn't be ready to abandon COM+ straight away. Considering everything that happens when you make a call to a Web service, you won't be surprised to learn that the price you pay for the new functionality is performance. If method calls to Web services are an integral part of the processing load of your system, you simply won't achieve the throughput you might expect to see if you were using COM+, even if you are calling Web services hosted on your local network. If the Web service server is located on a distant node of the Internet, the round-trip time for a method call could be as high as 5 or 10 seconds, or worse.

Here's a checklist to refer to when choosing between COM+ and Web services.

REASONS TO CHOOSE WEB SERVICES

- ◆ Current or future need to access service over the Internet
- ◆ Current or future need to interoperate with non-Microsoft tools and technologies
- ◆ Requirement to provide services to, or access services from, businesses or organizations outside of your own
- ◆ Requirement to exchange data with other businesses or organizations

REASONS TO CHOOSE COM+

- ◆ Provider (server) and consumer (application) of service reside on the same network
- ◆ All components of the system are built using Microsoft technologies
- ◆ Speed is the primary design consideration, and component method calls are involved in the regular processing of your application's workload.

Consuming Web Services

After we build the Web service, the next step is to actually use it. So far, we've tested our example Web service using the browser. The URL for our sample Web service is http://localhost/Ch7-Ex1/Service1.asmx. If you view this page in your browser, you will get a standard test user interface, provided by .NET.

You can also make direct calls to a Web service using HTTP GET from your browser. To do so, first append */MethodName* to the Web service URL, where *MethodName* is the name of the method you want to invoke. Then append query string parameters for each parameter (if any) to that method. Recall that the first query string parameter is introduced by a question mark, and subsequent query string parameters are introduced by an ampersand. To divide 5 by 2, we would request the following URL:

```
http://localhost/Ch7-Ex1/Service1.asmx/Divide?dblA=5&dblB=2
```

The Web service will perform the division and return the result as an XML message, as shown here:

```
<?xml version="1.0" encoding="utf-8" ?>
<double xmlns="http://tempuri.org/">2.5</double>
```

As you can see, the value enclosed in the returned tag is 2.5, which is the result of dividing 5 by 2. Although we've demonstrated a number of ways to access a Web service using the browser, we haven't yet attempted to call a Web service programmatically. We'll now create a Web page that uses the sample Web service to perform calculations.

If you've developed COM objects in Visual Basic 6, you've probably written test applications to call the methods of your COM objects. You did so by writing a simple Visual Basic application, adding a reference to the component's type library to your Visual Basic project, and writing code to call the various methods of the component. Because you added a reference to the component, you were able to use early binding in your test application. You can test your Web services in Visual Studio .NET using pretty much the same technique. You can write a simple ASP.NET Web form application to serve as your test UI. Of course, with a Web service, there is no DLL to which to add a reference. However, there is a feature called *Web references*. In this section, we'll write a simple test application for the Web service that we created earlier. We'll add a Web reference from our test application to our example Web service.

Let's begin by creating the project for the test application:

1. Return to Visual Studio .NET. Select File, Close Solution to close the Web service project you've been working with up to this point.

2. Select File, New Project. In the New Project dialog box, do the following:

   ■ Leave Visual Basic Projects as the selected Project Type. Click ASP.NET Web Application under Templates.

   ■ Enter http://localhost/Ch7-Ex1Client in the Location field. Click OK to create the project. A new, empty Web application will be created for you.

3. Our next step is to add some controls to the Web application. The IDE will come up with grid layout mode of WebForm1.aspx. You'll be familiar with the appearance of the grid from the Visual Basic IDE.

4. Hover your mouse over the toolbox icon on the left side of the screen until the toolbox appears. A list of Web controls appears in the toolbox. Locate TextBox in the list. Double-click TextBox, and the IDE will drop a new TextBox1 on your form in the upper-left corner.

5. Drag and drop a second text box onto your form. The IDE creates a new TextBox2. Drag it so that it is placed underneath the first text box.

6. Drag and drop a button onto the form. Place it underneath the second text box.

7. Drag and drop a third text box (TextBox3), and place it underneath the buttons.

8. To make everything line up nicely, select all three text boxes and the button. On the Format menu, select Align, Centers. On the Format menu, select Vertical Spacing, Make Equal.

   Now, we'll set the design-time properties of the controls.

9. Because you selected all four controls in the last step, click on a blank area of the form to unselect the controls. Then click to select TextBox1, the first text box at the top of the page. Set its ID property to txtNumberA. Leave its other properties unchanged.

10. Select TextBox2, and set its ID to txtNumberB.

11. Select the button. Set its ID to btnMultiply. Set its Text property to Multiply.

12. Select TextBox3, and set its ID to txtResult. Because we plan to use this field to display the result of a calculation, we don't want the user entering numbers directly. Set its Enabled property to false.

    At this point, your Web form should look something like Figure 7.5.

    Now, we're ready to add a reference to the Web service being tested.

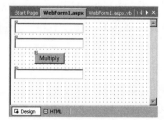

Figure 7.5   Web form design view of test application.

13. Right-click the Ch7-Ex1Client project in Solution Explorer and select Add Web Reference. The Add Web Reference Browser will appear. In the Address box, enter http://localhost/Ch7-Ex1/Service1.asmx? WSDL and hit the Enter key.

14. The Add Web Reference will display the WSDL document for the example Web service in the left pane and a list (consisting of a single item) of Web services defined within the WSDL document in the right pane.

15. Click the Add Reference button. Note that a new Web References folder appears in Solution Explorer. If you expand this folder, you'll see a subfolder for the host on which the Web service resides, localhost in this case. Within this folder are WSDL files for each Web service referenced. In our case, we have only a Service1.wsdl, as shown in Figure 7.6.

    In our test application, we'll only test the Multiply method of our Web service. We need to write some code to call the Web service's multiply method when the user clicks the test application's Multiply button.

16. Double-click the Multiply button on your form. Just as in Visual Basic, the system will throw down a blank Sub btnMultiply_Click for you.

17. In the On Click handler for the Multiply button, enter the following lines of code (an explanation of the Dim statement follows this example):

```
Dim objWebService As New Ch7_Ex1Client.localhost.Service1()


txtResult.Text = objWebService.Multiply(txtNumberA.Text,
txtNumberB.Text)
```

    We're now ready to run the test application.

18. Select Start from the Debug menu, or press F5. Note that your program compiles before it runs. After a brief wait, you should see your form in a browser window.

Figure 7.6 Web references for test application.

19. Enter an integer in each of the first two text boxes, and then click Multiply. You should see the result of the multiplication in the third text box. This may not seem spectacular, but the code *did* instantiate and use a Web service to perform the multiplication.

In our code, we referenced the Web service as Ch7_Ex1Client.localhost.Service1. The first component of this name is the name of our project, which is Ch7-Ex1Client. Because the hyphen is not valid in identifiers, Visual Studio converted it to an underscore character to produce Ch7_Ex1Client. This name is the root namespace for our project. You can view it by right-clicking the project in Solution Explorer, selecting Properties, and examining the contents of the Root Namespace field on the General page of Common properties. You might want to take a moment to explore the property pages for the your project at this time.

The second component is the name of the subfolder under Web references that contains the reference to our Web service. When we added the reference, the name of this folder defaulted to the name of the server on which the Web service is hosted, which in this case is localhost. We can rename this folder in Solution Explorer. Doing so would allow us to use more meaningful names in our references.

The final component of the reference is the name of the Web service itself. Our example Web service is named Service1.

If we needed to declare many instances of this service, the Dim statements could be cumbersome. To simplify things, we could import the namespace. To do so, add the following line to the top of WebForm1.aspx.vb, before the beginning of the class:

```
Imports Ch7_Ex1Client.localhost
```

We could then change our dimension statement in the event handler for the Multiply button to read as follows:

```
Dim objWebService As New Service1
```

Creating a Proxy

Now that we've seen the easy way to call a Web service, let's examine what goes on behind the scenes. Web references, as used in the previous example, hide the details of the communication between our client application and the Web service. When you make method calls to a Web service using a Web reference, you are really making calls to a proxy class running on your computer. The code for the proxy class was generated for your automatically when you added the Web reference. The IDE called the wsdl.exe command line utility to generate the source code for the proxy class. If you choose, you can run this utility directly. It accepts the URL of the WSDL document for a Web service and can produce proxy classes in either C#, Visual Basic .NET, or JScript.NET.

In this example, we'll demonstrate running wsdl.exe manually. We'll essentially create a Web reference "by hand". As in all previous examples, we'll call methods of our example Web service synchronously. This means that when we make a method call, we do not continue executing our program until that method call completes. This is not really a problem when we are running a sample Web page and the Web service is installed on the same machine as the client code.

If we were running a real application, and we were calling a Web service on a distant Internet site, we would need to allow for the possibility that the round-trip time for a method call may be multiple seconds, tens of seconds, or worse. Typically, users begin to wonder if an application has locked up if it stops responding for 0.25 seconds.

A proxy class allows the client application to make asynchronous calls to Web services. This means that the client application's code continues executing in parallel with the Web service's processing of the method call. You don't need to create the proxy class by hand to make asynchronous method calls. You can use the Web reference feature and allow the IDE to generate the proxy class for you.

Synchronous Method Calls

Our first example of using a manually generated proxy class will make synchronous method calls. Our first task is to use a command line utility to generate the source code for our proxy class:

1. Go to the command line and locate the wsdl.exe utility. This utility is located in the directory \Program Files\Microsoft Visual Studio .NET\FrameworkSDK\Bin.

2. Execute the following command, all on one line:

```
wsdl /language:vb /out:\temp\Service1Proxy.vb
  http://localhost/Ch7-Ex1/Service1.asmx?WSDL
```

3. The WSDL utility will respond with messages like the following:

```
Microsoft (R) Web Services Description Language Utility
[Microsoft (R) .NET Framework, Version 1.0.3617.0]
Copyright (C) Microsoft Corp. 1998-2001. All rights reserved.

Writing file '\temp\Service1Proxy.vb'.
```

Next, we'll create a test application that will call the Web service using the proxy class we just generated. As usual, we'll start by creating an empty Web application.

4. Return to Visual Studio .NET. Select File, Close Solution to close the Web form project you created in the previous example.

5. Select File, New Project. In the New Project dialog box, do the following:

   - Leave Visual Basic Projects as the selected Project Type. Click ASP.NET Web Application under Templates.

   - Enter http://localhost/Ch7-Ex1Client2 in the Location field. Click OK to create the project. A new, empty Web application will be created for you.

   Next, we need to add controls to the form and set the design-time properties of the controls. We want to implement the same UI that we did in the previous example. To add controls to the form, perform steps 3 through 8 from the previous example. To set the design-time properties of the controls, perform steps 9 through 12 from the previous example. Once you have completed these steps, your Web form should look like Figure 7.6.

   Although the UI of this example is the same as the previous example, the code that calls the Web service is very different. In the previous example, we used a Web reference to call the Web service. In this example, we'll use a proxy class. We've already generated the proxy class using the command line utility. Now, we just need to add the proxy class to our Web project.

6. In Solution Explorer, right-click Ch7-Ex2Client2, and select Add, Add Existing Item. The Add Existing Item dialog box appears.

7. In the File Name field, enter X:\temp\Service1Proxy.vb (where X is the drive on which you created the proxy class) and hit the Enter key. You'll see the proxy class added to your project, as shown in Figure 7.7.

   The code that was generated for us by the WSDL.EXE utility imports the System.Web.Services namespace. However, our project does not have a reference to the DLL that implements the classes in that namespace. Our next step is to add a reference to the correct DLL.

Figure 7.7 Proxy class added to test project.

8. In Solution Explorer, right-click References, under Ch7-Ex1Client2. Select "Add Reference". The Add Reference dialog box appears. On the .NET tab, scroll down to locate "System.Web.Services.dll". Double-click "System.Web.Services.dll". This component should now appear in the "Selected Components" box. Click the OK button to add the reference to your project.

    Our final task is to write the event handler for the Multiply button. The code we'll write for the event handler performs the goal of this example: using the proxy class to call the Web service.

9. Double-click the Multiply button on your form.

10. In the On Click handler for the Multiply button, enter the following lines of code:

```
Dim objWebService As New Service1()


txtResult.Text = objWebService.Multiply(txtNumberA.Text,
txtNumberB.Text)
```

    We're finally ready to run the program.

11. Select Start from the Debug menu, or press F5. Note that your program compiles before it runs. After a brief wait, you should see your form in a browser window.

12. Enter an integer in each of the first two text boxes and then click Multiply. You should see the result of the multiplication in the third text box. As before, we used the Web service to perform the actual multiplication. In this example, we created the proxy class ourselves rather than allowing .NET to do all the work for us.

Asynchronous Method Calls

When we created the proxy class, either using a Web reference, or using the WSDL.EXE utility, the system generated code for us that allows us to make both synchronous and asynchronous method calls. Now that we've seen an example of synchronous method calls, let's look at asynchronous method calls.

As mentioned above, an asynchronous method call allows our code to continue executing while we are waiting for the Web service method call to complete. Obviously, we will want to know when that method call does eventually complete. We can make this determination in one of two ways. The first technique is *polling*. Polling means that our code occasionally checks to see if the Web service has returned a result to us. If the results aren't available yet, we continue processing and check back later.

The second technique is *callback*. In this scenario, when we call an asynchronous method, we specify a function in our code that is to be *called back* when the Web service has returned a result to us. To those unfamiliar with the technique, this may seem to stand things on their head. It is almost as if code in our application is being called by the Web service. However, if you think in terms of an event handler, say for a button on a form, a callback isn't all that unusual.

Polling is simpler to implement and simpler to understand initially. Callbacks are more efficient because no processor time is wasted in polling and are more timely because your application is notified as soon as results are available. In this example, we'll go with the simpler solution and use polling.

The previous example used the synchronous methods of the proxy class, which are Multiply and Divide. The synchronous methods of the proxy class have the same names as the public methods of the Web service.

For each synchronous method, WSDL.EXE also creates two asynchronous methods, named Begin and End, followed by the name of the method. For example, for the synchronous Multiply method, the proxy class contains an asynchronous BeginMultiply and EndMultiply method.

The Begin method initiates an asynchronous method call. It accepts all of the same parameters as the synchronous version of the method, as well as two additional parameters that are used to implement callbacks. The Begin method does not return the return value of the method call. Rather, it returns an object of type IAsyncResult, which can be used to determine when the call is completed (using polling). Specifically, the IsCompleted property of this object returns true if the Web service has completed its processing of the request and false if the call is still in progress.

Once IAsyncResult.IsCompleted has indicated that the call has completed, the End method of the asynchronous method call can be used. It accepts a single parameter, which must be the IAsyncResult object returned by the corresponding Begin method. The End method returns the return value of Web service's method call.

The following example also illustrates how to create a copy of a Web project. This can be useful for experimentation and piloting of new ideas and designs.

Our first step is to create the proxy class, using the command line utility:

1. Once again, we'll use our arithmetic Web service. Because we've already created a proxy class, and the Web service's interface hasn't changed since the proxy was generated, we can simply reuse the Service1Proxy.vb file that we created in the previous example. If you have changed the interface, or if you didn't do the previous example, perform steps 1 through 3 of that example.

   You've already gone through the work of creating the same test application twice. Because the application is fairly simply, it's not too difficult to repeat the steps to create it. However, let's take this opportunity to learn

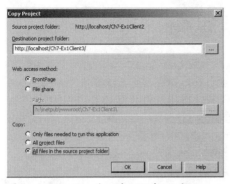

Figure 7.8   Copying the Web project.

how to create a copy of an existing Web application. This technique will be vital if you ever need to copy a large ASP.NET Web application.

2. Return to Visual Studio .NET. If the previous example (Ch7-Ex1Client2) isn't already open, open it.

3. Select Project, Copy Project. The Copy Project dialog box appears, as shown in Figure 7.8. In the destination field, enter http://localhost/Ch7-Ex1Client3. In the Copy section, select All files in the source project folder.

4. Make sure the options match those shown in Figure 7.8, and click OK. Visual Interdev will copy your Web project. The progress dialog box shown in Figure 7.9 will briefly display during the copy operation.

5. Select File, Close Solution to close the previous example.

6. In step 4, you created a copy of your Web project. However, Interdev duplicated the Web project and its files only. It did not create a new solution file for you. To do so, first select File, New,Blank Solution. The dialog box shown in Figure 7.10 will appear. Leave Visual Studio Solutions selected in the Project Types list, and Blank Solution selected in the Templates list. In the Name field, enter Ch7-Ex1Client3. Make sure the Location field displays the folder in which you store your solution files. In most cases, this will be the Visual Studio Projects folder under My Documents.

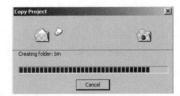

Figure 7.9   Progress dialog box for Web project copy operation.

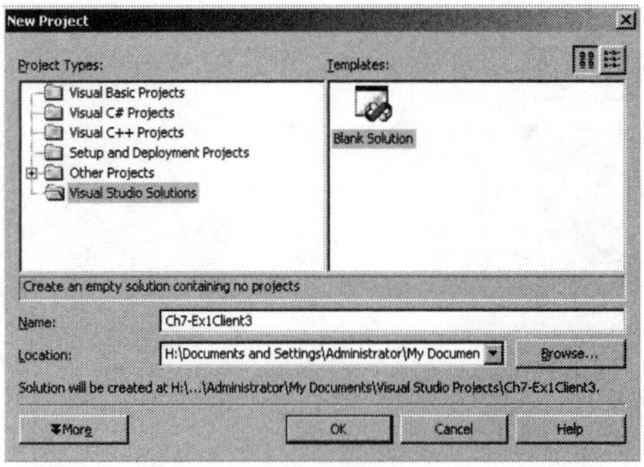

Figure 7.10 New Solution dialog box.

7. Click OK to create a blank solution. Solution Explorer will display your new solution with no projects, as shown in Figure 7.11.

8. Select File, Add Project, Existing Project from Web.... In the dialog box shown in Figure 7.12, leave the default value of localhost for the server from which to create the project.

9. Click OK. The Add Existing Project dialog box will appear, as shown in Figure 7.13.

Figure 7.11 New solution with no projects.

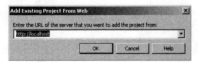

Figure 7.12 Selecting the server.

Figure 7.13   Add existing project.

10. Double-click Ch7-Ex1Client3. The dialog box will display the project files within the selected project. Note in Figure 7.14 that the project file still displays as client 2. When we copied the Web project, we created an exact copy of everything in the project. The new copy of the project resides in a new folder labeled client 3, but all of the contents of the client 2 and client 3 folders are identical.

11. Double-click Ch7-Ex1Client2.vbproj. Solution Explorer now displays the project, as shown in Figure 7.15. Note that it still looks like you're working with client 2.

Figure 7.14   Project file still listed as client 2.

Figure 7.15   Project listed as client 2 in IDE.

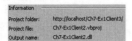

Figure 7.16 Information properties of project.

12. To verify that you really are working with a new *copy of* client 2, right-click Ch7-Ex1Client2, and select Properties. Note that in the information section, as shown in Figure 7.16, the project folder is definitely client 3. Don't close the properties dialog box yet.

13. Let's eliminate any possible confusion by renaming everything labeled client 2 to client 3. First, in the Properties dialog box you opened in the previous step, change both the Assembly Name and Root Namespace fields from Client2 to Client3. You should see something like Figure 7.17.

14. Click OK to close the Properties dialog box. Right-click Ch7-Ex1Client2 in Solution Explorer, and rename it from 2 to 3 as well. Finally, rename Ch7-Ex1Client2.vsdisco, again using Solution Explorer. You should see the project listed under its new name, as shown in Figure 7.18.

15. Finally, right-click WebForm1.aspx and select Set As Start Page.

You have completed the process of creating a new copy of the previous example. Now, we can begin modifying it to perform an asynchronous method call. Before you go on to the next step, you might want to run the Web application and verify that it works exactly as the previous example did.

We now have an exact copy of the previous example. We can begin modifying it to support the features we want in this example. First, we'll modify some controls' properties and add other, additional controls to the form:

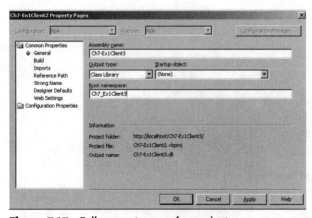

Figure 7.17 Full property page for project.

Figure 7.18   Project correctly listed as client 3.

1. Double-click WebForm1.aspx. Click to select the Multiply button. Change its Text property to Send Request.

2. Drag the third text box (txtResult) down a few rows to make room for two additional controls.

3. Add a fourth text box to the form. Place it just below the Send Request button. Set the new control's ID to txtStatus, and its Enabled property to false.

4. Add a second button to the form. Place it between the new text box you just created and the txtResult text box you moved earlier. Set the button's ID property to btnResult, its Text property to Show Result, and its Enabled property to false.

5. Select all six controls: Select Format, Vertical Spacing, Make Equal. Select Format, Align, Centers. Your Web form should look something like Figure 7.19.

   Finally, we'll write the code to make calls to the Web service asynchronously. This example is somewhat more complex than the earlier examples.

6. In Solution Explorer, right-click WebForm1.aspx, and select View Code. Edit the code-behind file to match the following. We'll discuss the code after the example is complete.

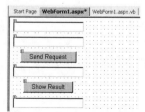

Figure 7.19   Modified Web form.

```
Public Class WebForm1
    Inherits System.Web.UI.Page
    Protected WithEvents txtNumberA As
System.Web.UI.WebControls.TextBox
    Protected WithEvents txtNumberB As
System.Web.UI.WebControls.TextBox
    Protected WithEvents btnMultiply As
System.Web.UI.WebControls.Button
    Protected WithEvents txtStatus As
System.Web.UI.WebControls.TextBox
    Protected WithEvents btnResult As
System.Web.UI.WebControls.Button
    Protected WithEvents txtResult As
System.Web.UI.WebControls.TextBox

  ' (Web Form Designer Generated code appears here)

    Private Enum enumState
        iStateNew
        iStatePolling
        iStateComplete
    End Enum

    Private m_objWebService As Service1
    Private m_objAsyncResult As IAsyncResult
    Private m_iState As enumState

    Private Sub SetState(ByVal iState As enumState)
        Select Case iState
            Case enumState.iStateNew
                btnMultiply.Enabled = True
                txtStatus.Text = "Waiting for Input"

            Case enumState.iStatePolling
                btnMultiply.Enabled = False
                btnResult.Enabled = True
                txtStatus.Text = "Waiting for Results"

            Case enumState.iStateComplete
                btnMultiply.Enabled = False
                btnResult.Enabled = False
                txtStatus.Text = "Complete"

                Session("objWebService") = Nothing
                Session("objAsyncResult") = Nothing
        End Select
```

```
          m_iState = iState
          Session("iState") = m_iState
     End Sub


     Private Sub Page_Load(ByVal sender As System.Object, ByVal e As
System.EventArgs) Handles MyBase.Load
          If Session("iState") Is Nothing Then
              m_iState = enumState.iStateNew
          Else
              m_objWebService = Session("objWebService")
              m_objAsyncResult = Session("objAsyncResult")
              m_iState = Session("iState")
          End If


          SetState(m_iState)
     End Sub


     Private Sub btnMultiply_Click(ByVal sender As System.Object,
ByVal e As System.EventArgs) Handles btnMultiply.Click
          m_objWebService = New Service1()
          Session("objWebService") = m_objWebService


          m_objAsyncResult =
m_objWebService.BeginMultiply(txtNumberA.Text, txtNumberB.Text,
Nothing, Nothing)
          Session("objAsyncResult") = m_objAsyncResult


          SetState(enumState.iStatePolling)
     End Sub


     Private Sub btnResult_Click(ByVal sender As System.Object, ByVal
e As System.EventArgs) Handles btnResult.Click
          If m_objAsyncResult.IsCompleted Then
              txtResult.Text =
m_objWebService.EndMultiply(m_objAsyncResult)
              SetState(enumState.iStateComplete)
          End If
     End Sub
End Class
```

7. Select File, Save All.

   You can now run the program.

8. Select Start from the Debug menu, or press F5. Note that your program
   compiles before it runs. After a brief wait, you should see your form in a
   browser window. The status field will initially display Waiting for Input.

Figure 7.20 Method call pending.

9. Enter an integer in each of the first two text boxes, and then click Send Request. The status will field will change to Waiting For Results.

   At this point, the test program has made an asynchronous call to the Web service's Multiply methods. The form should display in your Web browser as shown in Figure 7.20. The test program won't attempt to retrieve the result of the calculation until you click the Show Result button.

10. Click the Show Result button. Assuming the Web service has completed its calculation, the status changes to Complete, as shown in Figure 7.21.

Let's examine this example in detail. We declare an enum to define the state of our application: New, Polling, or Complete.

Refer to the Page_Load event handler. When the page is viewed for the first time, Session ("iState") will be Nothing. Our code sets the state to New and calls the SetState subroutine. SetState enables or disables the buttons on the form and sets the contents of the status text box, depending on the state value it is passed. When we initially pass it a state of New, it disables the Show Result button, enables the Send Request button, and sets the status field to Waiting for Input.

No further processing takes place until you enter values in the first two text boxes and click the Send Request button. The Send Request button is btnMultiply. Refer to the btnMultiply_Click event handler.

The btnMultiply_Click event handler first instantiates m_objWebService, which is a reference to an instance of the proxy class, and stores this reference in Session state. It then calls the BeginMultiply method of the proxy class. As described, this method initiates an asynchronous call to the Multiply method of the Web service. BeginMultiply returns a new instance of the IAsyncResult class. We store a reference to this object in Session state as well. (We must keep a reference to this object because we will later need to pass it to the EndMultiply method.) The last thing the event handler does is to call the private SetState method, with a new state value of Polling. This causes the SetState method to disable the Send Request button, enable the Show Result button, and change the status field to Waiting for Results.

Figure 7.21 Method call complete.

At this point, we have initiated an asynchronous call to the Multiply method of our arithmetic Web service. Because the call was asynchronous, we were able to continue processing and return control to the user. The asynchronous method call will remain pending until the Web service completes processing and our application requests the results of the computation.

No further processing takes place on our end until you click the Show Result button. In the meantime, the Web service is processing the multiplication request. Examine the btnResult_Click event handler. When you do click the Show Result button, this event handler first checks to see if the Web service has completed processing the request. The event handler does so by checking the IsCompleted property of the IAsyncResult object that we received as a return value from the BeginMultiply method of the Proxy class.

If the event handler determines that the call is still in progress, it does nothing. The Web page is rerendered to the user, and the state field still displays Waiting for Results. The user can wait a few moments and then click the Show Result button again.

When the event handler for the Show Result method eventually determines that the Web service has in fact completed processing, the event handler calls the EndMultiply method. The single parameter to this method is the IAsync-Result object that we received from BeginMultiply. The return value of the End-Multiply method is the same as the return value from the Web service's Multiply method—the results of the multiplication. btnResult_Click stores the result of the multiplication in the Text property of txtResult. It then calls the private SetState method with a new state value of complete. The SetState method disables both of the buttons and removes the references to m_objWebService (the instance of the Proxy class) and m_objAsyncResult (the asynchronous method call result object) from Session state.

Of course, in this example, it is very unlikely that the Web service method call will fail to complete before you can click the Show Result button. If you want to prove that things really are working as they should, you can insert a delay loop in the Multiply method of the Web service. To do so, open the Web service project (Ch7-Ex1), and add the following lines of code within the Multiply WebMethod:

```
Dim dtNow As DateTime

dtNow = Now()
While DateDiff(DateInterval.Second, dtNow, Now()) < 30
    ' Do nothing
End While
```

This will create an artificial delay of at least 30 seconds for each call to the Multiply method. Make sure you are in the Web service project rather than the client project, and recompile the Web service by selecting Build, Build. You can then retest this example and verify that the call is in fact asynchronous. Don't forget to remove the delay loop from the Web service, and recompile the Web service if you plan to do any further experimentation with any of the other earlier examples in this chapter.

Using Publicly Available Services

The final example for this chapter uses a Web service on the Internet, running on a non-Microsoft platform. As you'll see, you access the Web service just as you did the one you created on your machine in .NET. For this example, we'll use the simpler Web reference technique to call the Web service.

I located the Web service for this example by going to http://www.xmethods.com. One of the services listed gives the current temperature for any U.S. zip code. I hope this service will still be available when you read this book.

Once again, we'll begin by creating a new, empty Web Form project:

1. Return to Visual Studio .NET. Select File, Close Solution to close the Web form project you created in the previous example.

2. Select File, New Project. In the New Project dialog box, do the following:

   - Leave Visual Basic Projects as the selected Project Type. Click ASP.NET Web Application under Templates.

   - Enter http://localhost/Ch7-Ex2 in the Location field. Click OK to create the project. A new, empty Web application will be created for you.

   Next, we add controls to the form.

3. The IDE will come up with grid layout mode of WebForm1.aspx. You'll be familiar with the appearance of the grid from the Visual Basic IDE.

4. Drag and drop a text box onto your form. The IDE creates a new TextBox1. Drag it so that it is placed in the upper-left corner of the form.

5. Drag and drop a button on to the form. Place it underneath the text box.

6. Drag and drop a second text box (TextBox2), and place it underneath the button.

7. To make everything line up nicely, select both text boxes and the button. On the Format menu, select Align, Centers. On the Format menu, select Vertical Spacing, Make Equal.

We now set design-time properties of the controls to produce the behavior we require:

8. Click to select TextBox1. Set its ID property to txtZip. Leave its other properties unchanged.

9. Select the button. Set its ID to btnInvoke. Set its Text property to Get Temp.

10. Select TextBox2, and set its ID to txtResult. Because we plan to use this field to display the result of a calculation, we don't want the user entering numbers directly. Set its Enabled property to false.

We'll use a Web reference to call the Web service, as we did in an earlier example. Note that we are able to add a reference to the Web service, even though it was developed using non-Microsoft technologies and is hosted on a non-Microsoft Web server.

11. Right-click the Ch7-Ex2 project in Solution Explorer and select Add Web Reference. The Add Web Reference Browser will appear. In the Address box, enter "http://www.xmethods.net/sd/2001/TemperatureService. wsdl" and hit the Enter key.

12. The Add Web Reference will display the WSDL document for the example Web service in the left pane and a list (consisting of a single item) of Web services defined within the WSDL document in the right pane.

13. Click the Add Reference button. Note that a new Web References folder appears in Solution Explorer. If you expand this folder, you'll see a subfolder for the host on which the Web service resides, net.xmethods. www in this case. Within this folder are WSDL files for each Web service referenced. In our case, we have only a TemperatureService.wsdl.

14. Right-click the net.xmethods.www folder and select Rename. Change the name of the folder to xmethods.

Finally, we'll write the code that executes when the user clicks the Get Temp button:

15. Double-click the Get Temp button on your form.

16. In the On Click handler for the Get Temp button (btnInvoke), enter the following lines of code:

```
Dim objWebService As New xmethods.TemperatureService()


txtResult.Text = objWebService.getTemp(txtZip.Text)
```

The program is now ready to be tested:

17. Select Start from the Debug menu or press F5. Note that your program compiles before it runs. After a brief wait, you should see your form in a browser window.

18. Enter your zip code in the first box. Click the Get Temp button. After a few seconds, the outside temperature should appear in the second text box.

19. Go outside and see if the Web service returned the correct result.

This is incredibly impressive. In the space of a few minutes, you discovered a Web service on the Internet, created a client application to use it, and actually made a call and received data back.

Wrapping Up

In this chapter, we've taken a fairly in-depth look at Web services and the technologies on which they're built. We used a simple Web service to demonstrate the many techniques by which a client can interface with the Web service. We experimented with both synchronous and asynchronous calls to Web services. Finally, we even wrote an ASP.NET application that uses a non-Microsoft Web service.

In the next chapter, we'll start on an entirely new topic: Data Access with ADO.NET.

CHAPTER 8

ASP.NET Data Access Topics

Information networks straddle the world. Nothing remains concealed. But the sheer
volume of information dissolves the information. We are unable to take it all in.
Günther Grass

Most interactive Web sites would not be of much use if they didn't have data-bases behind them. Much of the work involved in creating a Web site for busi-ness purposes typically involves allowing the Web site to manipulate data.

This chapter discusses the technologies in Microsoft .NET that are oriented around data access. We'll discuss ADO.NET, which is Microsoft's evolution of ADO (ActiveX Data Objects) and why it works well for many mainstream types of Web development. But a discussion of data on the Web would not be complete without including XML, and this chapter also looks at the ways XML-formatted data can be accessed and manipulated from Visual Basic .NET.

To gain maximum benefit from this chapter, you should already be familiar with the basics of ADO and relational databases. This chapter will not make any attempt to explain basic concepts in these areas. There are a number of good references to learn more about data in general and ADO in particular. Take a look at *Programming ADO.NET* by Richard Hundhausen and Steven Borg (Wiley, April 2002).

It is not possible to cover all the capabilities for .NET data access in one chapter. That would take a whole book, and even then it would be hard to get them all in. This chapter concentrates on data access techniques that are (1) rel-atively simple and (2) needed for common tasks. There are many more alter-natives and options for the techniques than those presented in this chapter. Just because a technique is not included does not mean it is valueless or that you should not use it. However, once you have mastered the fundamentals as presented in this chapter, you are ready to experiment with more advanced techniques as presented in the documentation for Visual Studio .NET.

Some Logistical Guidelines for This Chapter

The examples in this chapter that require a database mostly use the Northwind sample database in SQL Server. If you are using a different data store (such as Microsoft Access, or Jet format), you will need to change some of the example code to compensate.

There are two ways to create most of the objects discussed in this chapter. You can create them by authoring code (much like you would with ADO), or you can create them using a set of wizards, controls, and designers that are included with Visual Studio .NET. This chapter will first present techniques for creating and manipulating the objects using code. That will communicate the essential structure of the ADO.NET classes.

After that, we will discuss some of the other tools that are available in the IDE to write such code for you. You should use these tools, especially for your early efforts. They can speed up the process of integrating ADO.NET technologies into your programs.

Using ADO.NET

Most developers coming from a Visual Basic background will gravitate to ADO.NET as their main data access technology. It has an object model that bears some resemblance to ADO, which was the primary data access tool for most Visual Basic developers before .NET came along. However, there are big conceptual differences that you'll have to understand before you can use ADO.NET effectively.

To understand these differences, we have to first talk about why we need a new data access model in the first place. Why not just continue to use ADO in .NET?

Why We Need Another Data Access Model

Data access techniques in Visual Basic have evolved quickly in the last few years. We have gone from local access using things like the Access Jet engine, to client-server access using databases such as Oracle and SQL Server, and then to Internet access, all since 1993.

In an attempt to keep up, Microsoft has introduced several models for accessing data. Data Access Objects (DAO) were introduced for local access.

DAO proved insufficient to work well with client-server architectures, so Remote Data Objects (RDO) came next. RDO proved less than ideal and was only used widely for a couple of years. Microsoft learned from that attempt and introduced ADO.

Like RDO, ADO was designed for connection-based, client-server architectures, but it was introduced just about the time the Web became an important factor in creating business systems. Microsoft responded with regular versions of ADO, rolling out new capabilities. The most significant distributed capability added to ADO was Remote Data Services (RDS).

Despite Microsoft's attempt to retrofit Web-oriented capabilities on ADO, developers began to see limitations in ADO for Web development. The most important were:

- Connection-based use of ADO required unacceptable overhead. Architectures to avoid continuous connections required more development work.

- RDS worked for distributed access but imposed a variety of limitations. Using it effectively involved a steep learning curve.

- XML became a de facto standard for data interchange on the Web, but ADO was designed before XML became important, and so ADO's integration with XML was weak.

- Early versions of ADO were mutually incompatible. This was fixed in later versions but only after developers had been forced to make many conversions to newer versions just to keep software systems on one server in synch with a single version of ADO.

We can summarize the most important problems into two areas. ADO is not ideal for distributed architectures, and it does not integrate well with XML. These are the biggest problems with ADO that Microsoft needed to address as it moved to .NET.

ADO and ADO.NET: A Comparison

There are some areas in which ADO and ADO.NET resemble one another closely and others in which they are wildly different. Let's first look at areas of similarity.

Both models require a connection to a data store to fetch data, and the code for getting a connection is similar for both. Both models have Connection and Command objects. The Connection object is extremely similar in both models. The Command object is conceptually similar in its function for both, but the object model changes. However, the similarity in these areas means that code to create and open a connection, and use a Command object to execute commands, will look immediately familiar to the experienced ADO developer.

Both models manipulate collections of rows and fields, but their techniques of manipulation are different, as we will see later in the chapter. Both models have support for transactions through the Connection object, and this functionality uses similar code in both models. And both models can be bound to controls for automatic data handling.

At that point the similarities begin to diminish. In ADO, the main construct for holding data to be manipulated is the Recordset. It is a set of rows or records holding data that was typically fetched from some data store. ADO.NET has no Recordset object. The functional equivalents to a Recordset in ADO.NET depend on the type of data access you need. The two main ones are called a DataReader and a DataSet.

There are other significant differences. For example, ADO.NET has no functionality at all for pessimistic concurrency, in which records are locked when they are accessed and remain locked until the lock is released by the accessing code. This type of concurrency has no place in a stateless Web environment because it depends on extensive maintenance of state information. The only type of concurrency available in ADO.NET is optimistic concurrency, in which records are checked for changes when an attempt is made to rewrite a record.

Because ADO.NET is quite different, and because there are things that ADO does that ADO.NET cannot, it will still be necessary for some design scenarios to continue to use ADO in .NET projects. ADO is still available through COM interop, and the code is almost exactly the same as ADO code in VB6. Because the code is the same as what you are probably already accustomed to, we won't discuss data access with ADO in this chapter. But we will point out places where using ADO is still a good choice.

The ADO.NET Classes

The main classes that make up ADO.NET are in three namespaces:

System.Data   General classes for disconnected access. The most notable class in this namespace is the DataSet. There are also classes for the elements that are related to DataSets, such as the DataTable and DataView.

System.Data.SQLClient   Classes that provide connection-based operations for SQL Server 7.0 and later versions. These classes do not use OLE DB for data access.

System.Data.OleDB   Classes that provide connection-based operations for generic OLE DB-compliant data stores. Supported databases include SQL Server, Oracle, Access Jet, and others.

The dichotomy between classes for connected access and those for disconnected access is important. We will first discuss connected operations in ADO.NET and then discuss disconnected operations and the relationships between connected and disconnected access.

Also, there are two different ways to set up and use these classes in projects. You can write all the code from scratch to create and use the appropriate classes, or you can use the wizards and other tools provided by the Visual Studio IDE. These tools will write much of the commonly used code for you and let you concentrate on the application.

Our initial discussion will focus on the object models (interfaces) for the classes and the code to manipulate them. Later in the chapter, we will spend some time discussing the various wizards and data tools to automate the creation of this type of code.

Data Providers and Connection Operations

The sets of classes that handle connected operations are referred to generically as data providers. (You'll also sometimes see them referred to as managed providers.) A data provider can be compared in many respects to what we used to call a database driver. It handles interaction with the database at the binary level and exposes an object model that we can manipulate to get at the data.

As the preceding list suggests, there are two groups of such providers in ADO.NET at present. One group is used specifically to access SQL Server databases, and the other handles more generic OLE DB access.

The OLE DB Data Provider

The OLE DB .NET data provider is a generic provider that is designed to work with any standard OLE DB provider. It has been tested with the following common ones:

SQLOLEDB   OLE DB provider for SQL Server

MSDAORA   OLE DB provider for Oracle

JOLT   OLE DBprovider for the Access Jet engine

The OLE DB .NET data provider does not work with the OLE DB provider for ODBC (MSDASQL). A data provider for ODBC is available as a separate download at http://msdn.microsoft.com/downloads. Since this is an optional and infrequently used capability for new projects, this book will not discuss ODBC data access in .NET.

Because OLE DB providers are COM-based software, the OLE DB data provider must use COM interoperability to work with them. However, the ability to interoperate with COM is well integrated into .NET, so you don't normally need to worry about the details. The OLE DB data provider takes care of them automatically.

The SQL Server Data Provider

The SQL Server .NET data provider provides access only to Microsoft SQL Server version 7.0 or later. It is implemented totally in the .NET Framework.

Because it does not go through a COM-based OLE DB provider, it yields superior performance. If you know that your code will only need to work with SQL Server, the SQL Server data provider is typically your best choice. If you suspect that your code may need to access multiple data stores other than SQL Server through OLE DB, you should probably use the OLE DB data provider, which as mentioned is capable of working with the SQL Server OLE DB provider.

For consistency, most of the examples in this chapter use the SQL data provider. Because the object model of both data providers is quite similar (as you can begin to see in Table 8.1), you should be able to translate examples to the OLE DB provider without much trouble.

Classes in the Data Providers

Both data providers have substantially similar classes in them. Table 8.1 lists the main classes in these namespaces, along with their basic purpose and how the classes in the two groups correspond.

Table 8.1   Classes in Data Provider Namespaces for Connected Access to Data in ADO.NET

TYPE OF CLASS	PURPOSE	NAME IN SYSTEM.DATA. OLEDB NAMESPACE	NAME IN SYSTEM.DATA. SQLC NAMESPACE
Connection	Establishes and manages a connection to a database. Very similar to the Connection object in ADO.	OleDbConnection	SQLConnection
Command	Carries out an operation while connected to the database. Conceptually similar to the Commandobject in ADO, but it contains a different object model and has new functionality.	OleDbCommand	SQLCommand

TYPE OF CLASS	PURPOSE	NAME IN SYSTEM.DATA. OLEDB NAMESPACE	NAME IN SYSTEM.DATA. SQLC NAMESPACE
DataReader	Presents a stream of data generated by a query operation on a database. Fulfills similar function as a forward-only, read-only rRecordset in ADO.	`OleDbDataReader`	`SQLDataReader`
DataAdapter	Fetches data from a database and transfers it into a DataSet and then later transfers changes in the data back into the original data store.	`OleDbDataAdapter`	`SQLDataAdapter`

Because the classes are similar in both data providers, we will not discuss them separately. That is, we won't discuss, for example, the OleDbConnection class and then turn around and duplicate most of that discussion for the SQL-Connection class. Instead, we will have one topic for each of the four types of classes and note a few small differences in the classes between the data providers.

Sticking with One Type of Data Provider

The classes in the different data providers are not compatible with each other. For example, you can't create your connection with a SQLConnection object and then switch namespaces to use an OleDbCommand object to generate queries against the database. If you begin using a SQLConnection object, you must only use classes in the SQL Server data provider set. And if you begin using an OleDbConnection, you must stick to other classes in the System.Data. OleDb namespace to interact with it. However, either type of data provider can be used to generate a DataSet, as we will see later in the chapter. The DataSet class and the related classes in the System.Data namespace can work with either type of data provider.

OleDBConnection/SQLConnection Class

The first ADO.NET class to be used in a data operation is typically a connection class. The OleDBConnection and SQLConnection classes are both such connection classes. Both strongly resemble the Connection object in ADO, so we won't go into a lot of detail on the object model.

Both classes are initialized with a connection string, and the string is close to identical to a connection string in ADO. Here is an example of a connection string for the SQLConnection object that we will use throughout the examples in this chapter:

```
Dim sConnectionString As String = "User ID=sa; " & _
        "Initial Catalog=Northwind;Data Source=MYSERVER"
```

In the following examples, you will need to change MYSERVER to the name of your SQL Server. You may also need to change the User ID and add a password if you are not using the typical developer setup, in which the User ID is set to sa, and the password is blank.

Here is the corresponding string for an OleDBConnection class that connects to a SQL Server database:

```
Dim sConnectionString As String = _
        "Provider=SQLOLEDB.1; User ID=sa; " & _
        "Initial Catalog=Northwind;Data Source=MYSERVER"
```

The main difference is that the OleDBConnection class requires a parameter to tell it which OLE DB provider to use. Because the SQLConnection class does not use an OLE DB provider, it has no such parameter.

Lots of other parameters can be included, such as a connection timeout period. Many of these parameters can also be accessed as properties of the Connection objects. As mentioned, because these parameters work the same way as the ADO Connection object, we will not go into detail on them.

Once a connection string is created, a Connection object can be instantiated and opened. Here is some sample code:

```
Dim sConnectionString As String = "User ID=sa; " & _
        "Initial Catalog=Northwind;Data Source=MYSERVER"
Dim myConnection As New _
        System.Data.SQLClient.SQLConnection(sConnectionString)
myConnection.Open()
```

This code uses the standard Visual Basic .NET technique of both declaring and initializing an object in the same line of code. Note that we are explicitly referring to the namespace for the SQLConnection object. If we placed the following line at the top of our module:

```
Imports System.Data.SqlClient
```

the code to get a Connection object could be made more concise, like this:

```
Dim sConnectionString As String = "User ID=sa; " & _
      "Initial Catalog=Northwind;Data Source=MYSERVER"
Dim myConnection As New SQLConnection(sConnectionString)
myConnection.Open()
```

To keep our examples concise, we will assume for the remainder of the chapter that the following lines are at the top of the modules that use the example code:

```
Imports System.Data
Imports System.Data.SqlClient
```

Methods of Connection Classes

As with the ADO Connection object, the primary methods needed to work with connection classes are the Open and Close methods. A Connection object must be explicitly opened before it can be used. We saw an example in the preceding code. The Close method should be called as soon as you are finished with a Connection object to release the resources used by the object.

Note that you can't set parameters on a Connection object when it is open. If you need to set properties on a Connection object after it is instantiated, you must do so before you call the Open method.

Pooling Connections

By default, connections in ADO.NET are automatically pooled. That is, once a connection is established to a database, and then released, it does not immediately go away. It is available for other code to use. However, a connection can only be reused from the pool if a new connection has exactly the same connection string. For this reason, if you want your connections to be automatically pooled, take care to make the connection strings identical.

You can turn off pooling for a connection. The parameters in the connection string to do this vary between a SQLConnection and an OleDbConnection. They are:

SQLConnection   Uses Pooling parameter in connection string

OleDbConnection   Uses OLE DB Services parameter in connection string

There are a couple of reasons you might want to turn off pooling. If you're sure a Connection object will not be needed again, there is no need to hold onto its resources by pooling it. Or if you want to use COM+ Services (which we will not discuss in detail) and let it manage pooling, the internal ADO.NET pooling can be turned off.

Connection objects have other properties to fine-tune the use of pooling. If you are particularly interested in getting maximum performance, you can investigate these properties in the documentation for the Connection objects.

OleDBCommand/SQLCommand Classes

Once a connection is established, you'll need classes to interact with and manipulate data. The classes that are the key to such interaction are the OleD-BCommand and SQLCommand, which we refer to generically as the command classes.

As we mentioned earlier, ADO.NET command classes are conceptually similar to the command object in ADO, but the methods and properties are different. There are also more ways to create a command object in ADO.NET.

Instantiating an ADO.NET Command Class

There are two properties for a command object that must be set before the command object can be used. One is the connection to use. (We saw earlier how to create a Connection object.) The other is the SQL statement to carry out some desired operation.

You have a choice about when you supply these property values. You can supply one or both at initial instantiation. Or you can set one or both via properties after the command object has been instantiated.

In most data access code, you know the SQL statement and the connection you want at instantiation time. In that case, it's good practice to supply both pieces of information. An example of creating a SQLCommand object this way is:

```
sSQL = "SELECT * FROM Customers"
Dim myCommand As New SQLCommand(sSQL, myConnection)
```

This example assumes that myConnection was already instantiated and opened as shown in the preceding section on connection classes.

Here's one alternative, in which properties are used to supply the information:

```
sSQL = "SELECT * FROM Customers"
Dim myCommand As New SQLCommand()
myCommand.CommandText = sSQL
myCommand.Connection = myConnection
```

The end result of either of these techniques is the same. You have a SQLCommand object that is ready to be used.

Methods of the Command Classes

You'll recall from your VB6 development that the most commonly used method of an ADO command object is the Execute method. This method executes a SQL statement, and the results (or lack of results) of the operation can be used in various ways.

The Execute method does not exist in ADO.NET command classes. Instead, it has been replaced with a number of methods to accomplish connected operations. The most frequently used ones are listed in Table 8.2.

We will see examples at this point for the ExecuteNonQuery and the ExecuteScalar methods. The ExecuteReader method is shown in the DataReader example later in the chapter.

Here is an example for ExecuteScalar. Suppose we want to find the count of all customers in the Northwind database whose name begins with the letter H. We could get that count into a variable named nCustomersBeginningWithH using this code:

```
Dim sConnectionString As String = "User ID=sa; " & _
        "Initial Catalog=Northwind;Data Source=MYSERVER"
Dim myConnection As New SQLConnection(sConnectionString)
myConnection.Open()

Dim sSQL As String
sSQL = "SELECT COUNT(CustomerID) AS CustomerCount " & _
        "FROM Customers WHERE (CompanyName LIKE 'H%')"
Dim myCommand As New SqlCommand(sSQL, myConnection)

Dim nCustomersBeginningWithH As Integer
nCustomersBeginningWithH = CInt(myCommand.ExecuteScalar)
```

If you have the standard Northwind sample database loaded, this code should result in a value of 4 being placed in nCustomersBeginningWithH. Obviously, if the database has been changed since SQL Server was installed, the count might be different.

An example for ExecuteNonQuery is similar. Suppose we want to delete all the customers whose name begins with the letter H. Our example would change to look like this:

```
Dim sConnectionString As String = "User ID=sa; " & _
        "Initial Catalog=Northwind;Data Source=MYSERVER"
Dim myConnection As New SQLConnection(sConnectionString)
myConnection.Open()

Dim sSQL As String
sSQL = "DELETE FROM Customers WHERE (CompanyName LIKE 'H%')"
Dim myCommand As New SqlCommand(sSQL, myConnection)

myCommand.ExecuteNonQuery()
```

Table 8.2 Frequently Used Methods for Command Object

METHOD OF COMMAND OBJECT	PURPOSE
ExecuteNonQuery	Used to execute a SQL statement that does not return a value. A typical example would be a DELETE statement.
ExecuteReader	Return a reference to a DataReader object. As we saw earlier, this is an object to get fast, read-only, forward-only access to a set of rows. We will cover the DataReader in more detail later.
ExecuteScalar	Executes a SQL statement and returns only the first field in the first row of the result. This is often helpful when accessing aggregate SQL functions such as COUNT. Using ExecuteScalar is faster than getting back a DataReader and then looking at the first row in it.
ExecuteXMLReader (only available for SQLCommand class)	Like ExecuteReader but returns rows in XML format. This is an easy way to get XML straight out of a SQL Server database.

Associating a Command Object with a DataAdapter

The preceding examples all have to do with connected access to data. But another use of a command object is to help get data into a DataSet for disconnected access. A DataAdapter is the intermediary in this operation. We are going to cover DataAdapters and DataSets in detail later in the chapter, and in that section we'll see the code for a command object to be used in that fashion.

OleDBDataReader/SQLDataReader Classes

We have previously touched on DataReaders as a means to get fast, read-only access to data. We saw in the preceding that a DataReader class is returned from the ExecuteReader method of a command object. Now we are ready to talk about DataReaders in more detail.

DataReaders classes (OleDBDataReader or SQLDataReader) can only be created with the ExecuteReader class. You can't create one with a New statement, nor can you inherit from these classes to make your own specialized DataReader. So don't try to use code like this:

```
Dim MyDataReader As New SqlDataReader()  ' This will not work!!
```

Instead, once you've created a Command class, as previously covered, you create an object variable of the appropriate type (OleDBDataReader or SQLDataReader) and then use ExecuteReader to initialize it as an active DataReader, like this:

```
Dim sConnectionString As String = "User ID=sa; " & _
        "Initial Catalog=Northwind;Data Source=MYSERVER"
Dim myConnection As New SQLConnection(sConnectionString)
myConnection.Open()

Dim sSQL As String
sSQL = "SELECT * FROM Customers WHERE (CompanyName LIKE 'H%')"
Dim myCommand As New SqlCommand(sSQL, myConnection)

Dim myDataReader as SqlDataReader
myDataReader = myCommand.ExecuteReader()
```

At this point the DataReader is ready to use. You can loop through it with a While loop, and the Read method of the DataReader supplies you with the next row.

This is similar to the way a forward-only, read-only ADO Recordset would be used, but there is one key difference in code. When a Recordset is initialized, the first row (if the Recordset has any rows) is already active, and you can refer to its fields right away. By contrast, a new DataReader, such as the one created by the preceding code, has no active row when it is created. The Read method must be invoked to get to the first row. That means the code for looping through the rows in the DataReader looks like this:

```
While (myDataReader.Read)
    Console.WriteLine("customer name: " & myDataReader("CompanyName"))
End While
myDataReader.Close
myConnection.Close
```

I think this is an improvement over ADO because it's not possible to forget the MoveNext method at the end of the loop that ADO required. (Forgetting MoveNext would send the code into an infinite loop as the first row was processed over and over again.) Instead, the Read method of the DataReader must be done at the top of the loop or an error will result as soon as you attempt to run your code.

The major attraction of the DataReader is speed. Once the connection is established, the loop shown runs blazingly fast. The drawbacks are that (1) you must maintain the connection as long as you are using the DataReader, and (2) you have no way to back up through rows or modify rows in any way. Note that the connection cannot be used for anything else as long as the DataReader is active. You must explicitly close the DataReader, using the Close method, before the connection can be accessed for any other purposes.

These limitations turn out not to matter in many ASP.NET scenarios. When ASP.NET is building a Web page based on some data, forward-only, read-only access is all that's needed. And because the page is built and sent out as fast as possible, maintaining and monopolizing the connection is not a problem because it is only necessary to do so for a short period.

In fact, DataReaders are so useful for construction of Web pages in ASP.NET that they can be data-bound to ASP.NET server controls. (Note that DataReaders *cannot* be data-bound to controls in Windows Forms because those controls require an in-memory representation of the data for scrolling.) If we created a DataReader using the preceding code, but did not implement the While loop (which would use up the access to the data), we could use the DataReader to fill up an ASP.NET DataGrid. Here's code that would do that, assuming our ASP.NET page contained a DataGrid control named DataGrid1:

```
DataGrid1.DataSource = myDataReader
DataGrid1.DataBind
```

This allows ASP.NET pages to separate data related logic from layout logic very effectively. The cosmetics for the grid can be done with properties, whereas the data is derived with a DataReader and just plugged in. Even if you have been leery of using data binding in the past, this use for data binding in ASP.NET is something you should definitely try.

Working with DataSets

As useful as DataReaders are, inevitably data applications need to modify data and place the modifications in the original data store. The construct that ADO.NET contains to allow this functionality is the DataSet.

Unlike all the classes we have looked at, there is only one DataSet class. It is used by all types of data providers and can even be constructed on the fly independent of any data provider. You should think of it as a generic container for data, with the data coming from any source or even from multiple sources.

Another key difference from the classes discussed earlier is that the DataSet is designed to be used in a disconnected mode. As discussed, all the classes that make up a data provider can only be used with an active connection to the database. A DataSet requires no such connection.

DataTables

It may help to think of a DataSet as a miniature relational database in which the data is kept in memory. It contains a collection of small sets of rows called *Data-Tables*. It may also help to think of a DataTable as the closest analog in ADO.NET to a Recordset in ADO because a DataTable contains a set of rows that are typically extracted from a database using a SQL statement or a stored procedure.

A DataSet can contain as many DataTables as is appropriate for a given application. For example, a single DataSet might contain one DataTable for customers, another for orders, and a third for order details.

The DataSet can also contain the relationships between these DataTables. For example, if the DataSet contained DataTables for customers, orders, and order details, it could also contain two relationships, with one describing the relationship between customers and orders and another describing the relationship between orders and order details.

This virtual local relational database is totally disconnected from the original source of the data, yet it has very flexible relational capabilities. We'll see later in the chapter how you can access all the orders associated with a single customer, for example.

XML as the Foundation

The foundation technology for a DataSet is XML. As we'll see later in the chapter, XML is used to store DataSets on disk for extended periods and to pass DataSets around between application tiers. As befits an XML-based technology, once the data has been placed in a DataSet, the original source does not matter. The data is operated on identically regardless of how it was put in the DataSet. In fact, data in a DataSet might come from several original sources. A DataSet might contain, for example, one DataTable that was derived from a SQL Server database and another DataTable that was derived from an Oracle database. Operating on the DataSet involves exactly the same techniques, even if the data comes from disparate sources.

The Life Cycle of a DataSet

As discussed earlier, data used in ADO.NET usually starts in a traditional relational data store such as SQL Server or Oracle. From there, we've seen how a data provider allows us to connect to the database and extract data. Once the data has been extracted and placed in a DataSet, there is no longer a need to continue a connection to the database. This disconnected design for the DataSet contrasts with the connected design of an ADO Recordset.

The way a DataSet is used also varies quite a bit from typical usage of a Recordset. The life cycle of a DataSet is more complex; it can also vary a lot depending on circumstances. However, here are the stages in the life cycle of a typical DataSet:

1. Set up a connection to the database, using the Connection object.

2. Create a Command object.

3. Create a DataAdapter object to transfer data from the database.

4. Create a DataSet to hold the data.

5. Place the desired data into DataTables in the DataSet using the DataAdapter.

6. Close the connection to the database once all needed data has been fetched.

7. Set up relationships among multiple DataTables, if necessary.

8. Manipulate the data as necessary (adding, changing, or deleting rows).

9. Go back to a connected mode and set up the Connection, Command, and DataAdapter objects again.

10. Use the DataAdapter to write any changes in the DataSet back into the Database.

11. Close the connection.

This quick overview leaves out a number of options and details that we'll cover later, but it is sufficient for our discussion at this point. The key ideas are that the DataSet is created while connected to the database, but it can be manipulated without any active connection because the data is held locally in in-memory storage. Only when changes need to be written back to the database is it necessary to reestablish a connection.

It may help to understand these steps if they are laid out graphically. In Figure 8.1, we follow the life cycle of a DataSet that contains a Customers DataTable and an Orders DataTable. Most of our examples in this chapter will involve just such a DataSet.

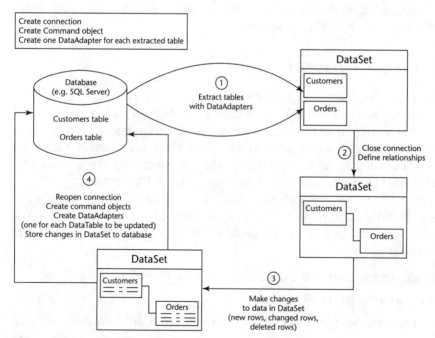

Figure 8.1   A typical life cycle for a DataSet.

It is important that you understand the life cycle of a DataSet and how it varies from the way you work with Recordsets in ADO. This life cycle gives you a conceptual structure into which you can fit the various techniques that we are now ready to cover.

Constructing a DataSet

There are a number of ways to construct a DataSet, but the most common way, as discussed with the DataSet life cycle, is to use a DataAdapter. We touched on the DataAdapter previously because the DataAdapter classes are part of data providers. Before we get into creating and using DataSets, let's talk in some more detail about DataAdapters.

OleDbDataAdapter/SqlDataAdapter Classes

The two currently available DataAdapter classes are the OleDbDataAdapter (from the OleDB data provider) and the SqlDataAdapter (from the SqlClient data provider). They work very much alike. Here is how to create a Sql-DataAdapter in code:

```
Dim sConnectionString As String = "User ID=sa; " & _
                "Initial Catalog=Northwind;Data Source=MYSERVER"
Dim myConnection As New SqlConnection(sConnectionString)
myConnection.Open()

Dim sSQL As String
sSQL = "SELECT * FROM Customers WHERE (CompanyName LIKE 'H%')"
Dim myCommand As New SqlCommand(sSQL, myConnection)

Dim myDataAdapter As New SqlDataAdapter(myCommand)
```

As this code demonstrates, creating a DataAdapter is much like creating a DataReader. It is necessary to get a connection established and then set up a Command class (in this case a SqlCommand) that contains the information on fetching the desired data. However, whereas the DataReader is created by calling the ExecuteReader method of the Command class, a DataAdapter is instantiated like any other object, and the associated Command class is included as an argument in the constructor for the DataAdapter.

Once you have created a DataAdapter, it can be used to transfer data from a database into a DataSet. Each DataAdapter can fill up one DataTable in the DataSet, so you may need multiple DataAdapters if your DataSet needs to contain several DataTables.

The method of a DataAdapter that is used to transfer data to a DataTable in a DataSet is the Fill method. To continue the preceding code, we can create a DataSet and fill a DataTable named Customers inside the DataSet with this code:

```
Dim myDataSet As New DataSet()
myDataAdapter.Fill(myDataSet, "Customers")
```

Notice that our SQL statement in the earlier code fetched all records in the Customers table that began with the letter H, so those are the records that will end up in our Customers DataTable after these two lines are executed.

Getting Multiple DataTables into a DataSet

We can repeat the preceding procedure to get more DataTables into a DataSet. For example, to add a DataTable based on the Orders table in Northwind to the preceding DataSet, we would use the following code:

```
sSQL = "SELECT * FROM Orders "
Dim myOrdersCommand As New SqlCommand(sSQL, myConnection)

Dim myOrdersDataAdapter As New SqlDataAdapter(myOrdersCommand)
myOrdersDataAdapter.Fill(myDataSet, "Orders")
```

Of course, in a real application, the SQL statement for fetching orders would have a WHERE clause to only get the desired orders, but we are leaving that off for simplicity. (The Orders table in Northwind is small, so it won't cause a problem in this instructional example.)

When we are finished getting all the data we need into our DataTables, the connection to the database should be closed. This would be done with the line:

```
myConnection.Close
```

Setting Up Relationships between DataTables

At this point, we have two DataTables with data in them. Our DataSet is ready to use, and we could access the rows containing customer and order information. However, if we want to access the data in a relational fashion (getting orders associated with a given customer, for example), we must add the relationship between the DataTables. This is done with the DataRelation class.

Each DataSet has a Relations collection to hold DataRelation objects. The collection may be empty, of course, which means there are no relationships set up among the DataTables in the DataSet. That's where we stand right after creating our DataTables for Customers and Orders.

To create a DataRelation, we need to point to the columns in the DataTables that need to be related. For example, in our Customers/Orders example, the Customers DataTable has a primary key called CustomerID. The Orders table has a field named CustomerID also, and this field is used to point to the customer for this order. (In database parlance, a primary-foreign key relationship exists between the Customers table and the Orders table in the Northwind database.)

To specify the columns to use for a relationship, the DataColumn class is used. Each DataTable already has a collection of DataColumns, which was created by the DataAdapter as part of the DataTable's structure. We just need to point to the DataColumns that we need for our relationship.

To bring it all together, here's how we create a DataRelation and add it to the Relations collection:

```
Dim ParentColumn As DataColumn
Dim ChildColumn As DataColumn
ParentColumn = myDataSet.Tables("Customers").Columns("CustomerID")
ChildColumn = myDataSet.Tables("Orders").Columns("CustomerID")

Dim myRelationship As New DataRelation("CustomersToOrders", _
ParentColumn, ChildColumn)
myDataSet.Relations.Add(relRelationship)
```

Now the DataSet can be used in a relational fashion. We'll see soon how to use this capability in code in the section *Accessing Data Using For...Each Loops.*

The name of the relationship (CustomersToOrders in our example) can be set to any value desired, and it is used to refer to the relationship in later code.

Accessing Data in a DataSet

You can randomly access individual DataTables in a DataSet and then access the rows within them. That is done with collection-based syntax, like this:

```
sName = myDataSet.Tables("Customers").Rows(0).Item("CompanyName")
```

This line would first go to the DataTable in the Tables collection with the name Customers. Then it would access the first row in that DataTable (Row(0)). Then it would get the field named CompanyName using the Item collection. If we replace the zero in Row(0) with an index variable, we could loop through the rows with a For Next loop.

This is very different from ADO, which used a cursor to point at an active row. The ADO.NET DataSet has no cursor in that sense. You just indicate the table, row, and field in which you are interested in a random access fashion. This is easier to use than connected ADO Recordsets and also much more powerful than using disconnected Recordsets in ADO, which only support the minimal cursor operations of MoveNext, MovePrevious, MoveFirst, and MoveLast.

Accessing Data Using For...Each Loops

Because DataTables, rows, and fields are held in collections, For...Each syntax is another good way to get at data. Here is data to print out the Company-Name for all the rows in a given DataSet using a For...Each loop:

```
Dim rowCustomer as DataRow
For Each rowCustomer In myDataSet.Tables("Customers").Rows
    Console.WriteLine("Company name" & rowCustomer("CompanyName"))
Next
```

This would produce similar output to the DataReader example presented earlier. The difference is that a loop like this can be used to manipulate the data. Rows can be changed, added, or deleted. We will see how to do that later in the section *Manipulating Data in a DataSet.*

If we have set up a relationship between the Customers and Orders Data-Tables, we can use a nested For...Each loop to look at customers and their orders. Here is how it looks in code:

```
Dim rowCustomer As DataRow
Dim rowOrder As DataRow

For Each rowCustomer In myDataSet.Tables("Customers").Rows
    ' Access header information for customer
    Console.WriteLine(rowCustomer("CompanyName"))

    ' Now get orders associated with the current customer
    For Each rowOrder In rowCustomer.GetChildRows("CustomersToOrders")
        Console.WriteLine(rowOrder("OrderDate"))
    Next

Next
```

The nested For...Each loop for orders uses the GetChildRows method of a DataRow to get only the orders associated with a given customer. GetChildRows uses the information in the DataRelation that we set up earlier to do that.

This type of relational access to data is a big improvement over the way similar tasks are done with ADO code. Much of the code required to manually manage the relationships among tables in ADO is not needed with ADO.NET because the DataSet can be configured to automatically manage relationships between DataTables.

Manipulating Data in a DataSet

Manipulating data in existing rows of a DataTable uses syntax much like we've already seen. For example, to change the value of the CompanyName field in the first row of a DataTable, we would use code like this:

```
myDataSet.Tables("Customers").Rows(0).Item("CompanyName") = "ABC Company"
```

This resembles ADO code somewhat. The difference is that the changes made in this manner are not automatically placed back in the database as soon as a different row is accessed. Instead, they are stored in the local copy of the data, and changes are updated to the database in batch in another operation (detailed in the section *Storing Changes Back to a Database*). However, there are several additional techniques that you'll need, including:

- Adding a row to a DataTable
- Finding a particular row in a DataTable
- Deleting a row from a DataTable

Let's look at each of these.

Adding Rows to a DataTable

Unlike a Recordset, you don't create a new row in a DataTable with an AddNew method. Instead, you create a row as an object, set values for the fields in the row, and then add the row to the DataTable's Rows collection. Here is code to do this for a new customer in our Customers DataTable:

```
Dim rowNewCustomer As DataRow
rowNewCustomer = myDataSet.Tables("Customers").NewRow
rowNewCustomer("CustomerID") = "NEWCU"
rowNewCustomer("CompanyName") = "New Customer"
rowNewCustomer("ContactName") = "Clark Kent"
' Set values for all customer fields...

' New row is now complete. Add it to the DataTable
myDataSet.Tables("Customers").Rows.Add(rowNewCustomer)
MyDataSet.AcceptChanges()
```

The last line includes a method of the DataSet that we have not previously discussed. The AcceptChanges method is used after all the desired changes have been made to a row. Until the AcceptChanges method is invoked, you can easily throw away pending changes. That is done by using a method called RejectChanges instead of using AcceptChanges. These methods work when changing rows as well as when adding new ones.

Remember that the changes made by the preceding code, even after invoking AcceptChanges, are only in the local DataSet, not in the original database. If you take no action to restore the changes in the database (as described in *Storing Changes Back to a Database*), the changes are lost when your program ends. In fact, the changes are lost as soon as the DataSet falls out of scope and is destroyed.

As with ADO, you are responsible for placing valid data in the fields. You must match up data types, for example. If the DataSet has constraints on it, you must satisfy the constraints. (We look at constraints under *Advanced Topics* later.) If you fail to satisfy any of these conditions, you'll get an exception in your code.

Finding a Particular Row in a DataTable

You might think that you could get to a particular row in a DataTable by using a key to the Rows collection, like this:

```
myRow = myDataSet.Tables("Customer").Rows("NEWCU") ' This does not work!
```

Unfortunately, the Rows collection only takes a numeric index, so this technique does not work, even if rows have primary keys. Instead, the DataTable class has a Select method that is used to get the row or rows you want. To fetch the row we just inserted (which has a CustomerID value of NEWCU), we use the following code:

```
Dim rowsSelected() As DataRow
rowsSelected = myDataSet.Tables("Customers").Select("CustomerID =
'NEWCU'")
```

A Select method might return more than one row in a DataTable, so we have to declare an array of DataRow objects to hold the results of the Select method. In our case, we only have one row with the unique Customer ID of NEWCU, so our returned array will only have one element in it.

Now that we have the row, it is manipulated just as any other row would be. For example, we can put the ContactName from the row into a label with this line of code:

```
Label1.Text = rowsSelected(0).Item("ContactName")
```

Keep in mind that what is obtained in the array that is returned from a Select method is a set of object references to DataRow objects in the DataTable. The rows are still in the DataTable's Rows collection—we just have another means at this point to refer to them.

Deleting Rows from a DataTable

Deleting a row from a DataTable is easy. You just remove it from the Rows collection. The hard part is picking out the row you want, which we just covered.

If we have carried out the preceding select operation, we can remove our row (with CustomerID of NEWCU) with the following line:

```
myDataSet.Tables("Customers").Rows.Remove(rowsSelected(0))
```

We only need to pass any valid object reference to the row that we want to remove. In our case, the reference was obtained with a Select method of the DataTable object. But we could also remove a row using its numeric index, like this:

```
Dim myDataTable as DataTable = myDataSet.Tables("Customers")
myDataTable.Rows.Remove(myDataTable.Rows(0))
```

This example removes the first row in the Customers DataTable. (ADO.NET collections are all zero-based, so the first item in the collection has index zero.)

Storing Changes Back to a Database

Once data has been manipulated, it is often necessary to make the changes permanent. As we pointed out previously, changes to a DataSet are made to a local copy of the data, and those changes will be lost if they are not placed back into the database.

In a sense, resolving changes back to the database is the reverse of getting the data in the first place. We again need an active connection and a Command object. Then a DataAdapter object is created and associated with the Command object.

The actual method of the DataAdapter that is used to place changes back in the database is the Update method. Remember that a DataAdapter can only be associated with one DataTable in a DataSet. Resolving changes in a complex DataSet that has several DataTables will therefore require several DataAdapters.

DataAdapters can use appropriate SQL statements to perform the necessary database operations. That is, rows can be changed with an UPDATE statement, rows can be deleted a DELETE statement, and new rows can be inserted with an INSERT statement. You can create your own SQL statements for these operations, or a wizard (covered later) can generate the statements for you. Because it is extraordinarily tedious and error-prone to create your own statements, it is strongly advised that you use a wizard to do it. In the section on using the data tools in the IDE, we'll cover how to set up a DataAdapter with all of these statements automatically generated, and then we will return to the subject of updating data in the database using SQL statements.

Many production systems require such operations to go through stored procedures on the database. This allows the database to perform any necessary validation and also improves performance. To allow for this case, DataAdapters can be attached to stored procedures instead of SQL statements. We'll cover more on that later in the chapter.

Persisting a DataSet as XML

DataSets are manipulated while being held in memory. However, when necessary, DataSets can be saved as XML files. This allows the entire contents of the DataSet (including information such as which rows have pending changes) to be persisted on disk for an indefinite period of time.

This XML representation is also the way DataSets are passed between application tiers. The XML document for a DataSet contains both the schema and the data, so any tier can get a complete record of the data from any other tier.

Our Customers/Orders DataSet could be stored on disk in a file named C:\Data\CustomersOrders.XML with the following line of code, assuming that the directory C:\Data already exists:

```
myDataSet.WriteXML("C:\Data\CustomersOrders.XML", _
                   XmlWriteMode.WriteSchema)
```

The second parameter specifies that the schema for the DataSet should be included in the XML file. This contains information such as the fact that the FullName column is actually calculated from other columns. An XML file on disk can later be read back into a DataSet. We will see how to do this later in the chapter in the section that focuses more explicitly on XML.

The XML representation can also be output as a stream, and this is one way for DataSets to communicate between tiers. Another way is to just pass an argument of type DataSet. In that case, the serialization of the DataSet to XML so that it can be passed between components is automatic.

Using DataViews

DataSets are the local container for data in ADO.NET. We can display the information in them in a variety of ways. For example, we can bind a DataSet to a data grid to see the data within it. However, sometimes the way data is displayed needs to be different from the way it is stored. For example, we might only want a subset of the data, such as only customers that are in a given region. Or we might want to sort the data for display differently from the way the data is ordered in the rows of the DataTables in the DataSet.

To take care of such operations, ADO.NET includes a class called a DataView. A DataView is attached to a particular DataTable and applies filtering and/or sorting to it. You can arrange for a DataView to only return certain records in the DataTable and for the rows to be ordered by any field or combination of fields in the DataTable.

DataViews are often bound to Web forms controls to construct Web pages that view data. And, because several DataViews can be attached to a single DataTable, they can be used to provide multiple, simultaneous views of the same data in different controls. You can have one grid on your form that holds customers ordered by company name and another ordered by contact name, for example.

The DataView reflects a live view of the data in the underlying DataTable. If changes are made to any rows in the DataView, the changes are actually made to the corresponding rows in the DataTable. That means that any changes to rows in a DataTable are immediately available to all DataViews that are attached to that DataTable.

To create a new DataView, simply declare the DataView and indicate the DataTable that you want it to be attached to in the constructor. Here is example code:

```
Dim myCustomerDataView As New DataView(myDataSet.Tables("Customers"))
```

At this point, the DataView returns all the rows in the Customers DataTable in the order that they have in the DataTable. That is, if you data-bind the DataView to a grid at this point, you would not be able to tell the difference between it and the grid being bound directly to the underlying DataTable. So a DataView typically has properties set to enable its sorting and/or filtering functionality. Not only can you set such properties once, but the properties can be changed on the fly to dynamically alter the output of a DataTable.

Getting a Subset of Data into a DataView

There are two properties that enable a DataView to return a subset of rows in the underlying DataTable. They are the RowFilter and RowStateFilter properties.

The RowFilter property takes a filtering expression to subset the data. Suppose that our Customers DataTable in our previous examples had all the customers in it. (Remember that our example used a WHERE clause to only return a few customers. If that WHERE clause were eliminated from the SQL SELECT statement that fetched customers, all customers would be returned.) We want to set the DataView to return customers with contact names beginning with the letter D. The line of code to do that looks like this:

```
myCustomerDataView.RowFilter = "ContactName Like 'D*'"
```

This example is a simple expression with a single condition. But expressions can be much more complex than this, with multiple logical expressions connected with boolean operators (AND, OR, NOT, etc.); RowFilter expressions can also include arithmetic computations and constants in logical expressions and can reference as many fields as necessary.

The RowStateFilter property does not take an expression. Instead, it takes an enumerated value, with each value corresponding to a specific set of rows in the underlying DataTable. The enumerations for RowStateFilter are:

Added. Shows new rows that have been added to the DataTable since it was originally constructed from the database.

CurrentRows. Shows current rows, including unchanged, new, and modified rows. Deleted rows are not included in this filter.

Deleted. Shows deleted rows.

ModifiedCurrent. Shows rows that have a current version of data that is different from the original data in the row.

ModifiedOriginal.   Shows modified rows, but displays them with the original version of the data (even if the rows have been changed and have another current version of the data in them).

None.   Shows no rows at all. Could be used initially on a DataView for a control before the user has chosen viewing options.

OriginalRows.   Shows all rows with their original data version, including unchanged and deleted rows.

Unchanged.   Shows rows that have not been changed since the DataTable was extracted from the database.

You can get rows in more than one of these categories by combining the enumerated values with a logical OR. For example, this line of code causes the DataView to expose both new rows and unchanged rows:

```
myCustomerDataView.RowStateFilter = DataViewRowState.Added Or _
                            DataViewRowState.Unchanged
```

Sorting a DataView

To sort a DataView, you set the Sort property of a DataView to a string expression that specifies the sorting you want. You can sort on multiple columns, with each column sorted in ascending or descending order.

The string expression to describe the sorting contains column names to sort on, separated by a comma if there are more than one. By default, columns will be sorted by ascending values, but you can follow a column name with the letters DESC to make a descending column sort instead. Here is an example of a sort expression that sorts our Customers DataTable alphabetically by ContactName and then by descending phone numbers:

```
MyNewDataView.Sort = "ContactName, Phone DESC"
```

The order of the columns specified is important. In this case, the DataTable will be sorted first by ContactName, and then if there is more than one record with the same value for ContactName, those rows will be sorted by descending phone number.

More Details on DataSet-Related Classes

Now that we've seen the essentials of working with the main ADO.NET classes, we can look at them in detail and cover some advanced features. This section concentrates on those classes that are related to DataSets—the DataTable, DataRow, DataColumn, DataView, and Constraint classes. We begin by looking at the detailed structure of a DataSet.

Structure of a DataSet

A DataSet is made up of Tables and Relations collections. The Tables collection contains DataTables objects, which themselves contain collections of DataColumns, Constraints, and DataRows. Figure 8.2 is a diagrammatic representation of this.

For a DataSet to be functional, it must contain at least one DataTable object in its Tables collection, and to contain any data, the Rows collection of the DataTable must have some rows whose layout is described by the Columns collection. All the other elements of the object model are optional.

The layout of the data in DataTables, including information such as data types, is in the Columns collection. The constraints for a particular table are in the Constraints collection. The relationships between tables are in the Relations collection. The actual data resides in the Rows collection.

Understanding this structure and the relationship between the Columns collection and the Rows collection is key to manipulating DataSets. Each DataTable contains a Columns collection and a Rows collection. The Columns collection is accessed to get or set schema information about the fields in each row. The Rows collection contains individual DataRow objects, with each object representing a row or data record in the DataTable. Each DataRow has an Item property, indexed with column names from the Columns collection, to get to individual fields in the row.

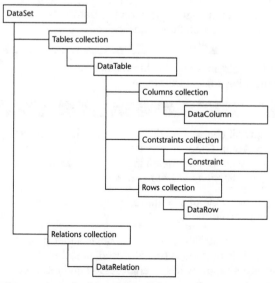

Figure 8.2 The hierarchy of classes contained in a DataSet.

DataTables

As discussed, a DataTable object contains one table of in-memory data. It has a collection of columns that contain the schema for the table and a collection of rows to contain the actual data.

The Columns collection to contain the schema for the DataTable is automatically created when a DataTable is initialized by a DataAdapter, using the DataAdapter's Fill method. But that's not the only way the schema for a DataTable can be created. In some cases, it makes sense to explicitly create the schema using code. Using that technique, each DataColumn in the Columns collection is created with code and then added to the collection.

As we have seen, new rows are added to a DataTable by creating the row with the NewRow method and then adding the row to the Rows collection. DataTables have several other useful properties and methods. The documentation contains a complete list, but some of the most important ones you should know about are listed in Table 8.3. Like all .NET classes, a DataTable must be declared using the WithEvents keywords to get access to its events.

Table 8.3   Commonly Used Properties, Methods, and Events for a DataTable

PROPERTIES	
HasErrors	A Boolean property that indicates whether the DataTable contains errors in any of its rows. Errors are typically present because a row violates the constraints that were placed on the DataTable. Note that individual DataRow objects also have a HasErrors property.
PrimaryKey	Gets or sets an array of columns that make up a primary key for the DataTable.
METHODS	
AcceptChanges	Accepts all changes made to the table since the last call of AcceptChanges. The impact of AcceptChanges is discussed in more detail in the section *Examining Different Versions of Data in a Row*.
Clear	Clears the table of all data (empties the Rows and Columns collections).
GetErrors	Returns a collection of DataRow objects that contain errors. This method is typically used after the HasErrors property has been accessed and returned true.

METHODS	
NewRow	Discussed earlier. NewRow creates a new DataRow object that is empty but has the structure needed for this DataTable and then returns a reference to this new object. Note that NewRow does *not* add the row to the Rows collection automatically. By design, this step is under the control of the programmer.
RejectChanges	Throws away all changes made to the table since it was loaded or since the last time AcceptChanges was called.
Select	Discussed previously. Takes a selection expression and returns an array of DataRow objects that match the selection expression.
EVENTS	
ColumnChanging, ColumnChanged events	ColumnChanging is fired when any data value in any row in the DataTable is being changed, but before the change actually happens. ColumnChanged is fired after the change actually takes place. The event arguments are identical for both, and they specify the row being changed, the column within the row, and the new value being proposed. ColumnChanging can be used to cancel a proposed change to a row, if necessary, by throwing an exception.
RowChanging, RowChanged events	Fired when a DataRow is being changed in any way (including deletion of the row or rollback of previous changes to the row). RowChanging is fired before the change, and RowChanged is fired after the change. Both feature the same event arguments, which specify the action that is taking place and the row affected. The change in the RowChanging event can be canceled by throwing an exception.
RowDeleting, RowDeleted events	RowDeleting cccurs when a DataRow is about to be deleted. The deletion can be canceled by throwing an exception in this event. RowDeleted occurs after a DataRow has been deleted.

DataColumns

Each field in a DataTable has a corresponding DataColumn object to contain the schema information for the field. The most important piece of information is the type of data contained in the field, and the DataType property of the

DataColumn indicates this type. Other properties of the column control other aspects of the field. These include the following Boolean properties:

AllowDBNull. Allows the field to contain a null value.

Unique. If true, requires the value in this field to be unique in the collection of rows in this DataTable

ReadOnly. If true, this field can only be read but cannot be changed.

A DataColumn can be set to automatically insert an incremented value for the column in new rows, similar to an Identity column in SQL Server or a Counter field in Access. The AutoIncrement property turns this feature on, and the AutoIncrementSeed and AutoIncrementStep properties control where the value starts and how it is incremented.

The most common use of a column is to hold a data value that has been extracted from a database. However, a column can be configured to hold a value that is computed or constructed from values in other columns. The Expression property holds the expression that is used for the calculation. For example, suppose you need a Contacts DataTable to have a column with a full name, but the database only has columns for FirstName and LastName. You could create a FullName column with code like this:

```
Dim clmFullNameColumn As New DataColumn("FullName")
clmFullNameColumn.DataType = System.Type.GetType("System.String")
clmFullNameColumn.Expression = "FirstName + ' ' + LastName"
myDataSet.Tables("Contacts").Columns.Add(clmFullNameColumn)
```

You can also do calculations in a derived column, including addition, subtraction, and so on. This could be used in an Orders table, for example, to apply a discount rate to a suggested retail price.

DataRows

We've already seen how DataRows in the Rows collection can be used to contain actual data in the DataTable and to manipulate that data. Recall an example we used earlier:

```
myDataSet.Tables("Customers").Rows(0).Item("CompanyName") = "ABC
Company"
```

This line of code sets the CompanyName field in the first row of our Customer DataTable to ABC Company. It works because the Item property of the DataRow class is indexed on the column name. Because the column name is part of the schema for the DataTable, it is held in a DataColumn object in the Columns collection. In this case, we have a DataColumn object with a Column-Name of CompanyName.

Because the Item property is the default property for a DataRow, and it is an indexed property, we can also perform the same operation with the following syntax:

```
myDataSet.Tables("Customers").Rows(0).Item(1) = "ABC Company"
```

In this case, we are using the numeric index of the CompanyName column, which happens to be 1, because CompanyName is the second column in our DataTable.

Changing Data with an Editing Mode

As we have seen, DataRows can be changed by simply accessing the columns and setting values. This works well if the volume changes are fairly small and we are not doing any event-handling on our DataTable. (Recall that a Data-Table can be set to generate events when rows are changed.)

However, if we are making many such changes, and each change is generating an event, we may be seriously affecting performance. There is an additional pitfall. If the event performs some validation that depends on other columns, and the other columns have not been set yet, the validation will fail.

What we need to remedy these problems is a way to suspend events for a row. This can be done by putting the row into an editing mode. While the row is in such a mode, changes will not generate events and validation will not be performed. Then, when the editing mode is exited, the events and validation take place.

A DataRow object has three methods to control the editing mode. Two of these will look rather familiar to a developer experienced in ADO programming:

BeginEdit Places the row in editing mode.

CancelEdit Cancels editing the row and throws away any changes made. Similar to CancelUpdate in ADO.

EndEdit Commits the changes to the row and takes the row out of the editing mode. Similar to the Update method in ADO. (Remember that changes to a DataSet don't automatically propagate to the original database. Changes committed with an EndEdit can still be lost if the changes in the DataSet are not saved to the database.)

Even though this looks a lot like editing rows in ADO, there is a key difference. Only one row can be in an edit mode at a time in ADO because the ADO cursor can only refer to one record at a time. In ADO.NET, you can have as many references to different DataRows as you need, and any of them can be in an editing mode simultaneously.

Note that if you use the AcceptChanges method of a DataTable, an EndEdit is automatically applied to each row that is in an editing mode.

Examining Different Versions of Data in a Row

DataSets are designed to hold data in a disconnected state, and that means the manipulation of the data in a DataSet may be extensive and spread out over time. It may be important to know what state a particular row is in so that a user has various options to undo or roll back changes.

We've also discussed the fact that there can be multiple versions of data in a DataRow simultaneously. A particular DataRow can have one or more of the following versions of data in it:

Current.   The current accepted data in the row. This can be the original data if no data has been changed, or it can be the value after changes have been made.

Default.   The default values for the row. These are the values that would be in a row when it had just been created by a NewRow method on the DataTable.

Original.   The data in the row when the table was first added to the DataSet or the data in the row after the last time an AcceptChanges was done on the *entire DataTable*. An AcceptChanges method on the individual DataRow does not alter the Original values—it just puts the Proposed values into the Current values.

Proposed.   The row has some new data that has not been committed with an AcceptChanges method on the DataTable or the individual DataRow. Such data can be rolled back with a RejectChanges method on the DataTable or DataRow and returned to its previous value.

By default, the Item property of a DataRow gets the Current version of the fields. However, you can get to other versions by using an optional parameter of the Item property. The parameter takes any of the following enumerated values, corresponding to the preceding version types:

- DataRowVersion.Current
- DataRowVersion.Default
- DataRowVersion.Original
- DataRowVersion.Proposed

Here is an example. Suppose I have changed the data in the first row of my Customers DataTable with the following line:

```
myDataSet.Tables("Customers").Rows(0).Item("CompanyName") = _
  "ABC Company"
```

Further suppose that I don't carry out an AcceptChanges method on myDataSet or on the Customers DataTable. Then, later in my code, I would like to get the proposed value of CompanyName column. The code to do that would look like this:

```
Dim sProposedCompanyName As String
sCompanyName = MyDataSet.Tables("Customers").Rows(0).Item("CompanyName", _
  DataRowVersion.Proposed)
```

If the row does not contain a Proposed version of its data (because no changes have been made), the second line would generate an exception. That can be avoided by first checking to see if a particular version is present. The DataRow has a property named HasVersion to do that.

Constraints

The final structural element of a DataTable that needs to be mentioned is Constraints. There are two types of constraints that can be imposed on fields in a DataTable:

Foreign key constraint.   Requires a field to contain a value that is present as the primary key in some row of another DataTable.

Uniqueness constraint.   Requires a field to be unique within the rows of this DataTable.

To impose a constraint on a DataTable, you create an appropriate constraint (from one of two constraint classes named ForeignKeyConstraint and Unique-Constraint), set the constraint's properties as needed, and then add the constraint to the DataTable's constraint collection.

Setting up a ForeignKeyConstraint object requires you to provide the following information:

- The related DataTable that has the primary key to which the foreign key points
- The column or columns containing the foreign keys in this DataTable (the one on which the constraint is being imposed)
- What action is to be taken if the constraint is violated

Some of this information is supplied to the constructor for the Foreign-KeyConstraint, and some is provided by setting properties for the class after it is instantiated. The following is some sample code that sets up a

ForeignKeyConstraint for our DataSet that contains a Customers DataTable and a related Orders DataTable. (This code assumes that the DataSet was created as we did earlier in the chapter, with one small exception. Because we are loading all Orders into the DataSet, we need to load all Customers as well, so the SQL statement for the DataAdapter that fills the Customers DataTable should have the WHERE clause dropped.)

```
Dim ParentColumn As DataColumn
Dim ChildColumn As DataColumn
ParentColumn = myDataSet.Tables("Customers").Columns("CustomerID")
ChildColumn = myDataSet.Tables("Orders").Columns("CustomerID")

Dim myFKConstraint As ForeignKeyConstraint
myFKConstraint = New ForeignKeyConstraint("OrderFKConstraint", _
ParentColumn, ChildColumn)

' If Customer is deleted, set corresponding foreign
' keys in Order table to null values
myFKConstraint.DeleteRule = Rule.SetNull

' If Customer row has primary key updated, cascade results to orders
myFKConstraint.UpdateRule = Rule.Cascade

' Add the constraint to the Constraints collection
myDataSet.Tables("Orders").Constraints.Add(myFKConstraint)

' Set the DataTable to enforce constraints
myDataSet.EnforceConstraints = True
```

There is one by-product of this operation that you should know about. A foreign key constraint requires a unique primary key in the associated table. So when a foreign key constraint is added to the Orders DataTable in the preceding code, a uniqueness key constraint is automatically added to the Customers DataTable for the CustomerID field. You can see that this is the case by examining the Count property of the collection myDataSet.Tables ("Customers").Constraints both before and after the preceding line that adds the constraint. Even though the constraint is added to the *Orders* DataTable, the constraint count for the *Customers* DataTable also increases.

The other type of constraint class is UniqueConstraint. It is much simpler. It is only necessary to set the columns in the DataTable that must contain unique values by associating them with a UniqueConstraint. Here is code for making the ContactName field in our Customers DataTable unique. This code would work if it were placed just before the last line in the preceding code that set the EnforceConstraints property to True for the DataSet:

```
' Force contact name to be unique (just for demo purposes)
Dim myUniqueColumn As DataColumn
myUniqueColumn = myDataSet.Tables("Customers").Columns("ContactName")

Dim myUniqueConstraint As New UniqueConstraint("UniqueContact", _
myUniqueColumn)

myDataSet.Tables("Customers").Constraints.Add(myUniqueConstraint)
```

As mentioned, the CustomerID field in the Customers DataTable already had a unique constraint imposed by the foreign key constraint on the Orders table. Therefore we have demonstrated the capability with the ContactName field instead, even though that would be a foolish thing to do in a real application.

Using the Data Tools in the IDE

The Visual Studio IDE is very well integrated with ADO.NET, and a number of tools are available in the IDE to simplify working with DataSets.

The Server Explorer

The Server Explorer was mentioned briefly in Chapter 2. Now let's take a look at some of the data-related functionality it includes.

You can display the Server Explorer with the View, Server Explorer menu option. It appears in the same section of the screen as the toolbox. It contains a tree-structured hierarchy of server-based resources.

When first opened, the Server Explorer contains two top-level elements—one for Data Connections and one for Servers. Let's look at the second one first. If you click on the plus sign next to Servers, you'll see some of the server-based resources that you currently have available to you. The screen looks something like Figure 8.3.

You can continue to navigate through the hierarchical tree of resources. If you are using SQL Server as your database, one of the most useful resources is under the section labeled SQL Servers. This section allows you to navigate among your databases, looking at or modifying the structure of your tables and examining and changing data. The information exposed is placed on the screen in the area where the code editor resides. Figure 8.4 is a screen that shows the Customers table in the Northwind database.

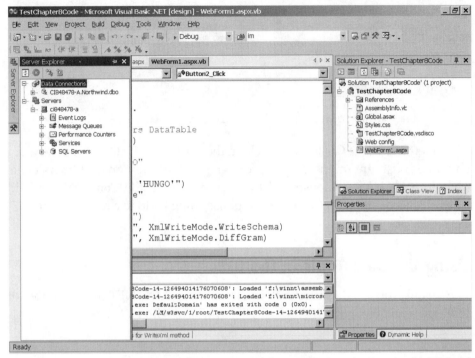

Figure 8.3   IDE with the Server Explorer open, and the Data Connections option highlighted.

With previous versions of Visual Studio, you would need to load SQL Enterprise Manager for much of this functionality. But now it is available from within the development environment.

Creating a Database Connection

The other element in the Server Explorer allows you to establish a database connection. If you right-click on the Data Connections item in the Server Explorer and select Add Connection, you'll get the configuration screen for creating a connection, which looks like Figure 8.5.

By default, the connection is for a SQL Server database. If you want to establish a connection for a different type of database (such as Access or Oracle), select the Provider tab and then you choose the type of provider you want to use. The configuration screen varies for different providers.

For SQL Server, you just select the server that contains the database you want, type in login information, and then select the database to connect to. All of our examples connect to the sample Northwind database, which is installed with SQL Server.

The connections that are established in the Server Explorer are available in a drop-down list in several of the other tools that we will discuss. It is a good idea to establish the connections you need at the beginning of a project using ADO.NET. Remember that you might need more than one connection if you will be fetching data from different data sources.

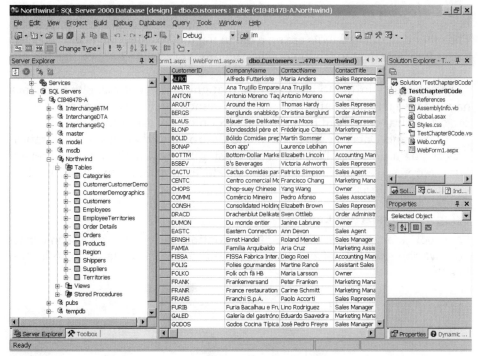

Figure 8.4 The Customers table in the Northwind sample database, accessed with the Server Explorer.

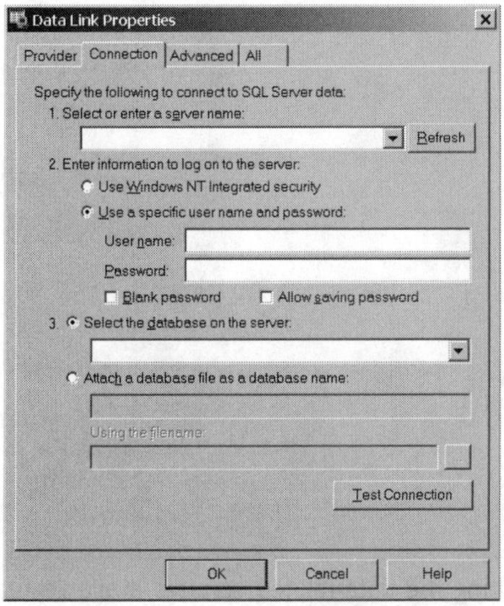

Figure 8.5 Dialog for setting up a new connection.

The Data Tab in the Toolbox

The other data-related tools are on a tab in the toolbox. The tab is labeled Data and is typically the top tab. If you click on this, you'll see a toolbox like the one in Figure 8.6.

The elements in the toolbox can be thought of as controls, although they have no visual manifestation at runtime. As such, they are incorporated into a project by dragging them from the toolbox onto the design surface.

DataSet and DataView each have one control, and there is a set of controls for each data provider. Because we are using the SqlClient data provider for our examples, we will only cover the SqlDataAdapter, SqlConnection, and Sql-Command controls.

Using a SqlConnection Control

Let's look at an example of one of these controls in action. We've seen earlier how we can establish a Connection object in code. The code to do so looked like this:

```
Dim sConnectionString As String = "User ID=sa; " & _
        "Initial Catalog=Northwind;Data Source=MYSERVER"
Dim myConnection As New SQLConnection(sConnectionString)
myConnection.Open()
```

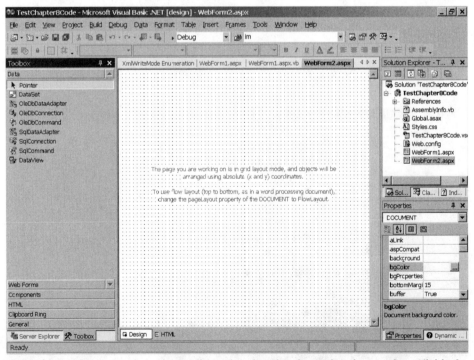

Figure 8.6 The Data tab in the toolbox, showing the data-related controls available for drag and drop onto the design surface.

As an alternative to creating a connection this way, we can drag a SqlConnection control from the toolbox to our design surface. It will receive the name SqlConnection1. This is no different from a Label control receiving the name Label1 when it is dropped onto a design surface. But because the SqlConnection control is not visible, it does not go on the form itself. Instead, it goes in a special area below the design surface called the component tray. Figure 8.7 shows the screen just after a SqlConnection control has been dropped onto the Web Form.

The new control (SqlConnection1) is highlighted in the component tray. Just as with any other control, that means that its properties are available in the Properties window. Instead of setting the connection string in code, you can just put it in the Properties window. Then you can get an active connection in code with only one line:

```
SqlConnection1.Open()
```

Of course, you could rename the control to anything you like in the Properties window. Just as with any other control, it's a good idea to give it an appropriate name.

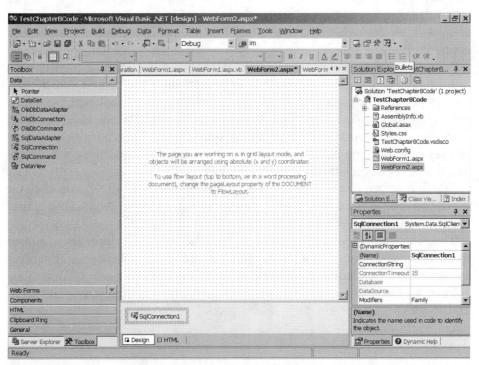

Figure 8.7   A design surface with a SqlConnection control dragged onto it and created as SqlConnection1.

The advantages of using such a control are (1) less code to write, and (2) it is easy to see the properties you can manipulate in a visual layout. You can examine all of the properties at once in the Properties window and change them as needed. Of course, as with other controls, any of the properties can be changed in code as well.

Using a SqlCommand Control

If you drag over a SqlCommand control, you will get a control named Sql-Command1. It too has properties you can set. The most important are the Connection property and the CommandText property.

The Connection property is where you hook a Command control to a connection. If you have already created Connection controls, you can select one of them to hook to the Command.

The Command property is where the SQL statement associated with the command object goes. It can be a SELECT statement for later use by a DataAdapter, or it can be a SQL statement to use with one of the execute methods of the command object that we discussed earlier.

Using a SqlDataAdapter Control

As we saw earlier, configuring a DataAdapter from scratch takes several lines of code. We also discussed the fact that a DataAdapter that will place changes into a database needs even more configuration. The entire configuration for a complex table can easily take over a hundred lines of code. Doing this by hand is prohibitively tedious.

To make the process easy, the DataAdapter control is configured with a wizard. When you drop a SqlDataAdapter control onto the design surface, the wizard begins automatically. It configures not only the DataAdapter but also the Connection and Command objects needed by the DataAdapter. It is not necessary or appropriate to create a Connection control and a Command control (as we did in the preceding examples) to use a DataAdapter control. You just drag over a SqlDataAdapter and let the wizard do it all.

The first screen of the wizard is just a welcome screen. When you click on Next, you'll be asked to select the connection to use for the DataAdapter. That wizard screen looks like Figure 8.8.

The connections that you added earlier in the Server Explorer are available in the drop-down list. A new connection can also be established right here by pressing the New Connection button.

Once you've chosen a connection, click on Next to get the screen shown in Figure 8.9.

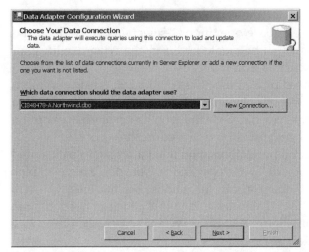

Figure 8.8   The first option screen in the DataAdapter configuration wizard.

We learned earlier that a DataAdapter can use either SQL statements or stored procedures to communicate with the database. This is where we specify which we want to use.

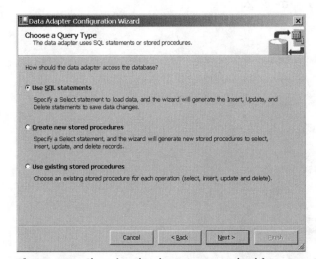

Figure 8.9   Choosing the data access method for a DataAdapter.

If you pick Use SQL statements, the DataAdapter will be configured with SQL statements for all of the database operations—select, insert, update, and delete. The SELECT statement will be created later in the wizard with your input, and the others will be created automatically.

If you pick Create new stored procedures, the wizard will create complete, but minimal, stored procedures for each of the four database operations. If you are working on a project with a new database that you just created, this option could make sense to help you get your stored procedures up quickly.

If you pick Use existing stored procedures, you'll get a screen to pick stored procedures for each of the four database operations. You don't have to pick stored procedures for all of them. You can just choose for the ones you will need when data is updated. But if you leave one out and it is needed later, you'll get a runtime exception. Figure 8.10 is the wizard screen used to choose stored procedures for the database operations.

Once you select the stored procedures you want to use, you can map the parameters for the stored procedures to the fields in your DataSet. Figure 8.11 is a version of the preceding screen with the stored procedures selected and the mapping grid filled up on the right for the Insert operation.

Selecting a Source Column (on the far right-hand part of the screen) gives you a drop down list to use in configuring your mapping.

If you do not use a stored procedure to select the rows you want, or if you select Use SQL statements, you will need to specify the SQL statement that you need to select records. You can enter a SQL statement manually into the wizard screen, which looks like Figure 8.12.

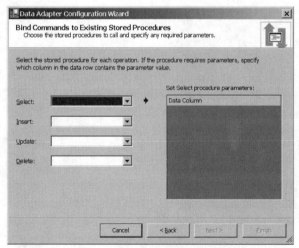

Figure 8.10 The screen in the DataAdapter configuration wizard for selecting the stored procedures to use for database operations.

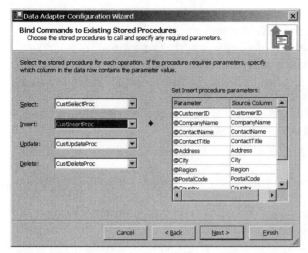

Figure 8.11   The screen from Figure 8.10 after stored procedures have been selected. The mapping of data columns to stored procedure parameters is shown in the grid on the right.

You can also design your SELECT statement graphically with a query builder. The query builder in the wizard is very much like query builders in other Microsoft tools that you have probably used before, such as Microsoft Access. You can add the tables you need to the query and then check off the

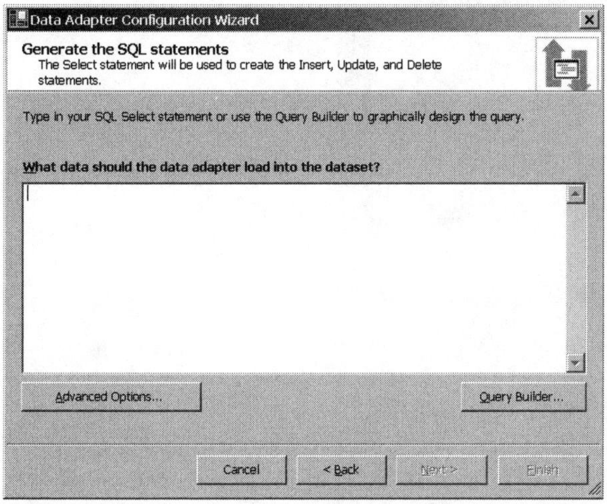

Figure 8.12   Specifying a SQL statement to use for selection of records in a DataAdapter.

fields you want. You can also include selection criteria used to build a WHERE clause, or you can type in a WHERE clause manually. The query builder looks like Figure 8.13 with a Customer table already added in.

Once you have completed selecting stored procedures and/or a SELECT statement, you are finished. The fully configured DataAdapter will be added to your project. A SqlConnection control will also be added for use by the DataAdapter control. (A Command object is optional for a DataAdapter, so a Command control is not included.)

Using a DataSet Control

When you drag over a DataSet control, you get a dialog box that looks like Figure 8.14.

We are not going to discuss typed data sets in this chapter. They are an optional, advanced technique used to work with data-related code. You must already have a DataSet configured in the project to use a typed data set.

If you select Untyped data set, you get a simple DataSet control named DataSet1 on your design surface. As with the other controls, you can manipulate it with the Properties window. It is used in code the same way a DataSet declared in code would be. For example, you can create a DataTable in a DataSet control by using the Fill method of a DataAdapter.

Using a DataView Control

Dragging over a DataView control works much like the untyped data set. You get a DataView that can have its properties manipulated in the Properties window. At a minimum, you must set the Table property. Accessing this property shows a list of the DataSets that are available to use with the DataView. Then you can set sorting and filtering properties as desired.

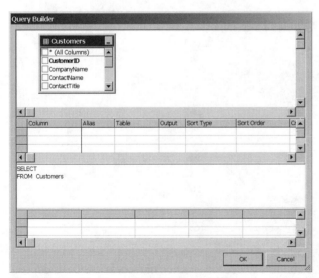

Figure 8.13 The query builder accessed from the DataAdapter configuration wizard.

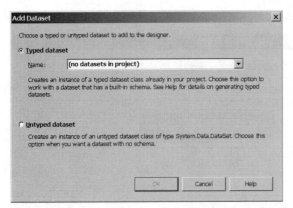

Figure 8.14   The dialog box for creating a DataSet control.

Advanced Topics

The ADO.NET classes are quite flexible. In the preceding sections, we've discussed the bare minimum of capabilities needed to use them for common database situations. It's just not possible in a single chapter to cover all the capabilities of ADO.NET, but there are some somewhat more advanced techniques that are needed frequently enough that you need to see how they work.

Updating Data Back to the Database

Now that we have covered creating DataAdapters with the IDE tools, we are ready to return to the topic of using DataAdapters to update changes in a DataSet back to the database. In this section, we'll allow the DataAdapter to work through SQL statements.

Let's step through an example that goes all the way from creating a DataSet through changing it and then getting the changes back in the database. We will use the IDE tools whenever we can to simplify the example. If you are interested in the detailed code generated by the tools, you can look at that code in the editor.

1. Start a new ASP.NET Web application project. In the location for the project, set the last directory name as CompleteCycle.

2. Place the controls in Table 8.4 on the blank WebForm1 that is automatically created for your project, and set the properties as indicated.

Table 8.4   Controls to Place on WebForm1 and Properties to Set for Each Control

CONTROL TYPE	PROPERTIES
Button	ID = btnLoadGrid
	Text = "Load grid"
Button	ID = btnMakeChanges
	Text = "Make Changes"
Button	ID = btnSaveChanges
	Text = "Save Changes to database"
Datagrid	ID = CustomerGrid

When you are finished, the screen should look something like Figure 8.15.

3. If you do not have an existing connection to the Northwind sample database, create one in the Server Explorer. We covered that operation earlier in the chapter.

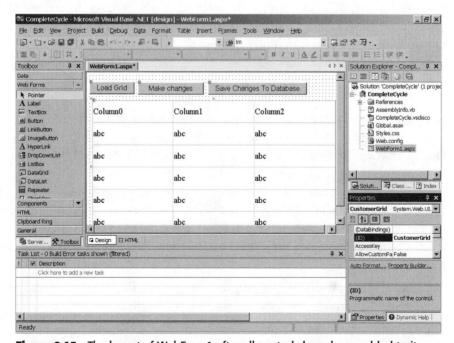

Figure 8.15   The layout of WebForm1 after all controls have been added to it.

4. Open the toolbox, select the Data tab, and drag a SqlDataAdapter control onto WebForm1.

5. In the wizard that comes up, click on Next, then select the connection to the Northwind database, and click on Next again.

6. Select the option to Use SQL Statements and click on Next.

7. Type in the SQL statement SELECT * FROM Customers and click on Next.

8. Click on Finish. The SqlDataAdapter1 control will show up in the component tray.

9. In the Properties window, change the name of the control to Cust-DataAdapter.

10. Drag a DataSet control from the toolbox onto WebForm1.

11. Select Untyped dataset on the dialog screen and click on OK.

12. In the Properties window, change the Name of the control to Customer-Dataset.

13. Double-click on btnLoadGrid, and in the click event routine, place the following code:

```
CustDataAdapter.Fill(CustomerDataset)
CustomerGrid.DataSource = CustomerDataset
CustomerGrid.DataBind()
```

14. Double-click on btnMakeChanges, and in the click event routine, place the following code:

```
CustDataAdapter.Fill(CustomerDataset, "Customers")

' Delete the first customer
Dim myDataTable As DataTable = CustomerDataset.Tables("Customers")
myDataTable.Rows.Remove(myDataTable.Rows(0))

' Add a new customer
Dim rowNewCustomer As DataRow
rowNewCustomer = myDataTable.NewRow
rowNewCustomer("CustomerID") = "NEWCU"
rowNewCustomer("CompanyName") = "New Customer"
rowNewCustomer("ContactName") = "Clark Kent"
' Set values for all customer fields in real application...

' New row is now complete. Add it to the DataTable
myDataTable.Rows.Add(rowNewCustomer)

' Change the contact for customer with ID "NORTS"
Dim rowsSelected() As DataRow
```

```
rowsSelected = myDataTable.Select("CustomerID = 'NORTS'")
rowsSelected(0).Item("ContactName") = "Lois Lane"
CustomerDataset.AcceptChanges()
CustomerGrid.DataSource = CustomerDataset
CustomerGrid.DataBind()
```

15. Double-click on the button btnSaveChanges, and in the click event routine, place the following code. This code is exactly like that in the previous step except that there is an additional line, just before the data grid is bound, to save the changes back to the database.

```
CustDataAdapter.Fill(CustomerDataset, "Customers")


' Delete the first customer
Dim myDataTable As DataTable = CustomerDataset.Tables("Customers")
myDataTable.Rows.Remove(myDataTable.Rows(0))


' Add a new customer
Dim rowNewCustomer As DataRow
rowNewCustomer = myDataTable.NewRow
rowNewCustomer("CustomerID") = "NEWCU"
rowNewCustomer("CompanyName") = "New Customer"
rowNewCustomer("ContactName") = "Clark Kent"
' Set values for all customer fields in real application...


' New row is now complete. Add it to the DataTable
myDataTable.Rows.Add(rowNewCustomer)


' Change the contact for customer with ID "NORTS"
Dim rowsSelected() As DataRow
rowsSelected = myDataTable.Select("CustomerID = 'NORTS'")
rowsSelected(0).Item("ContactName") = "Lois Lane"
CustomerDataset.AcceptChanges()


CustDataAdapter.Update(CustomerDataset, "Customers")


CustomerGrid.DataSource = CustomerDataset
CustomerGrid.DataBind()
```

16. Now run and test the program. Select Load Grid to see the original data. Select Make Changes to see the grid with the changed data. However, if you click on Load Grid again, you'll get the original data back because the code behind Make Changes did not save the changes to disk. Then select Save Changes to Database. Now if you go back to Load Grid, the changes will be there.

The preceding example would be quite similar even if the DataAdapter used stored procedures instead of SQL statements. The Update method of the DataAdapter uses whatever means that are configured for the DataAdapter to communicate with the database.

Optimistic Concurrency

There was one big aspect of the preceding code that is different from what you would want to do for a real system. That code has no exception handling or problems with the database.

The most likely problem you would encounter is one with concurrency. ADO.NET uses optimistic concurrency to deal with changes in the underlying database. That means that if someone changes the data in the database while you are manipulating your DataSet and making changes to the same rows, that fact must be detected. ADO.NET does this by maintaining the original version of the data and checking this version against the database before attempting to write the changes to the database. If it is discovered that the data has indeed changed in the interim (between the time you fetched the data and the time you tried to put changes back), an exception will be generated. You'll have a chance to look at the rows that are causing the problem and deal with them in some appropriate manner. A sample application later in the book uses exception handling in this fashion.

Transactions in ADO.NET

If you have done a lot of database-oriented programming, you are probably familiar with the concept of transactions. If there are several related database operations that must either all succeed or all fail, a transaction is the way to make that happen. An example might be entering all the items in a customer order. You would like to make sure that either all the items are ordered, or the customer is informed that there is a problem, and the whole order is saved so that another attempt can be made later.

There are two main ways of handling transactions in ADO.NET. One is to use the transaction management of COM+ Services. Doing transactions this way is beyond the scope of this book, but if you have a complex Web site with a lot of traffic, you should consider that option.

The other way is to use the transactional capabilities of the ADO.NET classes. The Connection classes of both data providers have a BeginTransaction method to begin a transaction and return a reference to a Transaction object. That Transaction object then has methods named Commit and Rollback that commit or roll back the transaction.

We will not see an example of a transaction because it would be necessary to explain the associated concepts. If you already understand using transactions in other contexts, the preceding information will steer you to information in the documentation that covers other details of transaction-based programming in ADO.NET.

Where You Should Still Use ADO

We have discussed ADO.NET extensively in this chapter, and you might be getting the feeling that it is a complete replacement for ADO. That is not true. ADO.NET is very flexible, but it is designed for disconnected scenarios. There are still some connection-based scenarios for which classic ADO remains the best option. For example, if you need to work on a large set of rows on a server using a server-side cursor, ADO is necessary because ADO.NET doesn't support server-side cursors. Or if you need pessimistic concurrency, in which records are locked when accessed and remain locked until updated or released, again ADO will handle it but ADO.NET will not.

If you do need to use ADO, you just refer to the ADO libraries to make them available in your code. Then your write ADO code very much as you would in earlier versions of VB6.

XML for Data in .NET

XML has become the lingua franca for data interchange in the Internet world. ADO.NET is built on it and so are Web services. In many cases, you use XML technologies without being aware of it. .NET does a great job of hiding the implementation of many features so that you can write an XML-based Web service, for example, without seeing a lick of XML.

There are times, though, when you need to go a bit deeper. You may need to explicitly work with data in ADO.NET in terms of XML, or you may occasionally need to work with XML directly. This final section of the chapter covers these topics.

Using XML with ADO.NET

We've already discussed the fact that ADO.NET is based on XML and that you can persist an ADO.NET DataSet as an XML file. Let's look at some of the other XML-related capabilities of ADO.NET.

Reading a DataSet from an XML File

We saw earlier that we could save our Customers DataSet with code like this:

```
myDataSet.WriteXML("C:\Data\CustomersOrders.XML", _
                XmlWriteMode.WriteSchema)
```

Of course, we need to be able to come back and load a DataSet from this file as some future time. Here is the logic that does that:

```
Dim myNewDataSet As DataSet
myNewDataSet.ReadXML("C:\Data\CustomersOrders.XML")
```

The resulting DataSet can be used just as any other DataSet would be. It can be bound to a grid, for example, or have a DataView imposed on it. In fact, the ReadXML method of the DataSet will work with any well-formed XML file. Suppose you have the following XML file in a file named C:\Data\Test.xml:

```
<?xml version="1.0"?>
<Customers>
<Customer>
    <CompanyName>That Big Old Company, Inc.</CompanyName>
    <CompanyID>TBOCI</CompanyID>
    <ContactName>Bubba Olds</ContactName>
    <Order>
        <OrderDate>2-19-2002</OrderDate>
        <ShipDate>2-24-2002</ShipDate>
    </Order>
    <Order>
        <OrderDate>3-4-2002</OrderDate>
        <ShipDate>2-12-2002</ShipDate>
    </Order>
</Customer>
<Customer>
    <CompanyName>Little Bitty, LLC</CompanyName>
    <CompanyID>LBLLC</CompanyID>
    <ContactName>Jack Small</ContactName>
    <Order>
        <OrderDate>1-22-2002</OrderDate>
        <ShipDate>1-24-2002</ShipDate>
    </Order>
</Customer>
</Customers>
```

Now suppose you place the following code in a project:

```
Dim myNewDataSet As DataSet
myNewDataSet.ReadXML("C:\Data\Test.XML")
```

After executing this code, you have a DataSet with two DataTables in it, namely, a Customers table and an Order table. The DataSet also has a relationship set up between the two DataTables, and there are new ID fields in the DataTables to use for the relationship. The ReadXML method reads the structure of the XML file and realizes the appropriate structure, so the resulting DataSet has that structure.

Manipulating XML with ADO.NET

Because you can read an XML file into a DataSet and then later save it into the same or a different XML file, ADO.NET gives you a way to manipulate the data in an XML file without using complex syntax. You can use the same syntax that you learned earlier in the chapter to add rows, change data in rows, and delete rows. The results will be stored in the output XML file. However, not all XML files can be transparently edited with ADO.NET this way. If the XML file is constructed in such a way that a complete schema cannot be abstracted from it, an exception will be raised.

Working with XML in the IDE

The preceding technologies for interpreting XML and placing the results in an ADO.NET DataSet are used by the Visual Studio IDE to create a slick XML editor. To see this editor in action, do the following:

1. In the Solution Explorer, right-click on a project and select Add, Add Existing Item.
2. Navigate to the C:\Data\Test.xml file that you created earlier (or any convenient XML file). To see the filename, you may need to change the file type in the dialog box.
3. Click on OK, and the XML file will appear as an item in the project.
4. Double-click on the XML file in the Solution Explorer.

At this point, you'll see the XML file and be able to edit it, just as you would in a normal XML editor. However, notice that just below the editor are two tabs. The currently active one is XML. Click on the Data tab, and you'll see the exact same data, placed into an editable grid.

The grid is the same one used in Windows forms programs, and it allows navigation through the hierarchy of the data. That is, if you click on the plus sign next to a customer records, you'll see a link to Customer Order. If you click that, you'll see the orders associated with the customer.

If you make changes in the grid, they are reflected in the underlying XML file. Of course, the XML file must be saved before the changes propagate to disk.

Using DataSets and XML within Web Services

A Web service in .NET can have a return data type of DataSet. Such a Web service is a good way to send a container of data to another process. As long as the consumer of the Web service is another .NET program, the Web service can return the data right into a declared DataSet in the consuming code. The Web service in code looks almost exactly the same as a function that returned a DataSet, and the consuming code also looks the same as if it were using a local function returning a DataSet.

But what if the process consuming the Web service is not based on .NET? After all, Web services are a standard and can be produced and consumed by any type of computer or operating system.

Because a DataSet is serialized as XML, when a non-.NET process uses a Web service that returns a DataSet, the DataSet just looks like XML to the non-.NET process. The XML stream that comes from the Web service can be parsed like any other XML.

You can see this in action if you create a Web service that returns a DataSet and then run the Web service in the Internet Explorer test bed. You'll see the DataSet as XML, and that's exactly the way a non-.NET program would see it.

Manipulating XML Data with System.Xml

In the long run, we will probably reach the point where routine application development does not require getting into the internals of an XML file. We are already shielded from this in some common cases by ADO.NET.

But for the present, there are still cases where an XML file needs to be parsed and interpreted in code. To do that, the System.Xml namespace contains various classes to read, manipulate, and write XML. The technology in System.Xml is the replacement for (and descended from) the MSXML libraries that are distributed with recent versions of Internet Explorer. If you are familiar with using the MSXML libraries, you'll find that you can write very similar code in .NET with System.Xml.

We will not cover the System.Xml classes completely. That's another subject about which there are entire books. But we will review some of the main classes and see a quick introduction to using them. Note that all the examples in this section assume that you have placed the following line at the top of your code module:

```
Imports System.Xml
```

XMLReader/XMLWriter Classes

To read or write an XML file one node at a time, the XMLReader and XML-Writer classes are available. For example, the following code reads through the C:\Data\Test.xml file that was created earlier and places only the contact names in a label on a Web form, using a subclass of XMLReader called XML-TextReader:

```
' Declare the XMLTextReader and point to the XML file
Dim myReader As New XmlTextReader("C:\Data\Test.xml")

' Move to beginning of XML document
myReader.MoveToContent()

' Go through the nodes in the XML document
While myReader.Read

    ' See if we have Contact Name
    If myReader.NodeType = XmlNodeType.Element Then
        If myReader.Name = "ContactName" Then
            ' When we find a ContactName element,
            ' we need to read the next node to
            ' get the value
            myReader.Read()
            Label1.Text &= myReader.Value & " - "
        End If
    End If

End While
myReader.Close
```

Although simple, this example shows the basic mechanism for using an XMLReader. The reader is declared and initialized to an XML file. Then the nodes are read sequentially, with decision making done on the type of node encountered.

The XMLReader base class can't be instantiated directly—it must be inherited into a subclass and extended. System.XML includes three subclasses of the XMLReader for specialized purposes:

XMLTextReader. Provides a stream of nodes, with no validation except that the XML is well formed. This generic reader is very fast. This is the class used in the preceding example.

XMLNodeReader. Can read subtrees of the XML hierarchy. This reader can have a text stream representing a node with all of its subnodes passes in (rather than an entire file), and it can parse through that. Like the XMLTextReader, it provides no validation except that the nodes are well formed.

XMLValidatingReader. Like an XMLTextReader, but it also has validation to a schema.

In addition to these types, you can subclass the XMLReader class and create your own specialized XML reader.

The XMLWriter is the converse of the XMLReader. Instead of reading a node at a time, it writes a node at a time. The input can be anything—a text stream from a flat file, an array, or any other input source that generates multiple records that need to be output as XML.

Like the XMLReader, the XMLWriter class cannot be used directly. There are several subclasses that can be used. For our example, we will use the simplest, which is the XMLTextWriter. The example takes an array of color names and outputs them as an XML file:

```
Dim sColor(5) As String
sColor(0) = "Red"
sColor(1) = "Blue"
sColor(2) = "Green"
sColor(3) = "Yellow"
sColor(4) = "Black"
sColor(5) = "White"

Dim myWriter As New XmlTextWriter("C:\SharedFiles\Colors.xml", _
                                  System.Text.Encoding.ASCII)

' Write the beginning of the XML doc
myWriter.WriteStartDocument(True)

' Write the root element
myWriter.WriteStartElement("Colors")

' Write the elements with the colors
Dim iColorIndex As Integer
For iColorIndex = 0 To 5
    myWriter.WriteElementString("Color", sColor(iColorIndex))
Next

' Write the end of the root element
myWriter.WriteEndElement()

' Write end of doc and close the writer
myWriter.WriteEndDocument()
myWriter.Close()
```

The XML file that will be generated by this code looks like this:

```
<?xml version="1.0" encoding="us-ascii" standalone="yes"?><Colors>
    <Color>Red</Color>
    <Color>Blue</Color>
    <Color>Green</Color>
    <Color>Yellow</Color>
    <Color>Black</Color>
    <Color>White</Color>
</Colors>
```

XMLDocument

The XMLReader and XMLWriter classes only offer sequential access to data. To get more complex types of access, you need the XMLDocument class.

XMLDocument implements an in-memory representation of the entire XML file, allowing navigation both up and down through the nodes. Nodes can be modified and new nodes inserted, and the changes can be saved.

Using an XMLDocument is very complex, but we will look at a simple example to show the capability to change elements. Here is code to look through the C:\Data\Test.xml XML file that we created earlier and change Jack Small to John Small whenever it is in a ContactName node:

```
Dim myXmlDoc As New XmlDocument()
myXmlDoc.Load("C:\SharedFiles\CustSample.xml")
Dim IndexNode As XmlNode
For Each IndexNode In myXmlDoc.GetElementsByTagName("ContactName")
    Dim DataNode As XmlNode
    For Each DataNode In IndexNode.ChildNodes
        If DataNode.InnerText = "Jack Small" Then
            DataNode.InnerText = "John Small"
        End If

    Next
Next
myXmlDoc.Save("C:\SharedFiles\CustSample.xml")
```

The XMLDocument class has many useful properties and methods, and we are only using a few in this example. The Load method creates the in-memory representation of the XML file, and the Save method saves the current state of the in-memory copy to an XML file on disk. The GetElementsByTagName method finds a collection of nodes with a given tag name. You can then navigate from these nodes through their child nodes.

XMLDataDocument Class

The XMLDataDocument class is derived from the XMLDocument class, and it adds the capability for the XML data to be used as a DataSet in ADO.NET. Because we've talked already about using XML in ADO.NET, we won't go into further detail on the XMLDataDocument class.

XSLTransform Class

Experienced XML developers are familiar with the idea of coupling an XML file full of data with an XSLT file that contains formatting information. When the transform described in the XSLT file is applied to the XML data, the output is a specially formatted version of the data. Such output can be HTML, fixed-length records, and various other formats.

Creating XSLT transforms is a programming art in itself, so we will not go into detail on constructing transforms. The format for a transform is a W3C standard and is thus the same in .NET as it was before. But we can take a look at code to apply a transform to an XML file.

Applying an XSLT transform in .NET is straightforward. The class to use is the XSLTransform class. It is loaded very much like the XMLDocument class is loaded, using a Load method that can point to a filename. (There are other ways of loading these classes, such as from a stream, but we will not pursue details in this book.)

Once the XSL document on disk has been loaded into the XSLDocument class, the class has a Transform method to create the transformed output. The output can be sent to a normal text file, or if the output is going to be XML, it can be sent to an XMLWriter.

Here is an example. Suppose our XSL document containing the transform logic is a file named C:\xml\CustOrders.xsl and the XML data is in a document named C:\xml\SeptData.xml. We want the output to go to a file named C:\xml\SeptData.htm because our transform outputs HTML. Here is code for the simplest case:

```
Dim myXSLTransform As New XSLTransform()
myXSLTransform.Load("C:\xml\CustOrders.xsl")
myXSLTransform.Transform("C:\xml\SeptData.xml", "C:\xml\SeptData.htm")
```

Wrapping Up

Creation of interactive Web sites is one of the most important uses of ASP.NET. That means manipulation of data, and in this chapter, we've seen the basics of doing that with ADO.NET. We've also covered the fundamentals of direct access to data in XML files.

The material in this chapter should be sufficient for you to understand the sample application later in this book and to start writing data-related code in your own ASP.NET projects.

In Chapter 9, we'll explore some in-depth capabilities of ASP.NET, such as configuration and security. Then we'll be ready to walk through an entire application in Chapter 10.

ASP.NET Web Application Services

Knowledge is not information, it's transformation.
Osho

Precision is absolute in the business of software development, and for the most part there is very little room for error. Some of the most sophisticated technological instruments in the world are written with software developed by a team of experts who count on the ability of their teammates to write flawless code. Technology has found a way to permeate its malleable backbone into all sectors of every market, making it imperative that mistakes, ones that could cost companies millions of dollars or individuals their lives, do not happen.

The approach to writing flawless code should always include writing secure code. Essentially, these tasks should go hand in hand, although they can be very mutually exclusive. For instance, it is possible to write good code that is not susceptible to failure under any circumstances, *even under a successful internal or external hack*. For this reason, it is important to apply the proper configuration to an application, preventing a successful attack against even the most well thought out lines of code. As any developer can attest, configuration and deployment issues have traditionally been the cause of many a headache. Fortunately, ASP.NET simplifies both of these areas by improving the deployment process for both code and ASP.NET pages and by providing extensible application configuration. In this chapter, you'll learn how to configure the application data, where it can be stored, and how to modify configuration handlers through the use of the Web.config file. We'll discuss authentication and authorization, application and session level objects, the new events added to the global.asax file, caching data, and Microsoft Passport.

Web.config

The Web.config file is used to store configuration information about a specific application. Up until now, ASP applications used the global.asa file to manage state-aware configuration information encompassing Web applications, but the Microsoft Development Environment 7.0 includes a true configuration file that allows you to store stateless system and application configuration information.

The default Web.config file is automatically generated when you create a new project, and it contains settings that will allow you to personalize the behavior of your application. It will also allow you to draw on the extensibility of this file by adding your own configuration sections and event handlers.

The following sections discuss the Web.config's structure, default tags and properties, how to create a configuration file, and how to obtain the values from a configuration file and apply them in an application.

Structure

The ASP.NET Web.config file has an XML hierarchical design structure. The file is a text-based document that contains pairs of tags that outline basic attributes of the application and define the characteristics of how the application is to behave. The element tags can also contain nodes that further define a structure under the root tag. An XML node is an entity that contains attributes. The attributes identify specific information that the application is looking for. The root tag is a universal base that is expected by a reading application. In the case of ASP.NET, the reading application is the compiler.

The structures of the XML element tags are almost identical to the structure of the tags found in HTML. The difference is that XML tags are user-defined, signifying that applications transacting with files or other applications using XML will need to know the meaning of each tag in order to communicate. Microsoft is making significant advances in the way XML is being used in the browser. If you are using Microsoft Internet Explorer 5.0 or later, copy the following configuration example, located in the next paragraph, into a text editor and save it with an .xml extension. Open the file in the IE Web browser and review the contents. The browser has the ability to validate XML files for a well-defined structure. Had our document not been well formed, the browser would have generated a meaningful error that would have guided us to correcting the problem in the XML file.

Let's take a look at an example. The following code is an example of a configuration section taken from the Web.config file of the Microsoft Development Environment 7.0:

```
<configuration>
    <authorization>
        <allow users="*" />
        <!-- Allow all users -->
        <!--
        <allow users="[comma separated list of users]" roles="[comma
        separated list of roles]"/>
        <deny users="[comma separated list of users]" roles="[comma
        separated list of roles]"/> -->
    </authorization>
</configuration>
```

Even though the XML format is recognized and validated in the browser, the data contained in the XML is not validated for authenticity or integrity. The browser will have no way to determine if the information included in the XML structure is true or false. This is because the actual XML node names, attributes, and values are user defined and not identified by the browser. For any processing to occur, a communicating application would need to assimilate this file; define what each node, attribute, and value means; and respond to it. In the case of the default structure in Web.config file, the .NET IDE compiler understands the meaning of each tag and can act in response to the settings.

Configuration

The configuration section handler, such as DictionarySectionHandler, can be supplied by the Microsoft .NET Framework or by the developer; in this case it is known as a custom handler.

Each configuration section contains nodes that define the settings for that particular area of ASP.NET. For example, the authentication node configuration attribute shown in Table 9.1 demonstrates the mode attribute defaulting to Windows authentication. However, if you look at the Microsoft Definition column in the table, you will see the other recognized values for this attribute. In this case, Cookies, Passport, and None will also work as valid authentication values in this node.

You can change the way the application authenticates by changing the value of the mode attribute in the authentication node and user node of the Web. config file, as shown later in the chapter.

Later on in this chapter we will talk about the different modes of authentication and demonstrate how they are used.

Table 9.1 Web.config Tags and Default Properties

DEFAULT CONFIGURATION ATTRIBUTES	MICROSOFT WEB.CONFIG DEFINITION
`<compilation defaultLanguage="vb" debug="true" />`	The defaultLanguage attribute denotes the default language for the applications running under this configuration file. Setting the debug attribute to true will turn on ASPX debugging. Setting it to false will improve runtime performance.
`<customErrors mode="RemoteOnly" />`	Values for the mode attribute are RemoteOnly, On, and Off. RemoteOnly allows remote users to see detailed error message or custom error pages. Something more informative than a simple error number and description. On: Shows the Custom Error Page, but never a detailed description of the error. The detailed error page is shown, but never a custom error page.
`<authentication mode="Windows" />`	Allows the developer to set the type of authentication. The choices are Windows, Forms, Passport, and None.

`<authorization>`
`//<allow users="*" />`
`    <deny users="?" />`
`</authorization>`
	Allows the developer to determine the authorization policies for the application. The developer can choose to allow or deny everyone, only anonymous users, specific users, and groups.

`<trace enabled="false" requestLimit="10" pageOutput="false" traceMode="SortByTime"localOnly="true"/>`	Application-level tracing allows an output log for every page in the application. If the pageOutput attribute is set to "True", then trace login ensues and displays information at the bottom of the page. If set to false, then it is stored in the trace.axd page in your applications root directory.

DEFAULT CONFIGURATION ATTRIBUTES	MICROSOFT WEB.CONFIG DEFINITION
| ```
<sessionStatemode="inproc"
stateConnectionString="tcpip=
127.0.0.1:42424"
sqlConnectionString="datasource=
127.0.0.1;userid=sa;password="
cookieless="false"
timeout="20"
/>
``` | The mode attribute can contain one of three values: inproc, sqlserver (database-based), and stateserver (memory-based).<br><br>The cookieless attribute supports a boolean entry. If true, then the cookie identier is stored in the URL. If false, then regular cookies will be used if supported by the client.<br><br>The timeout is the time, in seconds, for which the session is valid for each request.<br><br>The sqlConnectionString is the connection to the SQLServer Database, which will be maintaining state if you choose this option.<br><br>The stateConnectionString is the IP Address of the server or PC allocated to maintain state information in memory. The Port attribute follows the colons in the IP Address. The Port is a reserved number that is assigned to the listener on the State Server. |
| ```
<httpHandlers>
<add verb="*" path="*.vb"
type="System.Web.
HttpNotFoundHandler,
System.Web" />

<add verb="*" path="*.cs"

type="System.Web.
HttpNotFoundHandler,
System.Web" />


<add verb="*" path="*.vbproj"
type="System.Web.
HttpNotFoundHandler,System.Web" />
``` | This section provides information to prevent specific types of source code from being downloaded. |

continues

Table 9.1 (Continued)

DEFAULT CONFIGURATION ATTRIBUTES	MICROSOFT WEB.CONFIG DEFINITION
```<add verb="*" path="*.csproj"``` ```type="System.Web.``` ```HttpNotFoundHandler,System.Web" />```	
```<add verb="*" path="*``` ```.webinfo"``` ```type="System.Web.``` ```HttpNotFoundHandler,System.Web" />``` ```</httpHandlers>```	
```<globalization requestEncoding="``` ```utf-8" responseEncoding=``` ```"utf-8" />```	Sets the globalization settings for application requests and responses. There are five attributes that can be used in this section, including the request-Encoding and responseEncoding as we just mentioned. Also, there is fileEncoding, culture, and uiCulture. See the MSDN Web site for further details.

Getting/Setting the Values of Attributes

Aside from being able to view and modify the values of the attributes during the design, it is sometimes worthwhile to be able to see and manipulate the values of the attributes during runtime. For example, if you built a chat application and were monitoring the incoming text for inappropriate text, you might want to have the power to automatically disable someone who violates the rules from using the application. However, before you can a person's authorization capabilities, you will need to know who the person is. To acquire this information, your application will probably need some form of initial user authentication. Once the user's identification has been established, it is possible to store and control the user's abilities within the application.

In this case, we will use Windows authentication in the Web.config file as shown in this example:

```
<authentication mode="Windows" />
```

We will also deny unauthenticated users by using the following code. This, following alteration to the authorization node in the Web.config file, will force users to authenticate before using the application.

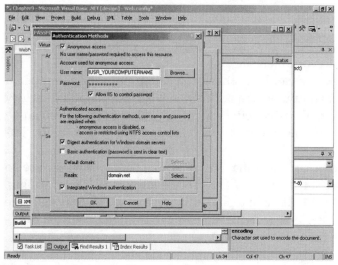

Figure 9.1 Authentication methods.

```
<authorization>
    <deny users="?"/>
</authorization>
```

Our Web.config settings now dictate that any .aspx file that spawns from this relative path of the virtual directory will require basic network authentication and deny access to anonymous users. So, if you are coming in via HTTP, you will encounter a standard Windows Network Authentication dialog box and be forced to log in before you can continue using the application.

Consequently, keep in mind that the Web.config file attributes are modified to override the machine-level configuration file, keeping the developer from having to modify the Directory Security Settings in IIS directly, as shown in Figure 9.1. Overriding the security settings of the IIS server can be achieved by placing the Web.config file in the application's root directory. It is as equally important to keep in mind that all subdirectories automatically become heir to these settings. However, it is possible for subdirectories to have their own individual Web.config file as well, and the child configuration files will override their parent directory's settings in such cases. Please Visit http://msdn.Microsoft.com/library/enus/cpguidnf/html/cpconconfiguringnetframeworkapplications.asp for more details on this matter.

Application Root Directory

The *application root directory*, also known in IIS as the local path, is the user-folder that typically contains all of the primary application files. Each Web site has a root virtual directory and might even have an ancillary structure below the root virtual directory. You can add supplemental virtual directories, directories, and files to the root structure through IIS. These ancillary directories might house include files, other directive material, and pictorial files that add visual embellishments to your Web site.

The virtual root directory can be a physical location on your computer, a shared drive on another computer, or a redirection URL. The default directory is <Your Harddrives default drive letter>:\InetPub\wwwroot, but it can be made to look at any one of the aforementioned locations to find your application's root directory.

Your application's root directory has an alias that Web browsers use to locate, access, and process file content. The process known as URL mapping, or the ability to associate a URL with a physical directory, helps to resolve the physical path when a user, who is requesting a page from your virtual directory, types your URL in their Web browser.

Creating a Configuration

In the following code example, you will create a configuration that will force a user to authenticate through windows and will not authorize them to use the application until they successfully log in:

1. Once the IDE is up and running, click on File, New, Project, and the wizard in Figure 9.2 will appear and assist in the creation of a new .NET application. Click on ASP.NET Web Application in the Templates window and type in a new name and location for the new Web service.

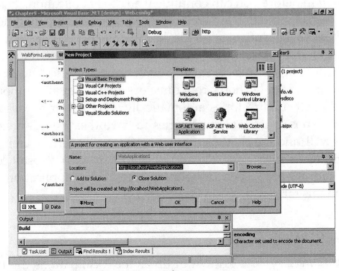

Figure 9.2 Creating a new project.

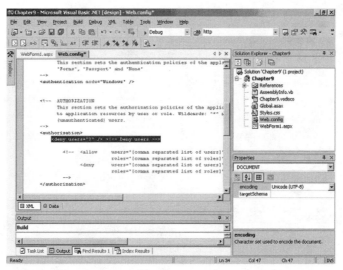

Figure 9.3   The Web.config file.

2. Double-click on the Web.config File in the Solution Explorer pane, and modify the authorization node as shown in Figure 9.3. We are changing the line containing <allow users="*" /> to <deny users="?"/>. This will force the authentication of anonymous users.

3. The default authentication method in IIS is Anonymous Access and Integrated Windows Authentication. We will discuss these in further detail later in the chapter, but for now we are going to deselect both the default authentication method checkbox and the Integrated Windows Authentication checkbox. Then, check the Basic Authentication box as Figure 9.4 shows, and click the OK button to accept these changes. This will force us to log in under the Windows Account Login each time we run our application, as shown in Figure 9.5.

4. Double-click on your WebForm1.aspx file and rename it MyAuth.aspx in the FileName Properties pane. Next, using the controls in the Web form section of the Control toolbox, copy in a textbox control and name it txtStatus. Expand it a bit, and set it's TextMode property to multiline. Then, double-click on the Web form, and you will be taken to the MyAuth.aspx.vb* file. Place the code in the paragraph below in the Page_Load Event. Rerun the application and satisfy the authentication dialog box by entering your user identification and password. You should now see a form that looks like Figure 9.6.

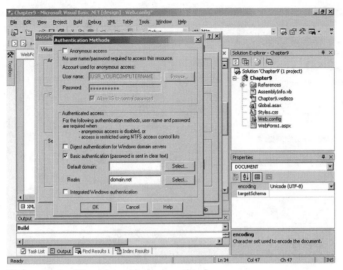

Figure 9.4   IIS authentication methods.

5. Copy the following code into the Page_Load Event of the aspx.vb* file:

```
'Obtain the authentication type.
Dim strAuthMethod As String
'Determine the authentication type.
strAuthMethod = User.Identity.AuthenticationType
Select Case Len(strAuthMethod)
    Case Is > 0
        'If authenticated then obtain the user name.
        Dim strUserName As String
        strUserName = User.Identity.Name
        txtStatus.Text = "Domain and User Name: " &
strUserName & vbCrLf & _
            "Authenticated Via: " & strAuthMethod
    Case Else
        'The code should not get here, but handle
        'it if it does.
        txtStatus.Text = "Failed!"
End Select
```

6. We can also manipulate the expiration of the cache by adding the following lines of code to the top of the Page_Load Event. The location of these two lines should be the same as the location of the code in Figure 9.7. Once you add the following lines of code, start the Web application, and you will be forced to log in.

```
Response.Cache.SetExpires(DateTime.Now.AddSeconds(15))
Response.Cache.SetCacheability(HttpCacheability.Public)
```

Figure 9.5 Windows account authentication.

Immediately stop the application and restart it. You should notice that you weren't required to log in because the page has been cached on the Web server for 15 seconds. Stop the application once more and wait at least 15 seconds. Then, restart the Web application and you will see that you are required to log in once again. This is because your cached server page expired.

Try different expiration settings with the cache, for instance an expiration of 1 second. The expiration happens so quickly that you will have to log in each time.

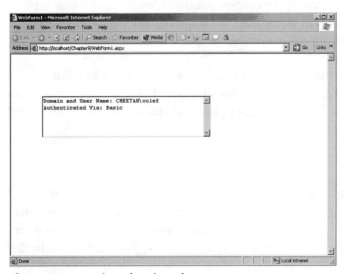

Figure 9.6 User is authenticated.

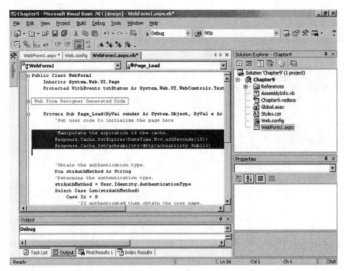

Figure 9.7 Manipulating the cache.

Performance and Scalability

Concentration is a card game that forces its participants to rely upon memory to achieve victory. The greater the collaborative memory of the players in a game, the shorter the duration of the game being played. This same philosophy about memory applies to building scalable, high-performance Web applications.

By storing things in memory, the performance of an application and Web server can increase because the application doesn't need to make trips to the server to obtain information it previously acquired. In turn, the less busy a server is handling redundant tasks, the freer it is to satisfy a greater number of meaningful requests by a greater number of users, thereby making the server more scalable as well.

There are several methods that allow us to take advantage of information retention, thereby increasing performance and scalability of our application and Web server; they include caching, application and server variables, static objects, and the global.asax file.

Caching

Caching is the ability to store page output and data in memory the first time it is requested, eliminating the need for the Web server to re-create this information every time a client request is made. There are several ways to cache information, and the cache can be stored on the client, the Web server, or in the request stream of a browser. In effect, caching can reduce the number of round trips from the client to the server or, at a minimum, reduce the amount of work the server needs to perform to summons the information. ASP.NET provides two powerful types of caching. There is output caching which is new in .NET, and HttpCachePolicy class caching.

Output caching enables the Web server to store dynamic page content and user control responses on the Web server. The output cache will handle all the requests. After a page has been cached, subsequent requests are satisfied by the cached version for as long as the duration is set. Try this out by placing the following line of code at the top of your .aspx page we just created:

```
<%@ OutputCache Duration = "30" VaryByParam="None" %>
```

The duration of the OutputCache is stored in seconds. Run the application from the IDE the first time, and you will encounter the Microsoft Network Authentication dialog box. Log in and immediately close the browser or click the stop-debugging icon on the toolbox. Quickly, run the application from IDE once more. Now you should be able to enter the application without having to authenticate through the Microsoft Network Authentication dialog box. Once again, stop the browser and wait for the duration to expire, and then start the application. You should now be forced to authenticate through the Microsoft Network Authentication Dialog box. This example demonstrates the effectiveness of the OutputCache method; it allows the server to cache Web pages in the server's memory and avoids server-side processing of pages that are continually accessed within the duration you supply.

Additionally, the VaryByParam parameter is a required OutputCache parameter; it gives you the ability to vary the number of documents that are cached for a single page. For instance, suppose your application accessed a database table that contained all of the states in the United States. This information is for the most part constant, so it does not make sense to have your Web server query the database to populate a drop-down listbox for each person who visits your site. To eliminate this problem, you can simply add the following line of code to the OutputCache directive:

```
<%@ OutputCache Duration = "3600" VaryByParam="state" %>
```

For the next hour, anyone who attempts to access the site using a state that was used by anyone else in the same duration will receive an immediate response from the server. The trip to the database to acquire the information will have been eliminated.

Additionally, there is also something known as HttpCachePolicy class caching, or programmatic caching, which allows you to set the cache in code. So, instead of supplying the directive at the top of the page, like we did using the OutputCache, we could use the following code in a server-side event. Remove the OutputCache Directive we included in our application, and copy these lines of code in the Page_Load Event of the WebForm1.aspx.vb file:

```
Response.Cache.SetExpires(DateTime.Now.AddSeconds(90))
Response.Cache.SetCacheability(HttpCacheability.Public)
```

Once you run the code, you will realize that the HttpCachePolicy class caching reacts the same way the OutputCache Directive did. However, the benefit is that you have more control over the HttpCachePolicy class because it is declared programmatically. Leaving the last lines as they are in the application, copy the following lines to Button1_Click Event:

```
Response.Cache.SetExpires(Now)
Exit Sub
```

Now try running the application once again. If you beat the expiration limit of the previous example we created, you will bypass the authentication process. But, if you wait for the previous cache to expire, then click the Send Message button. You are now forced to reauthenticate because we programmatically expired the cached page with the code we just included.

You can also add items to the cache object. Add the following lines of code to the Page_Load Event, just underneath the code you wrote that set the expiration and cacheability of the cache object:

```
txtMessage.Text = ""
If Len(Cache("MyMessage")) > 0 Then
Cache("MyMessage") = "Old Cache"
txtMessage.Text = Cache("MyMessage")
Else
Cache("MyMessage") = "Cache expired...New Cache."
txtMessage.Text = Cache("MyMessage")
End If
```

Run this code the first time, and you will see the message stating that this is a new cache. Press the F5 key, and you will now see that we are dealing with the new cache, which has become the old cache. Items stored in the cache object will continue to persist as dictionary objects.

An advantage to using HttpCachePolicy class caching OutputCache Directive is the ability to manipulate the properties, methods, and events of the cache directly in the code. The advantage to using either of these methods to control caching is reducing the number of times a Web server is required to access static information. For more information about the cache, visit http://msdn.microsoft.com/library/default.asp?url=/library/en-us/cpguidnf/html/cpconaspoutputcache.asp. There are also other ways to increase the performance and scalability of our application and Web server, including a feature called State Maintenance.

State Variables, Application and session-level variables are all server-side variables, meaning that their values are stored and accessed only on the Web server. The primary difference between session and application variables is the type of data they store. Session variables store values that are user specific, such as a user ID or other information that is specific to each individual accessing a Web application. Application variables, on the other hand, are used to store information that is site specific in application variables. This means that all users on a Web site will share application variables because they are not tied to each individual user.

Traditionally, session state has always been considered evil for several reasons. For one, session variables consume server memory. As each individual user stores unique information in a session variable, memory resources are depleted. Also, there is a question about how long a session variable should persist in the Web server's memory. If session variables persisted for too long in a Web server's memory space, there might be a chance that a large number of concurrent users could completely deplete a Web server's memory, forcing it to crash.

Session variables also used to be considered evil because of their limitations in Web farms. Because session variable data is stored on the Web server that fulfills the user's page request, there was no way for each Web server to pass along session variables in a Web farm. So, session variables had serious scalability limitations.

Furthermore, session variables were cookie dependent. So without the assistance of a cookie, session variables were completely stateless and useless. The responsibility of the session variable is to store unique information for each user who is accessing the Web site, and the responsibility of a cookie was to help identify who the users were. So, if a user's browser did not support the use of cookies, session-level variables were in fact worthless.

Because of this, Microsoft has changed the way in which session state is handled. Session state is handled in an out-of-process fashion, meaning the session state is separated from the process. Session information can be stored on a separate server that is accessible to every Web server in a Web farm, completely refuting the old scalability issues. Also, the users no longer need to support cookies on their PC in order for Session Variables to work properly. We will further expound on cookies a little later in this chapter.

Likewise, if the server that has been selected to store the session variables is dedicated to doing nothing more than handling out-of-process Web server session requests, memory management issues are suddenly alleviated as well. In addition to this, the .NET session variables do not require cookies to support state. The session ID, a unique identifier that is assigned to a user by a Web server when a Web site is first accessed, becomes part of the URL, allowing even a browser with disabled cookie support to maintain session-state on a Web server.

Keep in mind that you must set the .enableSessionState property in the .aspx file to true to provide session variable support to a client. Also, you must set the sessionState mode property equal to StateServer in the Web.config file to cookie-less session IDs.

Once this is done, copy the following code into the Page_Load Event of a new .aspx page. Then run the code in the .NET IDE. It will display the session variables on the page, and the session ID will be visible in the URL.

```
'Declaring the session variable.
Session("MyAddress") = "1111111 Sullivan Avenue"
Session("MyCity") = "GASullivanville"

'Accessing the session variable.
Response.Write Session("MyAddress")
Response.Write Session("MyCity")
```

Like session-level data, application-level data is also stored in name/value pairs on the Web server. Copy the following code into the Page_Load Event of a new .aspx page. Then run the code in the .NET IDE. It will display the application variable on the page. Everyone who accesses the page will see the same data because everyone shares it. Thus, the variables only have to exist once, making them less harmful than traditional session state variables and still using considerably less overhead than traditional session variables.

```
'Declaring the application variable.
Application("ThisSitesFavoriteURL") = "http://www.gasullivan.com"

'Accessing the application variable.
Response.Write Application("ThisSitesFavoriteURL")
```

There are also concurrency issues that should be thought about before you decide to use application-state variables. Keep in mind that the threads of a multiple or free-threaded application can access values deposited in application-state variables in a simultaneous manner. Occasionally, one thread collides with another thread while performing their individual pieces of work, sometimes leading to catastrophic errors in the application.

So, when using application-state variables, it is sometimes important to use the Application object's Lock and Unlock methods to prevent more than one thread from colliding with another as they concurrently attempt to access application-state variables. For example, if your application variable is responsible for keeping a count of the number of users accessing the Web server, you might want to lock the method, prior to incrementing the count. Users who access the application variable in its locked state cannot modify the application-state variables. When the method has been unlocked, after application variable after the increment is complete, you can then unlock the application variable for normal use.

The downside to this scenario is that you can lose data that you might have otherwise wanted to track, the request made by one thread to modify an application variable during it's locked state will simply be ignored. So, if you want to keep track of dynamic data, application variables are probably not what you will want to use. But, if you simply want a ballpark figure, or if you are keeping track of static data like we did in the aforementioned example, then the application variable will work just fine.

The following lines of code demonstrate the lock method of the Application object:

```
Application.Lock
Application("ServerPoll") = Application("ServerPoll") + 1
Application.Unlock
Response.Write "This Poll Has Been Visited: " &
Application("ServerPoll") & " Times."
```

global.asax file

The global.asax file is an optional ASP.NET application file. It responds to ASP.NET HTTPModules and application-level raised events and is generally housed in the root directory of the ASP.NET application. The contents of this file cannot be downloaded, as it is configured to reject any direct URL requests. If the file is not present, the ASP.NET framework automatically presumes that there is no predefined session or application event handlers.

NOTE This global.asax file does not replace the global.asa, where the global.asa already exists, and it cannot intrinsically communicate with a global.asa file, but it can peacefully coexist with it in the same directory if you decide to mix ASP with ASP.NET Technology in the same virtual directory.

The global.asax file does not really contribute to the performance or scalability of a Web application. Its true role is to provide built-in events that we can enlist when certain behaviors occur within our Web application. The traditional global.asa file offered four events, which were the session and application's Start and End events. But, the global.asax file supports more than 17 global events that you can participate in. The following is a list of each event of the Base and Global classes, as well as its usefulness:

- The Application_Error event occurs when an unhandled error is encountered.

- The Application_EndRequest event occurs when the application ends.

- The Application_AuthenticateRequest event fires just prior to any authentication attempts occurring.

- The Global_AuthorizeRequest event symbolizes that the request is preparing to be authorized.

- The Global_Disposed event fires after responding to a request and a reference to an object has been dereferenced.

- The Global_AuthorizeRequest event reacts when user authorization has been deemed verified.

- The Global_BeginRequest event occurs immediately before each new request has been responded to.

- The Global_PreSendRequestHeaders event transpires when right before headers are sent-off to the client.

- The Global_AuthenticateRequest fires when the user's identity has been acknowledged.

- The Global_BeginRequest fires once a response has been issued to pacify a request.

- The Global_EndRequest event happens immediately after each new request has been responded to.

- The Global_PreSendRequestContent happens right before content is transmitted to the client.

- The Global_PreRequestHandlerExecute and Global_PostRequest-HandlerExecute events fire just before a page or web service is about to execute and immediately after it has completed.

- The Global_ReleaseRequestState event happens when the application is through with the request state of an application.

- The Global_UpdateRequestCache event lets us know that the IIS is done fulfilling the request and that the page is now ready to be cached for future requests.

- The Global_AcquireRequestState event happens immediately before an .aspx page either acquires or reacquites state information from a running Web application.

- The Global_ResolveRequestCache event indicates that the cache could be out-of-date and need updating.

I should also point out that when the Global.asax is modified, the ASP.NET page framework will detect this modification and close all connections with users by sending the Application_OnEnd event to them. The application domain is then automatically restarted by the next request received, implementing the Application_OnStart event.

Security

Security can be a funny thing. Some individuals store their most valuable possessions within a million dollar vault at a financial institution but sleep in a domicile behind a twenty-dollar lock. Although sometimes this makes no sense, the point is that security is a very arbitrary thing, often justified by cost, convenience, and a sense of well-being.

It might make sense for an individual to allow a small-time Web hosting company to host his or her personal homepage, forced to succumb to the mercy of whatever authentication and other security measures that are available for a nominal cost each year. However, it might not be a good idea for a multibillion dollar corporation to do the same thing.

Determining the correct amount of security required to protect a site depends chiefly upon the value that is placed upon what being protected, as well as the likelihood that it could be stolen or damaged in the event of a successful break in. To prevent this from happening, it is often necessary to challenge a user through authentication before authorizing that user to do anything.

Authentication versus Authorization

The terms authentication and authorization sound so much alike, and without giving it much thought, it might easily be construed to mean the same thing. However, this is not the case at all. To authenticate someone means to acknowledge a relationship with them or to prove something. To authorize means to grant power or authority to do something.

Keep in mind that it is possible to authenticate a user without authorizing that user to do anything, and it is possible to authorize any user to perform an unlimited number of requests but to deny a specific authentication to keep that user from doing anything but attempting to log in.

With ASP.NET, all client communications are filtered through the Internet Information Server (IIS). It is the job of IIS to translate and, if optionally configured, to authenticate user requests before resources are returned to the client. Consider the Web service we built earlier in this chapter. The settings in the Web.config caused Network Authentication to take place before we could use the application. Once we were authenticated, we were then authorized. Because we have the ability to capture the name of users and their role, we can either authorize them to use the application or deny them access to the application. This can easily be achieved in very few lines of code.

ASP.NET uses IIS 5.0 as the primary host environment. There are five types of authentication methods available in IIS 5.0: basic, digest, Integrated Windows Authentication (with built-in NTLM or Kerberos support), anonymous, and certificate authentication. There are also three forms of built-in .NET authentication, including Windows, Forms, and Passport Authentication.

Basic authentication is a widely accepted method of authentication. A modal Network Login dialog box will appear in front of the Web form, forcing the user to authenticate with a valid Windows User Account through the Web server before being granted the ability to use the application.

Basic authentication is part of the HTTP specification, and is supported by most Web browsers. The only real downside to basic authentication is that user IDs and passwords are sent over the Internet in an unencrypted fashion. An individual with ill intentions and the correct equipment could possibly intercept this information.

Another form of authentication is digest authentication. New to IIS 5.0, this method of authentication sends the password information over the Internet in the form of a secure hash value. The downside to digest authentication is that it can only be completed if the domain server resolving the request possesses a plain-text copy of the requestor's password. Hence, the domain controller must be extremely secure from attacks.

The third form of authentication is Integrated Windows Authentication, which sends sensitive authentication information over the Internet in a cryptographic format. If the client is running IE 4.0 or higher and is on using a Windows-based system that is not connecting via proxy, IIS can be configured to use the built-in NTLM or Kerberos authentication systems.

A fourth method of authentication is anonymous authentication, giving users access to public areas of your Web site without prompting them for their username or password first. Windows uses the IUSR_YourComputerName Account, which is automatically included in the Guest Account of your PC's local users and groups. So, whatever security you have applied to the Guest Account, using the default settings or other ones, will also apply to the anonymous user, so be careful.

The fifth method of authentication is certificate authentication, which can use client certificates or server certificates for authentication through Secure Sockets Layer (SSL).

In the example we created earlier in this chapter, we took advantage of basic Windows authentication. It was a simple example that we created for our own use, so we weren't really concerned that our personal information was being sent in clear text. Also, we were accessing everything locally through the .NET IDE, so our requests were fulfilled on our own IIS servers and not strewn across our network to perform for URL or IP resolution.

In .NET, Forms Authentication is a means by which the application is responsible for authenticating a request. If the authentication is rejected, the request can be redirected to another form using client-side redirection. If the authentication is successful, a form that contains credentials for acquiring an identity is issued by the system. All requests made after a successful authentication will contain this form in the request header and are validated by an ASP.NET handler.

Passport Authentication is a very robust Microsoft Passport Single Sign-In (SSI) authentication system that offers customers an unparalleled level of security and interoperability between member sites. We will provide an example for configuring passport authentication later in this chapter.

Forms-Based Authentication

Upon the first request issued by any client to a server, that individual is redirected to a form that asks for an ID and password. Provided these two credentials match what the server is expecting, the server provides the client with a cookie that will be stored on the client's PC. The cookie is sent to the client in a cryptographic form and uniquely identifies who that person is.

Each time thereafter when the client makes a request to the server, this cookie is sent in the request header section and identifies that this user has been authenticated to use the site. The beauty of this is that it is established in the Web.config section of the ASP.NET solution:

```
<authentication mode = "Forms">
    <forms name="login.aspx" loginURL="A URL HERE"
           <credentials passwordFormat="SHA1">
                <user name="cole" password="MyPassword" />
           </credentials>
</authentication>
<authorization>
    <deny users="?"/>
</authorization>
```

In this example, the .NET application requires proof of authentication on a forms-based level, and if not found, the user will be redirected to the page shown in the loginURL attribute. If the user has already been authenticated, this information will have been included in the header section of the request.

In the following example, the users' credentials are checked before they are allowed to proceed:

```
Public Sub Login(ByVal sender as System.Object, ByVal e As
System.EventArgs)
     With System.Web.Security.FormsAuthentication
If(.Authenticate(txtUserID.Text, txtPassword.Text)) Then
.RedirectFromLoginPage(txtUserID.Text, False)
lblMySignOnStatus.Text = "Valid login"
             Else
lblMySignOnStatus.Text = "Invalid login"
             End If
     End With
End Sub
```

Cookies

Traditionally, cookies were HTTP text-only headers that were typically created by a hosting Web application and automatically stored on a user's hard drive by the user's browser. Cookies were ordered into memory and the HTTP header by the user's browser when requested by a hosting Web application.

As explained earlier in this chapter, cookies were a hit-and-miss sort of thing. If a user did not have cookies enabled as an option in their Web browser, then the attempt to read or write the cookie to and from the user's PC simply failed. If a cookie stored information like a username or password, and the option was disabled, the user would be forced to manually login each time the Web site required such credentials. To combat this issue, session variables were used to store the initial log in, so that the user was spared having to repetitiously log in each time the request for these credentials was issued by the Web server. But, an initial manual login would still be required each time a new session was used.

In ASP.NET, cookies have been retooled to work around those who disable cookies in their Web browsers. Cookies are now fused as part of the URL and can follow the navigation in this demeanor, similar to storing items in a QueryString, throughout the entire Web site. The example below shows you how to use cookies in ASP.NET by modifying the cookieless attribute in the sessionState tag of the Web.Config File:

```
<sessionState
mode="InProc"
stateConnectionString="tcpip=127.0.0.1:42424"
sqlConnectionString="data source=127.0.0.1;user id=sa;password="
cookieless="true"
timeout="20"
/>
```

Now, add the following lines of code into the Page_Load Event of an aspx.vb page and disable cookies in your Web browser.

```
Response.Cookies("MyUserName").Value = "Cole"
```

Run the page, and you will see something similar to the following in the URL of your Web browser:

```
http://localhost/WebApplication1/(ucgc1biy3jngowuo3zqi5m45)/WebForm1.aspx
```

If you view the source in your browser, you will also see the value of the cookie being used to identify the user.

Cookies are an ideal way to maintain state on the Web, because HTTP is a stateless protocol that does not inherently support persistence, making it difficult to distinguish one user from another. Thus, creating cookieless identifiers can assist in the proper identification of each user over the Internet, even if cookies are not supported in the client's Web browser.

Cookies store text-based information in name/value pairs as you saw in the previous example. Cookies are a great way of storing user identifiers and passwords so that the user can be easily identified the next time he or she accesses the Web site, eliminating the need for unnecessary reauthentications each time the Web site is visited.

Essentially, cookies can be anything you want to make them, because you are not limited to a specific genre of information that you can store in them, as long as what you are storing is text based. In a situation where cookies are enabled in the client's Web browser and used by the Web server, there are several essential parts of a cookie, including the name of the cookie, its value, the expiration date, the path, the domain, and the need for a secure connection in order to use the cookie.

The name and value attributes, better known as name/value pairs, and the path property are the most important of the aforementioned properties. You need to name your cookie, or you will never be able to locate it. Also, you'll probably want to supply a value to the name of the cookie; otherwise, there is really no point to creating it in the first place.

Additionally, the expiration property dictates how long the cookie will live before the information is no longer accessible, and the path property denotes the URL path within which the cookie is valid. If you store personal information in a cookie without setting this attribute, values might automatically stay in the HTTP header, so pages outside the path could potentially have access to your cookie information. If the path is not explicitly set, the path defaults to the URL path of the document that created the cookie.

Furthermore, the domain property extends the path property. By setting the domain property, you can allow multiple servers within the same domain to access the same cookie information or even assign cookies to be accessible to a single server on a domain.

Lastly, the secure connection property allows you to specify if the cookie property will only work over a secure connection, such as SSL. Because most sites do not use secure connections, the default value for this property is set to false.

Look at the code in the next paragraph. The class method, Values.Add, allows you to add a name and value to the HttpCookie object. The name/value pair will exist in the header of the Web documents that are passed between the client and server. You can expire the cookie by using the class method.Expires.AddMinutes(# of minutes). There are additional properties for the Expires method, including a range of expirations from .AddMilliseconds to .AddYears. You might even decide to never expire your cookie.

The following is an example of code that sets and gets traditional cookies. You can test this method by copying the following lines of code in the Page_Load event of an .aspx file, dropping a textbox control on the Webform, and running the code. The result should look like Figure 9.8.

```
'Declare local variables
        Dim objSetVoter As HttpCookie
        Dim objGetVoter As HttpCookie
        'Declare and set new reference to a Cookie.
        objSetVoter = New HttpCookie("OnlineVoterID")
        'Expire the cookie in one second.
        objSetVoter.Expires.AddSeconds(1)
        'Now create a voterID key and a
        'corresponding value.
        objSetVoter.Values.Add(txtOnlineVote.Text, _
            txtVoterName.Text)
        'Now append it to the response.
        Response.AppendCookie(objSetVoter)
        'Fill objGetCookie.
        objGetVoter = Request.Cookies("OnlineVoterID")
        'If populated, show the results in a textbox.
        If objGetVoter.Name <> "" Then
            txtMyResults.Text = objGetVoter.Value
        End If
```

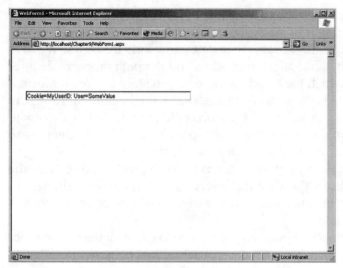

Figure 9.8 Expiring a traditional cookie.

As I mentioned in this section, for traditional cookies to work across HTTP, users must enable cookies in the Options Settings of the Web browser they are using. In the past, the single most frustrating thing about cookies was their dependence upon the settings of an individual's Web browser. If users decided to disable the use of cookies within their browser, you must have the ability to obtain the information elsewhere. In the case where a cookie was supposed to store a user ID and encrypted password for reauthentication on a machine the Enable Cookies property is disabled, the user will have to log in each time to recapture this information. This can be frustrating to a user who does not want to store cookies on their PC, as well as frustrating to a developer who watches the performance of their Web application deplete to some degree, as the application makes unnecessary trips to the database, or some other data storage medium, to look up the same values for a user, over and over again. ASP.NET allows us to overcome a situation where cookies use is not enabled in a user's Web browser, by adding the identifier to the URL.

Working with Passport Authentication

Microsoft Passport Authentication might be considered one of the easiest forms of authentication. The reason for this is that most of the authentication code is already taken care of for you behind the scenes. In order to test Passport Authentication, you must set up a Microsoft PREP Account. If you are familiar with a Microsoft Messenger Account, then a PREP Account should present no challenge to you. A PREP account is just like your Messenger Account, with the exception that it is for test purposes only.

In order to obtain a Microsoft PREP Account, please visit the following Web site: http://www.microsoft.com.

For more information, follow along with the section "Installing the Microsoft Passport SDK from the Web Site" later in this chapter.

It is important to remember that Microsoft Passport is still being developed. The information you will read is current as of the writing of this book. However, some of the information in this section might be outdated by the time the book is printed.

To test Microsoft Passport Authentication, log in to the PREP Account you created and modify the following lines of code in the Web.Config file of your .ASPX Page:

```
<authentication mode-"Passport">
    <passport redirectURL="internal"/>
</authentication>
<authorization>
    <deny users="?"/>
</authorization>
```

To learn more about becoming a Microsoft Passport member, please read the following.

Microsoft Passport is a single sign-in service and express purchase service that can be integrated into a participating Web site. There are many advantages to using the service, some of which follow. Microsoft Passport allows a Web server to offload authentication on an outside, yet central, source. A benefit to the client is that privileged information is provided to a single authority. User IDs and passwords need only be remembered by one site instead of many sites accessed on the Internet.

Imagine if users could sign on to every site on the Internet by using one user ID and password, without jeopardizing the integrity of their credentials. Microsoft Passport allows them to do just that by not forcing them to repeatedly enter confidential information into each Web site they visit. Their information is only entered at the time of the Passport sign up or when they edit personal information. Furthermore, from a server standpoint, Microsoft Passport offloads the responsibility of maintaining sensitive client information and allows for the *collection of shared information* that might normally be derived from several Web sites. Microsoft Passport also supplies shared information about members that can assist in marketing efforts. In addition, it provides other information that can assist in the personalization of a Web site, allowing users to feel catered to instead of canned, and it can gather information from users without annoying them.

This is possible because users sign up for Passport Services at a single location. They enter personal information only once. Much of the information requested is optional. Table 9.2 lists the information that must be supplied when creating a Passport account; the items that are not mandatory are indicated with an asterisk. It also shows the information that is shared across the Internet to Microsoft Passport-supporting Web sites. Most of the mandatory information that is shared applies to personalizing a site.

The users' language, your PUID (Passport Unique Identifier), and whether or not are under 13 years of age are the three items that are mandatory when signing up for Microsoft Passport, and they are shared across servers. This information allows a Web server to know what language format it should be using. The under 13 years of age allows a Web server to know if a child is accessing the Web site, allowing the host to tone down the content or deny the user if the content is too mature.

Currently, there are arguments that characterize Passport as being too intrusive. But, after careful examination, I have found this to be false. In Table 9.2, you gain an understanding of just how discrete the information you provide is to each participating Web site you visit. In reality, the only things that are shared are the PUID, whether or not you are under 13 years of age, and your language preference. Everything else is either optional or not shared.

The Passport Development Site

The following Web site, www.passport.com/SDKDocuments/SDK21/default. htm, is an MSN Web site that allows you to specify your system topology and automatically walks you through a step-by-step instructional tour for employing the Passport service on your Web site. The Express Purchase option on a subsequent Web site is platform independent. The benefit to using this site is that it will guide you through every step of the implementation, from getting started to after implementation.

A Final Walkthrough before Installation

Prior to installation, it is important to review the subsequent hardware, software, and operational requirements to ensure that the system that will be performing the installation of the Microsoft Passport Software Development Kit (SDK) is able to handle it. Also, it is important to remember that when you install the SDK, you should be logged on under the Administrator Account or at least make sure you have Administrative rights when installing under a User Account. This is because the SDK changes registry settings, installs files in the system folder, may stop and start critical services running on the PC, and installs virtual directories or ISAPI filters to the default Web site's root directory. So, if you are not an Administrator, or have Administrator privileges, these things cannot happen.

Installing the Microsoft Passport SDK from the Web Site

The best instructional methods for the installation of the SDK are on its Web site. To install the SDK from the Web site, access http://msdn.microsoft.com/downloads/default.asp?URL=/downloads/sample.asp?url=/msdn-files/027/001/644/msdncompositedoc.xml. There are several installation options to choose from, so be careful when choosing the ones that apply to you. It might be best to start with the Development/Test Site because you will probably test your site for functionality, accuracy, and integrity before actually deploying it for others to use. The remainder of our Passport examples will focus on the integration of a Web application with the Passport Deployment/Test Site.

Upon completion of the setup, the default.asp can be attempted. The next page is displayed. Click on the Microsoft Passport sign in and you are directed to the Microsoft Passport Member Service Sign In Screen. Type in the sign-in name and password you created to use for test, and click the Sign In button. Don't confuse this with your regular sign-in name and password, or you will be rejected and redirected to the previous page (see Figure 9.9).

Table 9.2 Shared Information

SHARED	NOT SHARED
Passport Unique Identifies (PUID)	Sign in Name
Zipcode, Region, Country*	Password
Birthdate*	Secret Question
Age Under 13 – Flag**	
Language Preference (LCID Format)	
Language Preference (LCID Format)	
Gender*	
Accessibility (ADA) (Boolean Value)*	
Nick Name*	
Preferred E-mail*	

* An optional field during Passport Member Registration. So, it is used only if it is provided.
**An optional field, so only if it was provided and only if the member is older than 13 years of age.

Figure 9.9   Member Services login.

For this example, we will use the SDK from the Web site and reboot when prompted. Look for the location of your installation on your hard drive. Then, open the Internet Services Manager and create a new virtual directory. From the wizard, browse to the location of the folder you created during the installation of the SDK. It will contain the following files: default.asp, logout.asp, LTDefault.asp, makefile, placefile, pleasewait.asp, signoutcheckmark (a quicktime player file), sources, and trans_pixel.

Open the Default.asp file in Internet Explorer. You should be taken to a site that forces you to log in with your MSPassport username and password. Figure 9.10 displays the results of your Microsoft Passport login. Listed below is what each of the labels means in the order they appear:

TicketAge is the difference in time between your last screen refresh and the time you initially logged in.

TimeSinceSignIn represents the total amount of time you have been logged on.

Accessibility denotes whether or not you allow other sites to share your public information.

Birthdate is the members entered date-of-birth.

Birthdate Precision represents the age range of the individual. Valid values are 0 through 5, depending upon the age of the individual and whether or not certain parts of their birthdate were not provided (e.g., the member might have withheld the month or day of their birth date).

City is the geographical identifier that corresponds with the member's entered city of residence.

Flags is a section that is reserved for network flags.

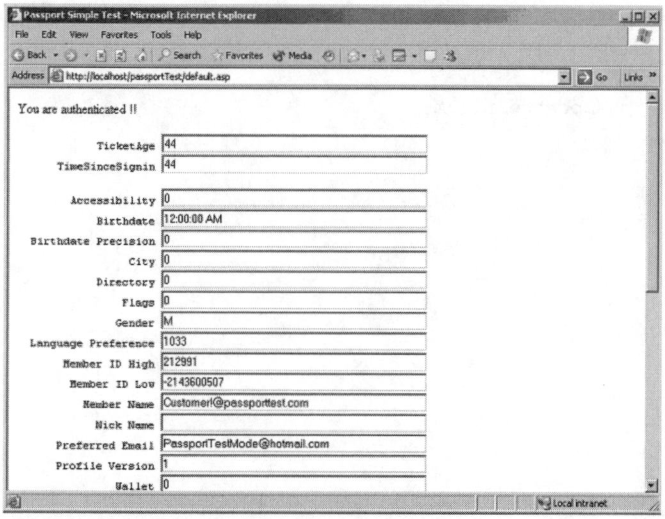

Figure 9.10 The default Passport screen.

Gender depicts the sex of the individual, "M" for male and "F" for female. This is an optional field, so other valid values are "U" for unknown and Null if the member did not supply gender information when signing up for a Passport Account.

Language Preference is the local identifier chosen by the user. It follows the LCID format.

Member ID High represents the upper portion of a member's PUID.

Member ID Low represents the lower portion of a member's PUID.

Member Name is the alternate name (i.e. nickname) specified by the user.

Preferred Email is the preferred email address as specified by the member during Passport signup.

Profile Version is the version of the profile used by the member.

Wallet is the result of whether or not the member has a wallet account associated with their Passport service.

Postal Code depicts the postal code in which the member resides.

Country ISO 3166-1 compliant country code that represents the zip code of the member.

Region the region in which the member resides.

For more information on the Microsoft Passport Core Profile Table, please go to http://msdn.microsoft.com/library/default.asp?url=/library/en-us/ppsdk14/Reference/miscref/r_profilecoretable.asp.

```
You are authenticatedILoveMyPassport
MemberIdLow:-910445580
MemberIdHigh:-1668754781
Member Name:Customer!@passporttest.com
Alias:ILoveMyPassport
Country:US
Postal Code:98052
Region:35841

Birthdate:2/11/1970
Gender:M


profileVersion:1
Flags:0

Your ticket is910 seconds old.
Now, modify the Web browser URL to point the default.asp file.
Congratulations, you are now an authenticated test site user and should
see a screen similar to the one in Figure 9.10. You are authenticated as
ILoveMyPassport!!
```

Your Passport Manager is currently in Test Mode (SiteID = 1). The Test Mode site is not yet known to the Login server's table of Site IDs, so it doesn't have the authority to sign out URLs. Therefore, clicking on the Sign Out link will redirect you to this test site.

Notice the message at the bottom of the screen. It says that Passport Manager is currently in Test Mode but that the Test Mode site is not yet known to the Login server's table of Site IDs to Sign Out URLs. For this reason, the Login server will be unable to log you out. Thus, the only way to log out at this point is to end the session by closing the browser. This will remain the case until Microsoft recognizes your site as a valid Passport Internet Site.

Right now, let's try out a nifty tool that will allow you to configure your test Passport site. Click on the Start button on the lower left-hand corner of your desktop, and then click Programs, Microsoft Passport, and Passport Administration Utility. This is the application that gives you the power to dictate the configuration of your Passport Web site. For convenience, we will use the default Web site that was provided with the SDK. Check out the default screen in Figure 9.11.

These are the defaults that command the site we accessed in Figure 9.10. Notice that the Install Dir points to the directory that contains the files created when you installed the SDK. You will also notice that the Time Window,

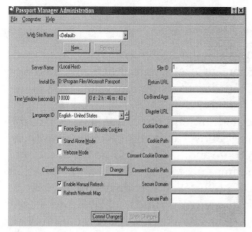

Figure 9.11 Passport Manager Administration.

shown in seconds, does not reflect the time that displayed in the http://localhost/passport/ltdefault.asp directory. However, if you attempt to modify the default site ID and commit the changes, the test site will no longer work properly. The site ID defaults to 1, denoting that the account is in test mode. Microsoft only grants the full core profile when you register your site with Microsoft on the Web.

Cobranding Your Site

Microsoft provides you with the ability to alter all the Microsoft Passport pages by applying cascading style sheets. This will allow you to apply your own look and feel to the Passport login screen.

Licensing Passport

To get approval to register your Passport Web site for public use, you will need to complete the following items:

1. Sign a non-exclusive service agreement with the Microsoft Corporation.

2. Make sure your site has been cobranded.

3. Provide Microsoft with the location of your Cobranding template file.

4. Make sure that your Web site complies with Microsoft's standards.

For additional details, please review the Microsoft Passport SDK.

Wrapping Up

Authentication can be applied by using a standard Microsoft Windows logon, basic authorization, forms authorization, or a standard Microsoft Passport logon, and security for a Web site can be driven using any one of the aforementioned authentication methods.

Microsoft Passport, the latest method of authentication added to the Microsoft Suite of authentication services, allows an integrated way of authenticating individuals logging on to a Web site and takes out some the additional code and hard drive space that is sometimes necessary to store authentication and personalized information. The SDK on the Web site makes it very easy to download and install Microsoft Passport service on almost all Windows-based PCs, and the development around the tool can be as simple or complex and the developer wishes to make it.

In the preceding example, the implementation of Microsoft Passport was extremely simplistic, but it gives you the idea of the fundamental tools and code that are necessary for getting a test site up and running. The templates and example that are installed with the SDK allow you to perform cobranding around your own custom Web site without having to start completely from scratch.

In Chapter 10, we will be walking through an entire application from start to finish, touching everything from a methodology for design and architecting a solution, to a project plan, and then right down to the development solution.

ASP.NET Application: A Walkthrough

If at first you don't succeed, get a bigger hammer.
Larry Brenner

This quote may seem out of place for the chapter, but I hope you'll see that it fits right in. We talked in Chapter 1 about the inherent difficulties with building traditional Web applications. We had to use the technological equivalent of bubble gum and baling wire to get the job done, and it wasn't always a success. After reading this book, you should be able to see how Visual Studio .NET, namely, Visual Basic .NET and ASP.NET, really is the bigger hammer for developers.

Now that we've explored the foundation and underlying parts of what you need to be productive with ASP.NET, its time to bring it all together. First, we're going to walk through the thought process and design documents behind the sample application. Next, will be a short look at why the planning process is very important, regardless of project size. Finally, we'll build some key parts of the Northwind Traders customer site to learn the why, what, and how.

The sample application I chose to build for this book is based on the Northwind Traders sample database that comes with SQL Server. Originally it was written in XML and used XSLT for rendering via XML for SQL Server (SQLXML.) Although the original sample application illustrates using XML from data to presentation tier, I thought this would be an interesting candidate for migration to .NET, showing that a Microsoft Visual Basic .NET application is more maintainable than a native XML application. The scenario is of a prototype for this fictional client, so that is the level of functionality that the sample has been designed for. Several outstanding examples of enterprise applications and books extensively cover this subject. One of the best that I've seen is the gasTIX demo application, which has been extensively tested and has some great features. You can find this application at gastix.net.

Why Plan?

It may seem ironic that we need to justify designing applications before building them. Ready, fire, aim appears to be the standard that sets our industry apart from other industries. A root cause might very well be that what we do is a blending of art and science, and that makes it difficult to tie down exactly what the requirements are at the beginning. Another root cause may be the tools themselves that allow us to rapidly create prototypes and proofs of concept, thereby empowering the user to exclaim "That's great! Let's just use this!"

It may appear, at first glance, that going through the design phase is a waste of time, especially given the ease with which we can now create the UI. And then there is the inevitable pressure from those who sponsor your projects, who might not always see the value, either. There are many great resources that cover this subject adequately, if not brilliantly. Check out the resources section for some recommendations. That said, I'm going to very briefly cover the topic and then illustrate the documentation and development mindset by focusing on several key parts of the Northwind application.

In the *Software Project Survival Guide* (Microsoft Press, 1997), Stephen McConnell illustrates why many, if not most, projects are doomed to failure. The main reason that approximately 70 percent of projects fail is that they suffer from a lack of planning and design. McConnell gives specific steps and practices to follow throughout the design and development phases. Here is an example of my recommended steps for the prototyping process:

Gather the Information.   It's important to gather the background information in order to understand and determine the problem. We have to figure out what the questions are before we can answer them, and gathering techniques that are available will help us do just that. In this example, we used user interviews and because there was an existing prototype on which to base our project, we give that a thorough examination.

Create the Vision/Scope.   We then take the information that was compiled and turn that into a vision statement. The vision statement is S.M.A.R.T.: It's specific, has a measured goal, is applicable to the problem, is realistic given available resources, and is time-based. The scope lists the feature set that will be included as we implement the vision statement and develop it into a solution. Any features not on this list will not be a part of this phase of the project.

Create the Functional Requirements/Specification. Based on the problem defined, the vision created, and the scope declared, we now move toward the actual design of the solution.

Build the Prototype. At this point, we begin the actual implementation and development work, creating and modifying stored procedures; building components; and developing forms, other user interfaces, and Web services. We'll also do some unit testing as well.

Conduct User Review. Once we've built the prototype and done an appropriate level of testing, we demonstrate it to the users and/or the project sponsors. Feedback is collected and, if the functionality of the prototype is acceptable, the user signs off. At this point, we put the feedback into the functional specification.

Amend Functional Specifications/Begin Development of Application. After making any necessary changes to the functional specification, we then begin development work on the application itself. It's important to realize that the prototype exists only to validate the proof of concept. Once that happens, it is thrown away and is not used in the actual application. We start development of the application from square one, using the functional specification as our guide.

As you can discern from these steps, the process enables the project team to create a successful prototype that fulfills the business requirement. The secret is in the process; having a plan allows you to answer the questions and also tells you what questions to ask. That said, let's walk through the design requirements for this project.

Northwind Traders Sample Application Documentation

For this walkthough, we're going to handle this project as I would any other—starting with the vision and scope and then working outward. Let's review the design documents created for this application, beginning with the business case.

Business Case

It's very important to build the business case. The relevance and necessity of the project must be laid out so that the project sponsor (the ones who have the funding) has a reason to fund it. Let's start out with the background.

Background

Northwind Traders, Inc., is a privately held food distribution company headquartered in Washington. Northwind has both domestic and international customers and suppliers. The company has a geographically distributed sales staff, with North American Operations and the Customer Service/Support Call Center located in Washington and European Operations located in London, England. Currently, the company relies on its quarterly catalog to transmit the bulk of its information to its customers, with additional telemarketing support provided by the Customer Service Support Call Center.

Northwind has relied heavily on its Distribution Information System (DIS). DIS is an Access database application that has been updated several times since its inception in Access 2.0. The current version of DIS is based on a client/server architecture, with most of the original functionality split between Microsoft Access 2000 as the client on the front end and a Microsoft SQL Server database as the server on the back end. The system is used for product inventory, sales analysis, invoice generation, order fulfillment and tracking, employee information, supplier information, and customer information. Although DIS has proven itself for Northwind's past requirements, it does not easily allow the sales staff access to current product and sales information in a timely manner, nor does it help to ease the load of the customer service and sales staff, whose primary vehicle for accepting customer orders has been email, fax, and over the phone.

Based on internal research by the company's executive staff, a Web-enabled n-tier architecture would allow the sales staff to be much more efficient by granting them access to up-to-date product information. It would also empower the management team to be more proactive in shaping Northwind's long-term market strategy through the use of real-time sales data and marketing information. This is a long-term goal. It has been decided by Northwind management that a business-to-consumer online presence is the most immediate need. However, it is crucial that the base functionality of the current system and the existing business processes be retained in the application.

The company has commissioned and developed a prototype of the consumer site that is written entirely using XML and related technologies. The prototype incorporates shopping cart functionality, the ability to check orders, and the assignment of a Northwind account representative to the new customer. Using Microsoft SQL Server 2000 native XML queries and extensible-style language transformations for flexibility, the overall site was impressive to the client in terms of overall appearance and site flow. The account management staff liked the ability to link contact information directly to the customer's session. The IT staff did not feel, however, that the site was maintainable or easily modifiable.

After learning about Microsoft Visual Basic .NET, Northwind commissioned a new prototype using .NET but retaining a majority of the existing functionality and overall look and feel of the original. The company would also like to add Web service functionality to this application to provide catalog information to clients directly.

Project Documentation

Here is the project documentation for the prototype. Countless books have been written on the subject of great design practices. I wrote the following as a quick but practical design guide.

Vision/Scope

The vision statement provides a high level guideline of the solution that is to be developed. The scope states exactly what features will be included in the vision implementation.

Vision Statement

Rearchitect the distribution information system consumer prototype into an n-tier architecture proof of concept that maintains the existing functionality, allows greater maintainability by Northwind personnel, and exposes a catalog web service prototype by the end of fiscal year 2002.

Application Scope

The Distribution Information System, Phase 1 will include the look and feel of the XML-based version and the following functionality:

- Ability to browse and order current products
- Ability to check account status
- Ability to get sales agent information
- A catalog Web service

Functional Specification

The functional requirements/specification lays out the information needed to develop the application. We include the architecture, data model, component functionality, and other related information, such as, in our case, a Web service.

Architecture

Figure 10.1 illustrates the architecture of the prototype. This diagram lays out the components and the respective tiers.

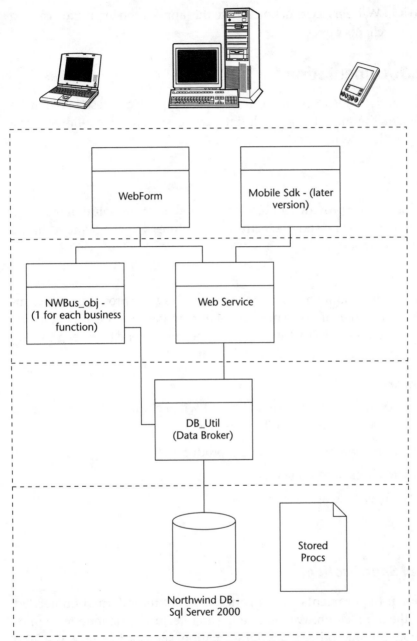

Figure 10.1 Architectural diagram of the Northwind prototype.

Components

Much of the core functionality will be included in the Northwind namespace, which will contain the backbone of the system. The architectural layout of the contained classes within it is as follows:

DBUtil.   Responsible for generic database functionality: data tier.

DB_Products.   Responsible for product-related functionality: business/data tier.

DB_Customers.   Responsible for customer-related functionality outside of ordering: business/presentation tier.

DB_Orders.   Responsible for order and order detail related functionality: business/presentation tier.

NWShoppingCart.   Responsible for shopping cart functionality: business tier.

Data Model

The Northwind data model consists of 13 tables, 14 views, and 27 stored procedures. In Figure 10.2, you can see the relationships of the tables as well as the tables themselves. As in many other databases you've worked on or developed, this database uses primary and foreign keys to establish the relationships. We'll look at the stored procedures and added database functionality in the next section.

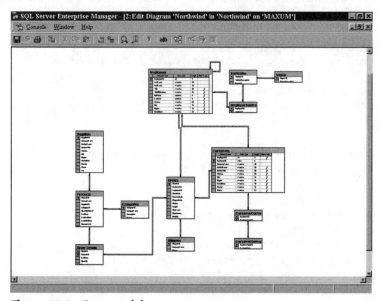

Figure 10.2   Data model.

Examining the Data Store

The data store for the prototype is based upon the Northwind sample database included with SQL Server 2000. Because this is based on an earlier prototype with an existing database, it's important to examine the data store as one of the first stages. We do this to understand if any additional changes need to be made. The Northwind database has been modified with the following changes:

- Agents stored procedure/functionality
- Stored procedures

Agent's Stored Procedure and Functionality

The purpose of the agent is to connect the customer with a Northwind sales representative on the Web site upon login. The GetCustomerAgentInfo stored procedure provides the information via SQLXML upon customer login. As outlined in the scope, this is a necessary requirement for successful implementation.

The SQL itself is relatively simple, using an alias on the employees table (agent) and tying it to the customers table by the customer ID. We'll use this information on the customer's personal shopping page to acquaint (or reacquaint) the customer with their sales rep as needed. The following is the Get-CustomerAgent stored procedure. Once again, we use stored procedures for our lower-level data access. This gives us the ability to secure the data because the stored procedures can be restricted to specific user accounts. Another advantage is that stored procedures are precompiled so that they can be accessed faster. We discussed data-related matters in Chapter 8.

```
CREATE PROCEDURE GetCustomerAgentInfo @@custid varchar(40) AS
     SELECT Agent.firstname, agent.lastname, agent.titleofcourtesy,
agent.extension, agent.photo
     FROM Employees As Agent, Customers
     WHERE Customers.CustomerID=@@custid AND
Customers.EmployeeID=Agent.EmployeeID
```

The information is extracted in the following code into the AgentInfo class and put into the highlighted fields in Figure 10.3.

```
Do While nwDataReader.Read
     'populate our agent object for return
     With AgentInfo1
         .FirstName = CStr(nwDataReader.GetString(0))
         .LastName = CStr(nwDataReader.GetString(1))
         .TitleOFCourtesy = CStr(nwDataReader.GetString(2))
         .Extension = CStr(nwDataReader.GetString(3))
         .Photo = nwDataReader.GetSqlBinary(4)
```

```
            End With
        Loop
        Return AgentInfo1
        nwDataReader.Close()
Public Class AgentInfo
    Public FirstName As String
    Public LastName As String
    Public TitleOFCourtesy As String
    Public Extension As String
    Public Photo As SqlBinary = New SqlBinary()
End Class
```

In keeping with the n-tier architectural philosophy, we'll retrieve our customer information in the following class. This allows us ready-made access to just the information we need.

```
Public Class CustomerInfo
    Public EmployeeID As Int32
    Public CustomerID As String
    Public CompanyName As String
    Public ContactName As String
    Public ContactTitle As String
    Public Address As String
    Public City As String
    Public Region As String
    Public PostalCode As String
    Public Country As String
    Public Phone As String
    Public Fax As String
End Class
```

Notice that all the information we need is contained in the class for easy access.

NOTE I chose to use custom classes, such as the one above, simply for convenience. Even though it maintains state, we have all the information needed without having to make another trip to the database.

In the following class, NWCustomerInfo, we retrieve and format all of the customer-related information that we'll need so that the customer can shop:

```
Public Class NWCustomerinfo
    Public Function GetCustomerAgentInfo(ByVal CustID As String) As
AgentInfo
        Dim nwDataReader As SqlDataReader
        Dim ds As DataSet = New DataSet()
        Dim AgentInfo1 As AgentInfo = New AgentInfo()
        Dim nwConn1 = New SqlConnection("user id=sa;password=;initial
```

```
catalog=northwind;data source=maxum;Connect Timeout=30")
        Dim nwCommand As SqlCommand = New SqlCommand()
        With nwCommand
            .CommandText = "GetCustomerAgentInfo"
            'set the type for stored procedure
            .CommandType = CommandType.StoredProcedure
            .Connection = nwConn1
            .Connection.Open()
            'create and add the parameters
            Dim mycParm As SqlParameter = .Parameters.Add("@@CustID",
SqlDbType.NVarChar, 40)
            'set direction for parms
            mycParm.Direction = ParameterDirection.Input
            'assign value to parms
            mycParm.Value = CustID
            'execute
            nwDataReader = .ExecuteReader(CommandBehavior.SingleRow)
        End With
```

NOTE Take notice of the use of the DataReader in this example. It gives better performance than a data set, and because we aren't updating, this makes a good choice. We then extract the data into the appropriate classes in the remaining part of this code (following) and send it on its way:

```
        Do While nwDataReader.Read
            'populate our agent object for return
            With AgentInfo1
                .FirstName = CStr(nwDataReader.GetString(0))
                .LastName = CStr(nwDataReader.GetString(1))
                .TitleOFCourtesy = CStr(nwDataReader.GetString(2))
                .Extension = CStr(nwDataReader.GetString(3))
                .Photo = nwDataReader.GetSqlBinary(4)
            End With
        Loop
        Return AgentInfo1
        nwDataReader.Close()

    End Function
```

In the Page_Load event for Default.aspx, we'll use the information that the customer-related classes provide. This allows us to initialize the content, extract the information provided by our objects, and populate the controls accordingly as needed.

NOTE We only want to load certain things once; hence the majority of the code is within the If Not Page.ispostback block, for performance sake.

```
Private Sub Page_Load(ByVal sender As System.Object, ByVal e As
System.EventArgs) Handles MyBase.Load
        'Put user code to initialize the page here
        If Not Page.IsPostBack Then
            Dim CustID As String = Response.Cookies("NWAppCustID").Value
            Dim nwCust1 As Northwind.NWCustomerinfo = New
Northwind.NWCustomerinfo()
            Dim nwCustInfo As Northwind.CustomerInfo =
nwCust1.GetCustomerInfo(CustID)
            Dim nwCustAgentInfo As Northwind.AgentInfo =
nwCust1.GetCustomerAgentInfo(CustID)
        'Extract the Information from the agent object and put it into
        'the appropriate controls
            With nwCustAgentInfo
                With nwCustInfo
                    litCompanyName.Text() = .CompanyName
                    litCustID.Text() = .CustomerID
                    litCustFullName.Text() = .ContactName
        'Use the DBObject to grab the photo directly from the database
                    imgAgent.ImageUrl =
"/enw/dbobject/Employees[@EmployeeID='" & .EmployeeID & "']/@Photo"
                End With
                litAgentFullName.Text() = .TitleOFCourtesy & "." &
.FirstName & " " & .LastName
                litAgentPicName.Text() = .FirstName & " " & .LastName
                litExtension.Text() = .Extension
            End With
        End If
    End Sub
```

The information is extracted from the stored procedure and then populated in an instance of the AgentInfo class, which is then returned to the Page_Load Event of CustomerPortal.aspx. The information is then loaded into each control, with strings loaded into literal Web service controls, and the photo is directly loaded into the image controls' ImageURL property via a SQLXML DBObject call. I chose the literal field because it is lightweight and designed for exactly this purpose.

The highlighted fields in Figure 10.3 illustrate the literal control placement within the template, which allows for customization for each customer and its corresponding agent.

Stored Procedures

Now let's take a look at the stored procedures in the Northwind data store. The ones currently in use in the prototype are listed fully with a short explanation of functionality.

CustOrdersDetail. This procedure is used to extract an existing order detail from the database. Notice that the discount is being factored in automatically.

```
CREATE PROCEDURE CustOrdersDetail @OrderID int
AS
SELECT ProductName,
    UnitPrice=ROUND(Od.UnitPrice, 2),
    Quantity,
    Discount=CONVERT(int, Discount * 100),
    ExtendedPrice=ROUND(CONVERT(money, Quantity * (1 - Discount) *
Od.UnitPrice), 2)
FROM Products P, [Order Details] Od
WHERE Od.ProductID = P.ProductID and Od.OrderID = @OrderID
```

CustOrdersOrders. This procedure is used to extract an existing order from the database. The information can then be combined with the order detail information.

```
CREATE PROCEDURE CustOrdersOrders @CustomerID nchar(5)
AS
SELECT OrderID,
    OrderDate,
    RequiredDate,
    ShippedDate
FROM Orders
WHERE CustomerID = @CustomerID
ORDER BY OrderID
```

Alfreds Futterkiste

Your Customer ID Code: ALFKI

Dear Maria Anders,

As a valued customer you are the most important person at our company.

Janet Leverling

If you have any questions that you do not find answered on our site, please do not hesitate to call your Northwind Trading personal agent, Sales Representative **Ms. Janet Leverling** at our international *toll free* number +**800-NORTHWIND** extension x3355 or by email.

Figure 10.3 Agent information panel.

GetCategoriesProductsParam. This procedure is used to extract products within categories from the database:

```
CREATE PROCEDURE GetCategoriesProductsParam  @@catid int  AS
SELECT
categories.categoryname,Products.ProductId,Products.ProductName,Produc
ts.QuantityperUnit, Products.UnitPrice FROM Categories, Products WHERE
Products.CategoryID=Categories.CategoryID AND
Categories.CategoryID=@@catid
```

GetCustomerAgentInfo. As previously discussed, this stored procedure links a given customer with its sales representative, called an agent:

```
CREATE PROCEDURE GetCustomerAgentInfo @@custid varchar(40) AS
     SELECT Agent.firstname, agent.lastname, agent.titleofcourtesy,
agent.extension, agent.photo
     FROM Employees As Agent, Customers
     WHERE Customers.CustomerID=@@custid AND
Customers.EmployeeID=Agent.EmployeeID
```

GetOrders. The GetOrders stored procedure will return all relevant order information, including order detail information, fully formatted as XML:

```
CREATE PROCEDURE GetOrders @@ordid varchar(40) AS
     SELECT 1 As Tag,
            NULL As Parent,
            Orders.OrderID as [Order!1!OrderID],
                 Orders.OrderDate as [Order!1!OrderDate!element],
                 Orders.RequiredDate as
[Order!1!RequiredDate!element],
                 Orders.ShippedDate as [Order!1!ShippedDate!element],
                 Orders.Freight as [Order!1!FreightCost!element],
                 NULL AS [ShippingAddress!2!Name!element],
                 NULL AS [ShippingAddress!2!Address!element],
                 NULL AS [ShippingAddress!2!City!element],
                 NULL AS [ShippingAddress!2!Region!element],
                 NULL AS [ShippingAddress!2!Country!element],
                 NULL AS [Shipper!3!ShipperID],
                 NULL AS [Shipper!3!CompanyName!element],
                 NULL AS [Agent!4!AgentID],
                 NULL AS [Agent!4!Name!element],
                 NULL AS [Agent!4!Photo]
     FROM Orders
     WHERE Orders.OrderID=@@ordid
     UNION ALL
     SELECT
2,1,NULL,NULL,NULL,NULL,NULL,Orders.ShipName,Orders.ShipAddress,

Orders.ShipCity,Orders.ShipRegion,Orders.ShipCountry,NULL,NULL,NULL,
NULL,NULL
     FROM Orders
```

```
    WHERE Orders.OrderID=@@ordid
    UNION ALL
    SELECT
3,1,NULL,NULL,NULL,NULL,NULL,NULL,NULL,NULL,NULL,NULL,Shippers.
ShipperID,Shippers.CompanyName,NULL,NULL,NULL
    FROM Orders INNER JOIN Shippers ON
Orders.ShipVia=Shippers.ShipperID
    WHERE Orders.OrderID=@@ordid
    UNION ALL
    SELECT
4,1,NULL,NULL,NULL,NULL,NULL,NULL,NULL,NULL,NULL,NULL,NULL,
Employees.EmployeeID,
    Employees.FirstName+'
'+Employees.LastName,'http://localhost/enw?sql=select+photo+from+
employees+where+employeeid='+convert(varchar,Employees.EmployeeID)+
'&amp;contenttype=image/jpeg'
    FROM Orders INNER JOIN Employees ON
Orders.EmployeeID=Employees.EmployeeID
    WHERE Orders.OrderID=@@ordid
    FOR XML EXPLICIT
```

GetProductListPhoto.   The GetProductListPhoto stored procedure returns product information along with a photo:

```
CREATE PROCEDURE GetProductListPhoto AS
            SELECT *
            FROM Products, Categories, Suppliers
            WHERE Products.SupplierID=Suppliers.SupplierID
                AND Products.CategoryID=Categories.CategoryID
              AND Products.Highlight=1
                AND DATALENGTH(Products.Photo) > 0
CREATE PROCEDURE GetProductSupplierInfo @@prodid varchar(40) AS
    SELECT *
    FROM Products, Suppliers
    WHERE Products.ProductID=@@prodid
      AND Products.SupplierID=Suppliers.SupplierID
    FOR XML AUTO
```

GetShippingOrderInfo.   This stored procedure returns complete shipper information, by order, in a custom format as XML:

```
CREATE PROCEDURE GetShippingOrderInfo @@shipid varchar(40) AS
    SELECT 1 As Tag,
          NULL As Parent,
          Shippers.ShipperID AS [Shipper!1!ShipperID!id],
                Shippers.CompanyName AS
[Shipper!1!CompanyName!element],
                NULL as [Order!2!ShippedBy!idref],
                NULL as [Order!2!OrderID!id],
                NULL as [Order!2!OrderDate!element],
                NULL as [Order!2!RequiredDate!element],
```

```
                          NULL AS [ShippingAddress!3!OrderID!idref],
                          NULL AS [ShippingAddress!3!Name!element],
                          NULL AS [ShippingAddress!3!Address!element],
                          NULL AS [ShippingAddress!3!City!element],
                          NULL AS [ShippingAddress!3!Region!element],
                          NULL AS [ShippingAddress!3!Country!element],
                          NULL AS [Items!4!OrderID!idref],
                          NULL AS [Item!5!OrderID!idref],
                          NULL AS [Item!5!ProductID!id],
                          NULL AS [Item!5!Quantity!element],
                          NULL AS [Item!5!ProductName!element]
        FROM Shippers
        WHERE Shippers.ShipperID=@@shipid
        UNION ALL
        SELECT 2,1,
                Orders.ShipVia,
                      NULL,
                      Orders.ShipVia,
                      Orders.OrderID,
                      Orders.OrderDate,
                      Orders.RequiredDate,
                      Orders.OrderID,
                      Orders.ShipName,
                      Orders.ShipAddress,
                      Orders.ShipCity,
                      Orders.ShipRegion,
                      Orders.ShipCountry,
                      NULL,
                      NULL,
                      NULL,
                      NULL,
                      NULL
        FROM Orders
        WHERE Orders.ShipVia=@@shipid AND ShippedDate IS NULL
        UNION ALL
        SELECT
3,2,Orders.ShipVia,NULL,Orders.ShipVia,Orders.OrderID,Orders.OrderDate
,Orders.RequiredDate,Orders.OrderID,Orders.ShipName,Orders.ShipAddress
,Orders.ShipCity,Orders.ShipRegion,Orders.ShipCountry,NULL,NULL,NULL,
NULL,NULL
        FROM Orders
        WHERE Orders.ShipVia=@@shipid AND ShippedDate IS NULL
        UNION ALL
        SELECT
4,2,Orders.ShipVia,NULL,Orders.ShipVia,Orders.OrderID,NULL,NULL,Orders
.OrderID,NULL,NULL,NULL,NULL,NULL,Orders.OrderID,NULL,NULL,NULL,NULL
        FROM Orders
        WHERE Orders.ShipVia=@@shipid AND ShippedDate IS NULL
        UNION ALL
        SELECT
5,4,Orders.ShipVia,NULL,Orders.ShipVia,Orders.OrderID,NULL,NULL,Orders
```

```
.OrderID,NULL,NULL,NULL,NULL,NULL,Orders.OrderID,[Order
Details].OrderID,[Order Details].ProductID,[Order
Details].Quantity,Products.ProductName
    FROM [Order Details], Orders, Products
    WHERE Products.ProductID=[Order Details].ProductID
      AND [Order Details].OrderID=Orders.OrderID
      AND Orders.ShipVia=@@shipid
      AND ShippedDate IS NULL
      AND Products.UnitsInStock >= [Order Details].Quantity
    ORDER BY
[Shipper!1!ShipperID!id],[Order!2!OrderID!id],Tag,[ShippingAddress!3!
OrderID!idref],[Items!4!OrderID!idref],[Item!5!OrderID!idref]
    FOR XML EXPLICIT
```

GetShoppingCartInfo.   If we chose to use the sqlserver state engine, the stored procedure would be useful for returning the shopping cart information. We are using the in-process state management, so this is not necessary.

```
CREATE PROCEDURE GetShoppingCartInfo @@sid varchar(40) AS
SELECT * FROM Cart,Products, Categories WHERE
Cart.ProductID=Products.ProductID AND
Products.CategoryID=Categories.CategoryID AND Cart.Session=@@sid FOR
XML AUTO
```

GetTop3Products.   This stored procedure displays the top three products that haven't been purchased by the customer. This is useful for moving merchandise that has been sitting around:

```
CREATE PROCEDURE GetTop3Products @@custid varchar(40) AS
        select top 3 Products.*
        from Products
        where Highlight=1
          and ProductID NOT IN (select OrderDetails.ProductID
                                        from [order details]
OrderDetails,Orders
                                                where
Orders.CustomerID=@@custid
                                                        and
OrderDetails.OrderID=Orders.OrderID)
        order by Products.UnitPrice
```

GetTop6Products.   This stored procedure displays the top six products that are regularly purchased by the customer. It is the data that is displayed upon login.

```
CREATE PROCEDURE GetTop6Products @@custid varchar(40) AS
select top 6
Products.ProductId,Products.ProductName,Products.QuantityperUnit,
Products.UnitPrice
```

```
                      from Products
                      where ProductID IN (
                                                select top 6
Products.ProductID
                                                from [order details]
OrderDetails,Orders,Products
                                                where
Orders.CustomerID=@@custid
                                                        and
OrderDetails.OrderID=Orders.OrderID
                                                        and
OrderDetails.ProductID=Products.ProductID
                                                group by Products.ProductID
                                                order by
SUM(OrderDetails.Quantity) DESC )
              OR ProductID IN (
                                                select top 3
Products.ProductID
                                                from [order details]
OrderDetails,Orders,Products
                                                where
Orders.CustomerID=@@custid
                                                        and
OrderDetails.OrderID=Orders.OrderID
                                                        and
OrderDetails.ProductID=Products.ProductID
                                                group by Products.ProductID
                                                order by
SUM(OrderDetails.Quantity) )
```

Login. This stored procedure verifies the username and password that has been entered by the customer:

```
CREATE PROCEDURE Login @@uid char(5), @@pwd varchar(10)  AS
SELECT CustomerID FROM Customers WHERE Customers.CustomerID=@@uid AND
Customers.[Password]=@@pwd
```

Ten Most Expensive Products. This stored procedure allows Northwind to get the most expensive stuff out in front on its clients. This data is the first they see upon entering the site.

```
CREATE procedure [Ten Most Expensive Products] AS
SET ROWCOUNT 10
SELECT     ProductName AS TenMostExpensiveProducts, QuantityPerUnit,
Photo, UnitPrice
FROM       Products
ORDER BY UnitPrice DESC
```

The Northwind database has other stored procedures that are not being used but were created as part of the original prototype. By browsing through them in the database, you may come up with some uses yourself.

Implementing the Data Tier

Our data tier primarily consists of the DB_Utils component. It's our custom data access component. By using a single point of access, we're providing a high level of maintainability by centralizing data functions and providing application longevity by abstracting data access from the other tiers. The data tier will communicate with parameterized stored procedures to return just the data needed. This provides greater control over who sees the data, and it provides for business rule storage in the data tier if the architecture should call for it.

Related to the data tier is the issue of where to store the connection string. In COM+, we'd use a constructor in the application package. In .NET, however, we'll use Web.config to hold this information. It's a good idea to keep this information in one spot where it can be easily updated. Let's take a look and see exactly how to do that. You begin by adding a section inside of the Web.config file for your connection string:

```
<configuration><appsettings>
<add key="NWconnection"
VALUE="server=MAXUM; uid=sa; pwd=; database=northwind" />
</appsettings>
</configuration>
```

You use it from your application code in the following manner:

```
StrNWConn = ConfigurationSettings.AppSettings.("NWConnection")
```

There is currently a single method in this component that is used for login purposes. It simply passes in the username and password as parameters to the GetLogin stored procedure and returns the customer ID as a string.

Implementing the Business Tier

The business tier contains the processing functionality that encapsulates the business rules for Northwind. We break this functionality into the following components, starting with the Customer component. Because the functional specification stated that the original functionality of the application needed to be maintained, we can accomplish this through these components.

Customer Component

The customer component deals with extracting and formatting the customer information to send to the performance tier:

```
Public Function GetCustomerInfo(ByVal CustID As String) As CustomerInfo
      Dim nwDataReader As SqlDataReader
      Dim CustInfo1 As CustomerInfo = New CustomerInfo()
      Dim nwConn1 = New SqlConnection("user id=sa;password=;initial
catalog=northwind;data source=maxum;Connect Timeout=30")
      Dim nwCommand As SqlCommand = New SqlCommand()
      With nwCommand
          .CommandText = "GetCustomerInfoPara"
          'set the type for stored procedure
          .CommandType = CommandType.StoredProcedure
          .Connection = nwConn1
          .Connection.Open()
          'create and add the parameters
          Dim mycParm As SqlParameter = .Parameters.Add("@@CustID",
SqlDbType.NVarChar, 40)
          'set direction for parms
          mycParm.Direction = ParameterDirection.Input
          'assign value to parms
          mycParm.Value = CustID
          'execute
          nwDataReader = .ExecuteReader()
      End With

      Do While nwDataReader.Read

          With CustInfo1
              .EmployeeID = CInt(nwDataReader.GetInt32(0))
              .CustomerID = CStr(nwDataReader.GetString(1))
              .CompanyName = CStr(nwDataReader.GetString(2))
              .ContactName = CStr(nwDataReader.GetString(3))
              .ContactTitle = CStr(nwDataReader.GetString(4))
          End With
      Loop

      Return custinfo1
      nwDataReader.Close()
   End Function
```

In this case, we use the GetTop6Products to retrieve the six most requested products by the given customer:

```
Public Function GetTop6Products(ByVal CustID As String) As DataSet
      Dim nwDataAdapter As SqlDataAdapter = New SqlDataAdapter()
      Dim CustInfo1 As CustomerInfo = New CustomerInfo()
      Dim nwConn1 = New SqlConnection("user id=sa;password=;initial
catalog=northwind;data source=maxum;Connect Timeout=30")
      Dim nwCommand As SqlCommand = New SqlCommand()
      Dim NWTop6 As DataSet = New DataSet()
      With nwCommand
          .CommandText = "GetTop6Products"
```

```
                   'set the type for stored procedure
                   .CommandType = CommandType.StoredProcedure
                   .Connection = nwConn1
                   .Connection.Open()
                   'create and add the parameters
                   Dim mycParm As SqlParameter = .Parameters.Add("@@CustID",
          SqlDbType.NVarChar, 40)
                   'set direction for parms
                   mycParm.Direction = ParameterDirection.Input
                   'assign value to parms
                   mycParm.Value = CustID
                   'execute
                   nwDataAdapter.SelectCommand = nwCommand
                   nwDataAdapter.Fill(NWTop6)
               End With
               Return NWTop6
           End Function
```

Product Component

The product component is what we use to populate product information in the Web site. It's important to note that this code is also used to retrieve product information for the entire site and return it to the calling page as a data set. The page then takes the information and can use it however it needs to.

```
Public Function GetProductsByCategory(ByVal CatID As Integer) As DataSet
        Dim nwDataAdapter As SqlDataAdapter = New SqlDataAdapter()
        Dim nwConn1 = New SqlConnection("user id=sa;password=;initial
catalog=northwind;data source=maxum;Connect Timeout=30")
        Dim nwCommand As SqlCommand = New SqlCommand()
        Dim NWCatProd As DataSet = New DataSet()
        With nwCommand
            .CommandText = "GetCategoriesProductsParam"
            'set the type for stored procedure
            .CommandType = CommandType.StoredProcedure
            .Connection = nwConn1
            .Connection.Open()
            'create and add the parameters
            Dim mycParm As SqlParameter = .Parameters.Add("@@CatID",
SqlDbType.NVarChar, 40)
            'set direction for parms
            mycParm.Direction = ParameterDirection.Input
            'assign value to parms
            mycParm.Value = CatID
            'execute
            nwDataAdapter.SelectCommand = nwCommand
            nwDataAdapter.Fill(NWCatProd)
        End With
        Return NWCatProd
    End Function
```

Shopping Cart Component

The shopping cart component holds the information as the customer shops online. The Add method is where items are added in preparation for check out, checking for like items and incrementing the quantity if necessary or adding a new entry. The LineTotal method computes and returns the total as a string. The shopping cart itself consists of CartItem objects, which contain the properties necessary for later purchase of the specific item.

```
Public arrNWShoppingCart As New ArrayList()
 Public Class CartItem
     Public ProductID As Integer
     Public ProductName As String
     Public Quantity As Integer
     Public UnitPrice As Double
     Private LineTotal As Double
 End Class

 Public Function LineTotal() As String
     Dim LineItem As CartItem
     For Each LineItem In arrNWShoppingCart
         LineTotal = LineItem.Quantity * LineItem.UnitPrice
     Next
     Return String.Format("{0:c}", LineTotal)
 End Function

 Public Sub Add(ByVal Line As CartItem)
     Dim LineItem As CartItem
     For Each LineItem In arrNWShoppingCart
         If Line.ProductID = LineItem.ProductID Then
             LineItem.Quantity += 1
             Return
         End If
     Next

     arrNWShoppingCart.Add(Line)
 End Sub
```

We started with the data store and then examined the components in the data and business tiers. We also included in the business tier a Web service to return the current catalog as a data set to customers so that they can use that information on their own Web sites or however they choose. The important point here, as we also learned in Chapter 7, is that Web services enable us to have the benefits of using resources and applications without having to be responsible for storing them.

Web Services

Part of the prototype was to add Web services functionality that would provide catalog information to customers. In our case, the customer will always have an updated catalog of the Northwind products to use for ordering without having to download or request the latest copy. As products are updated in the database, they are updated for the customer via the Web service that is provided.

Let's explore the steps to create a catalog data set that uses a data connection from within the Server Explorer. In our example, we are going to expose our product information for ease of ordering.

1. Create a new ASP.NET Web service Visual Basic project. Name it NorthwindService1.

2. In the Server Explorer, expand Servers, <NAME OF YOUR SERVER>, SQL Servers, < NAME OF YOUR SERVER >, Northwind, Tables.

3. Click and drag the Products table onto the Web service design surface.

4. Right-click on the Web service design surface and select Generate Dataset.

    Let's create an XML data set called NWCatalog. This is what the Web service will return.

5. In the Generate Dataset dialog box, enter NWCatalog in the New field for the data set name.

6. Click the OK button to add a data set that defines the data schema that we specified.

7. Double-click the NWCatalog.xsd file in the Solution Explorer window to preview the data.

8. Right-click on the Designer, select View Code.

9. Place your cursor on the line immediately following Inherits System.Web.Services.WebService, and type the following code:

```
<WebMethod()> Public Function GetNorthwindCatalog() As NWCatalog

        Dim NWDataSet As New NWCatalog()
        SqlDataAdapter1.Fill(NWDataSet)
        Return NWDataSet


    End Function
```

The <WebMethod> exposes the function through the Web service. We'll use this for testinf. Notice also that we're using an instance of our catalog data set, filling it, and passing the data set back. The end result should look like this:

```
Public Class NorthwindService1
  Inherits System.Web.Services.WebService
<WebMethod()> Public Function GetNorthwindCatalog() As NWCatalog
        Dim NWDataSet As New NWCatalog()
        SqlDataAdapter1.Fill(NWDataSet)
```

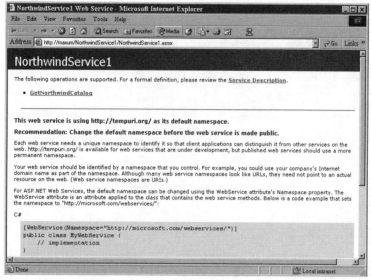

Figure 10.4 Web service diagnostic page.

```
        Return NWDataSet
    End Function

End Class
```

10. Build and run the application. The Web service will display a diagnostic page similar to Figure 10.4.

11. Click on the GetNorthwindCatalog link on the page and the screen shown in Figure 10.5 will appear.

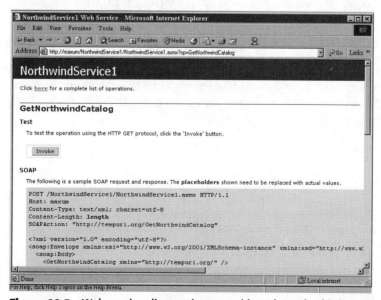

Figure 10.5 Web service diagnostic page with Web method information.

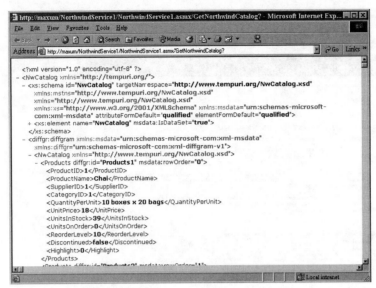

Figure 10.6 Web service return page.

12. Click Invoke. The Web service will return the results as XML, as displayed in Figure 10.6.

Implementing the Presentation Tier

The presentation layer within our prototype consists of several Web forms and a cascading style sheet. Let's examine each, starting with the style sheet.

The NorthWind Cascading Style Sheet

Cascading style sheets are very important within the presentation layer for maintaining a consistent look and feel throughout the entire application. Here is the style sheet used for the prototype, which helps to fulfill the look and feel requirement in the functional specification:

```
td.newsheader { font-size: 9pt; font-family: Tahoma; font-weight: bold }
table          { }
input          { font-weight: bold }
h1             { font-size: 24pt; font-family: Arial Black }
td             { font-size: 9pt; color:#506399 }
span.copyright { font-family: Arial; font-size: 8pt }
span.productname { font-family:Arial;font-weight:bold;font-size:10pt;color:white}
span.quantity {font-size:8pt;color:#DDDDDD}
span.price     { font-size:9pt;color:white}
td.news        { font-size: 8pt; font-family: Tahoma }
body { font-weight: bold;   background-image: url(Images/backgrd.gif); }
```

This is then saved in the project as NorthWind.css and implemented in each page in the header with the following line of code:

```
<LINK href="Northwind.css" type=text/css rel=stylesheet >
```

Web Forms

The presentation tier is responsible for communicating with the user. In the Northwind prototype, we are using several Web forms as the presentation tier. The Web forms included in the process are broken down as follows:

Default.   This is the main form in this application; everything else branches from here. The user can display categories and their associated products from this page and can log in as well. Upon login, users will also see their respective agent and a list of current orders, as shown in Figure 10.7.

Login.   A user who attempts to add a product to the shopping cart before being logged in will be directed to the login page. Authentication is based upon the customer's username and password. See Figure 10.8.

Check Out.   When users select the checkout link, they will be directed to this page. Summary information about the transaction will be displayed, and the user will be given an order number for this transaction.

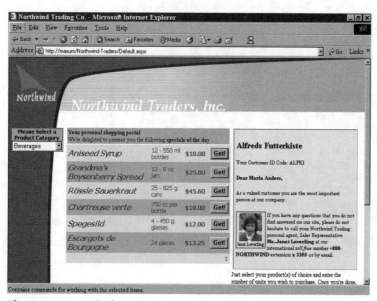

Figure 10.7   Default.aspx.

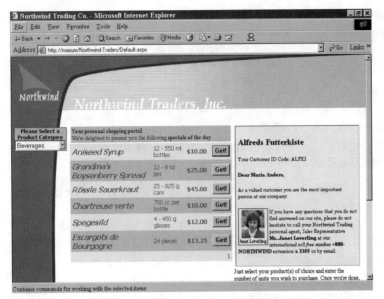

Figure 10.8   Login.aspx.

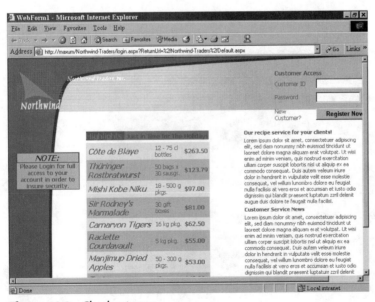

Figure 10.9   Checkout.aspx.

Implementing Authentication

As discussed in Chapter 9, ASP.NET can handle authentication in a variety of different ways. In this particular prototype, we are going to use forms-based authentication. It is easy to implement and allows us to store our information in a centralized location.

We'll use forms-based authentication to control who has access to certain sensitive areas of the site and to redirect users automatically to the login page if they want to place an order.

Let's start by setting this up in Web.config. We modify several different sections of the file to activate our authentication:

```
<!--    AUTHENTICATION
        This section sets the authentication policies of the
application. Possible modes are "Windows",
        "Forms", "Passport" and "None"
-->
        <authentication mode="Forms">
```

Here we specify the authentication mode, the URL, and the type of protection we desire. For a review of this, refer to Chapter 9.

```
                    <forms name="NWAuth" loginUrl="login.aspx"
protection="All" path="/" />
            </authentication>
```

The second part in Web.config only allows authorized users access to default.aspx, and denies everyone else:

```
<!-- set secure paths -->
<location path="default.aspx">
    <system.web>
        <authorization>
            <deny users="?" />
        </authorization>
    </system.web>
</location>
```

Open the Login.aspx page and insert the following code:

```
Private Sub cmdLogin_Click(ByVal sender As System.Object, ByVal e As
System.EventArgs) Handles cmdLogin.Click

        Session("custid") = txtCustID.Text
```

```
        Session("pwd") = txtPwd.Text
    If Page.IsValid Then
        pnlLogin.Visible() = False
        Dim nwCust1 As NWCustomerinfo = New NWCustomerinfo()
        Dim dbutil1 As DB_Util = New DB_Util()
        Dim CustomerID As String
        CustomerID = dbutil1.GetLogin(txtCustID.Text, txtPwd.Text)

        If (CustomerID <> "") Then
            FormsAuthentication.RedirectFromLoginPage(CustomerID,
False)
        Else
            pnlLogin.Visible() = True
        End If
    End If
End Sub
```

The purpose of this is to call the aforementioned customer component and authenticate. If there's a match, we are redirected to the default page. It works like magic.

Wrapping Up

This last chapter ties together the major concepts in the book in a practical way. We walked through the architecture, design rationale, and documents and then moved into the implementation of the application itself.

Following Chapter 10 are the reference and resource appendices. The reference appendix contains usage and syntax information on several of the most used assemblies within the .NET Framework. The resource appendix contains current Web sites and books that you'll find of value. You can check the book Web page at wiley.com/compbooks/alexander for updates and additions to the list and to download the most recent version of the Northwind application. I plan on continually revising it and checking the builds up through RTM, just in case.

.NET Framework Class Library References

This is an overview of the most used high-level namespaces of the .NET Framework class library. It's been broken down by functionality. For a drill-down, search on "class library" in Visual Studio .NET help.

General Functionality

System.   Elemental and base classes that contain definitions for common value and reference data types, events and their handlers, interfaces, attributes, and processing exception handling. Also includes services that support data type conversion, method parameter handling, mathematical operations, program invocation, application environment management, and managed/unmanaged supervision of applications.

System.CodeDom.   Contains classes used for representing source code document elements and structure.

System.Collections.   Contains interfaces and classes used for object collections such as lists, hashtables, queues, and dictionaries.

System.ComponentModel.   Contains classes that are used for components and controls run-time/design-time behavior implementation. It also includes base classes and interfaces for applying attributes and type conversion, data binding, and licensing.

System.Configuration.   Provides classes and interfaces that allow programmatic access of .NET Framework configuration settings and enables error handling in .config files.

System.Globalization.   Includes localization and culture-related information classes, including language, country/region, calendar usage information, corresponding date, currency, and number format, and string sort order as well.

System.Diagnostics.   Provides classes that allow interaction with system processes, event logs, and performance counters. It also provides debugging and trace classes.

System.Text.   Contains classes representing common character encodings; abstract base classes for converting blocks of characters to and from blocks of bytes; and a helper class that manipulates and formats String objects without creating intermediate instances of String. Provides access to the .NET Framework regular expression engine. The namespace provides regular expression functionality that may be used from any platform or language.

Microsoft.Win32.   Provides classes that handle operating system events and utilize the system registry.

Data Management Functionality

System.Data.   Contains classes that enable the ADO.NET architecture.

System.Data.Common. Provides functionality shared by the .NET data providers.

System.Data.OleDb.   Contains the OLE DB .NET Data Provider classes.

System.Data.SqlClient. Contains the SQL Server .NET Data Provider classes.

System.Data.SqlTypes.   Provides classes for SQL Server native data types.

System.Web.SessionState.   Furnishes classes and interfaces that provide session state data storage for a single client within a Web application on the server.

Graphics Functionality

System.Drawing.   Provides access to GDI+ graphics functionality.

System.Drawing.Printing.   Provides print-related services.

COM+/Component-Related Functionality

System.EnterpriseServices. Supplies COM+ service access infrastructure for .NET Framework objects. This namespace also enables the use of a COM+ Compensating Resource Manager (CRM) service in managed code, which allows inclusion of non-transactional objects in Microsoft Distributed Transaction Coordinator (DTC) transactions.

System.Reflection. Exposes classes that enable a compiler or tool to emit metadata and Microsoft intermediate language (MSIL) and PE file generation.

System.Resources. Provides classes and interfaces that enable the creation, storage, and management of application culture-specific resources.

System.Runtime.InteropServices. Provides classes for accessing COM objects, and native APIs from .NET. Also handles marshalling.

System.Runtime.Remoting. Provides classes and interfaces that support development and configuration of distributed applications.

System.Runtime.Serialization. Contains classes for object serialization and deserialization.

System.Threading. Provides multithreaded programming classes and interfaces, including functionality for thread scheduling, thread pool management, wait notification, deadlock resolution, and synchronizing mutually exclusive threads.

File I/O Functionality

System.IO. Enables synchronous and asynchronous reading and writing on both data files and streams.

Network-Related Functionality

System.DirectoryServices. Provides Active Directory access to managed code.

System.Management. Provides Windows Management Instrumentation (WMI) infrastructure access, management instrumentation application support, and exposure of management information and events through

WMI to consumers such as Microsoft Application Center or Microsoft Operations Manager.

System.Messaging.   Supplies classes for the connection, monitoring, and administration of network message queues and message sending, receiving, or peeking.

System.Net.   Provides programmatic access for many current network protocols, and exposes a managed implementation of the Windows Sockets (Winsock) interface.

Security Functionality

System.Security.   Provides the supporting infrastructure of the common language runtime security system, including permissions and policy management base classes, cryptographic services, and authentication.

System.Security.Principal.   Defines a security context object under which code is running.

Web Application Functionality

System.Web.   Supplies classes and interfaces that support browser/server communication, such as HTTP request and output management, server-side utility and process access, cookie manipulation, file transfer, exception information, and caching.

System.Web.Caching.   Provides classes for server resource caching. This could include ASP.NET pages, Web services, and user controls, hashtables, and other data structures.

System.Web.Configuration.   Contains classes that are utilized for ASP.NET configuration.

System.Web.Hosting.   Provides support functionality for ASP.NET managed application hosting external to Microsoft Internet Information Server (IIS).

System.Web.Mail.   Contains classes that enable message construction and delivery through an SMTP server.

System.Web.Security.   Contains classes that implement ASP.NET Web application security.

Web Service Functionality

System.Web.Services.   Supplies classes that support Web Services creation and development.

System.Web.Services.Configuration.   Provides configuration classes for XML Web services created using ASP.NET.

System.Web.Services.Description.   Contains classes that enable the description of an XML Web service through the use of Web Services Description Language (WSDL).

System.Web.Services.Discovery.   Supplies classes that allow XML Web service clients to discover available XML Web services on a Web server.

System.Web.Services.Protocols.   Consists of the classes that provide support for protocols used during communication between XML Web service clients and XML Web services created with ASP.NET.

Web Control Functionality

System.Web.UI.   Provides classes and interfaces that enable Web page user interface element creation, provide common functionality for all controls, support for data binding, view state, and page request management.

System.Web.UI.HtmlControls.   Provides classes that allow you to create HTML server controls on a Web page.

System.Web.UI.WebControls.   Contains classes that allow you to create Web server controls on a Web page.

XML-Related Functionality

System.Xml.   Provides standards-based processing support for XML utilization.

System.Xml.Schema.   Enables XML Schemas (XSD) support.

System.Xml.Serialization.   Contains classes that are used for object serialization into XML formatted documents or streams.

System.Xml.XPath.   Contains standards-based XPath parser and evaluation engine.

System.Xml.Xsl. Provides support for standards-based Extensible Stylesheet Transformation (XSLT) transforms.

Windows Forms Development-Related Functionality

System.Windows.Forms. Contains classes for creating Windows-based applications that utilize rich user interface Microsoft Windows features and that also extend design-time support for Windows Forms.

System.ServiceProcess. Provides classes that allow for implementation, installation, and controlling Windows service applications.

.NET Language Support Functionality

Microsoft.CSharp. Contains classes that support compilation and code generation using the C# language.

Microsoft.Jscript. Contains the JScript runtime and classes that support compilation and code generation using the JScript language.

Microsoft.VisualBasic. Contains the Visual Basic .NET runtime, utilized for application development and maintenance.

Microsoft.Vsa. Contains interfaces that enable .NET Framework script engine integration into applications, and for runtime code compilation and execution.

Resources

These are some resources that I've found helpful in my study of .NET and related technologies. A more up-to-date version can be found at the Web site for this book.

.NET Development

gasTix. (www.gastix.net) GasTIX.net is G. A. Sullivan's .NET-focused Web portal, designed to provide practical information and hands-on tools enabling you to learn about implementing enterprise-class applications utilizing Microsoft's .NET platform.

Dotnetmasters Site. (www.dotnetmasters.com) Site for .NET premier training.

Microsoft.com .NET site. (http://msdn.microsoft.com/net/default.asp) The .NET home site.

Visual Studio .NET site. (http://msdn.microsoft.com/vstudio/nextgen/) Product information for the rapid application development environment Visual Studio .NET.

MSDN SOAP Developer Info Site. (http://msdn.microsoft.com/soap/) Information about one of the key enabling technologies for the XML Web services model and .NET.

ASP.NET site. (www.asp.net/) Information about ASP.NET.

GOTDOTNET site.   (www.gotdotnet.com/) Run by the product team, this site contains tutorials and code samples that demonstrate ASP.NET and the .NET Framework.

MSDN Online XML Developer Center.   (http://msdn.microsoft.com/ xml/) Information about another of the key technologies for the XML Web services model and .NET.

.NET Enterprise Servers site.   (www.microsoft.com/servers/net/) Product information on the XML-enabled software servers that provide the infrastructure for running .NET solutions.

IBuySpy Solutions site.   (www.ibuyspy.com) The granddaddy of .NET sample sites, it demonstrates best practices for creating ASP.NET applications.

.NET Extreme.   (www.dotnetextreme.com/) A good site on .NET for beginners. Lots of articles and sample code.

Rational .Net Developers site.   (http://rational.devx.com/index.htm/ CONTENT_ID/5959) Information on how the Rationalproducts interact with .NET

Lutz Roeder's Programming .NET.   (www.aisto.com/roeder/dotnet/) Tools for Microsoft's .NET platform. Some very cool stuff here.

123ASPX.Com.   (www.123aspx.com) The biggest and baddest ASP.NET directory site on the planet.

scottgu: asp.net tips and tricks.   (www.eraserver.net/scottgu) Scott is the co-creator of ASP.NET. 'nuff said…

dotnetjunkies site.   (www.dotnetjunkies.com/) Lots of tutorials and code.

ASP.NET Pro Magazine site.   (www.aspnetpro.com/) Home of the only magazine devoted solely to the ASP.NET developer.

CodeSwap site.   (www.vscodeswap.net) CodeSwap is the largest pool of code samples produced by developers for developers.

4GuysFromRolla site.   (www.4guysfromrolla.com) These 4 guys are machines! This site rocks! (And they're in college.)

.NET Zone site.   (www.devx.com/dotnet) The .NET Zone site has a ton of different resources.

General Web Development

ArticleCentral site.   (www.articlecentral.com) This site monitors several sites around the clock and stores them in an index here.

Webmonkey site.   (http://hotwired.lycos.com/webmonkey/) A web developer's resource. It has a great HTML reference.

Web Developers Virtual Library.   (www.wdvl.com/) Another good resource for general Web development.

Index